WE ARE THE REVOLUTIONISTS

WE ARE THE REVOLUTIONISTS

German-Speaking Immigrants &
American Abolitionists after 1848

MISCHA HONECK

THE UNIVERSITY OF GEORGIA PRESS
Athens & London

Portions of chapter 3 appear, in a different form, as "An Unexpected
Alliance: August Willich, Peter H. Clark, and the Abolitionist
Movement in Cincinnati" in *Germans and African Americans:
Two Centuries of Exchange*, edited by Larry A. Greene and Anke
Ortlepp (Jackson: University Press of Mississippi, 2010).

© 2011 by the University of Georgia Press
Athens, Georgia 30602
www.ugapress.org
All rights reserved
Designed by Walton Harris
Set in 10.5/13 Garamond Premier Pro

Printed digitally in the United States of America

Library of Congress Cataloging-in-Publication Data
Honeck, Mischa, 1976–
We are the revolutionists : German-speaking immigrants and
American abolitionists after 1848 / Mischa Honeck.
       p.   cm. — (Race in the Atlantic world, 1700–1900)
Includes bibliographical references and index.
ISBN-13: 978-0-8203-3800-2 (hardcover : alk. paper)
ISBN-10: 0-8203-3800-1 (hardcover : alk. paper)
ISBN-13: 978-0-8203-3823-1 (pbk. : alk. paper)
ISBN-10: 0-8203-3823-0 (pbk. : alk. paper)
1. German Americans — United States — History — 19th century.
2. Antislavery movements — United States — History — 19th century.
3. Abolitionists — United States — History — 19th century.
4. Immigrants — United States — History — 19th century.
5. Germany — History — Revolution, 1848–1849 — Influence.
I. Title.
E184.G3H64 2011
973'.0431 — dc22   2010029557

British Library Cataloging-in-Publication Data available

For Elena

If the world separates itself from us,
it leads us to find a place in ourselves
and in each other . . .

—KARL (CHARLES) FOLLEN

CONTENTS

ILLUSTRATIONS

ACKNOWLEDGMENTS

RESEARCHING AND WRITING this book has been a privilege beyond expectation. But had it not been for the innumerable helping hands I have had the pleasure of shaking over the last years, this project would have remained just that: a project. The road to completion has been long, winding, at times stony, but always enchanting and full of life-changing experiences. Treading in the footsteps of my exiled countrymen led me across the Atlantic and back, from Heidelberg, Germany, through Washington, D.C., and Madison, Wisconsin, then on to Chicago, central Texas, Cincinnati, and Boston. Over the course of these travels, I have been exceedingly fortunate to meet a host of fine and generous scholars. If I was not a cosmopolitan earlier in my life, mingling with these wonderful individuals in various places has certainly made me one.

First thanks first. The idea for this book was hatched long ago, during my year abroad at Portland State University, where working with Tim Garrison made me keenly aware of some of the understudied realms of antebellum and Civil War history. Detlef Junker kindly admitted me to his flock of graduate students when my project had not even passed the proposal stage. A few months later, Manfred Berg stepped in as my first advisor and stayed in that position to the very end. His counsel, trust, and support continue to be of immeasurable worth to me. Among the many other mentors at the University of Heidelberg who have sharpened my thinking and broadened my horizon, Dietmar Schloss deserves special acclaim. I fondly remember the many sunny afternoons we spent on his veranda, sipping exotic tea and musing over the contested role of the intellectual in American culture. The ideas that sprouted from these conversations live on and resonate throughout this book.

I am no less grateful for the financial and institutional support I received at different stages of my project. The Kade-Heideking fellowship, awarded by the German Historical Institute (GHI) in Washington, D.C., and the University of Wisconsin–Madison, enabled me to mine a broad array of archives and research libraries in the United States. Upon my return to Heidelberg, a stipend from the Jacob G. Schurman Foundation provided ample leeway for writing much of this study. The Heidelberg Center for American Studies, my academic habitat, has been more than a workplace to me. Ably led by Detlef Junker and prudently managed by Wilfried Mausbach, the HCA has provided a splendid atmosphere for this project to blossom. It is refreshing and reassuring to have colleagues who genuinely want me to thrive and manage to create an environment conducive to success. I truly hope all benefactors take satisfaction from the result they have helped generate.

Happily, I can also name some of the people whose assistance and critical input have turned this study into a worthwhile enterprise. Bruce Levine, Michael Hochgeschwender, and Philipp Gassert showed enthusiasm for the project from the outset. Their uplifting words encouraged me to go ahead with it. In Washington, Christof Mauch, Dirk Schumann, Anke Ortlepp, Gerald Steinacher, and many other colleagues at the GHI taught me a great deal about academic perseverance. In one of those inevitable moments of gloom, Jon Powell, my fellow "archive rat" at the Library of Congress, was there to bail me out. Thanks, Jon, for buoying my spirits and initiating me into the redemptive powers of the diagram! Mark Louden and Cora Lee Kluge at the Max Kade Institute for German-American Studies were terrific hosts and made my sojourn in Wisconsin a rewarding one. Furthermore, although their names go unsung, I want to thank the librarians and archivists at the Library of Congress and the Smithsonian Institution in Washington, D.C., the New York Public Library, the State Historical Society of Wisconsin, the University of Wisconsin at Milwaukee libraries, the Center for American History at the University of Texas at Austin, the San Antonio Public Library, the University of Cincinnati libraries, the Cincinnati Public Library, the Cincinnati Historical Society, the University of Michigan Archives, the Boston Public Library, and the Houghton Library at Harvard University. In nearly endless quests through unknown bookshelves and microfilm reels, I could always rely on their gracious guidance.

When preparing this book for publication, I benefited enormously from the wisdom of some of the best scholars in the field. I cherish the support and friendship of Paul Finkelman, whose knowledge and valuable suggestions have improved this work inestimably. I am equally indebted to John David Smith, who took interest in this study almost from its inception and offered fabulous advice. Martin Klimke, John Stauffer, Martin Öfele, Kirsten Fischer, Frank Beyersdorf, Florian Pressler, Barbara Loomis, Richard Blackett, Jim Stewart, Bob Cherny, Bill Issel, Caleb McDaniel, Jeremi Suri, Anja Schüler, and Andrew Zimmermann read the entire manuscript or segments of it. I sincerely appreciate their constructive comments and razor-sharp criticism. I shudder at the thought of what this book would look like without them. Manisha Sinha, editor of the University of Georgia Press's Race in the Atlantic World series, has been passionate about the project ever since we first touched base. So were Beth Snead, Jon Davies, and my first-rate copy editor Barb Wojhoski, who did much to furbish my prose. Their performance has more than lived up to the reputation of the press. I must, with all humility, acknowledge my project editor, Derek Krissoff. Derek skillfully and judiciously navigated the manuscript through the initial phases of the editorial process and together with his coworkers helped turn the book into a product of which I am now proud.

Tracking down sources and "making them speak" can be a lonely business, but I was blessed with friends and relatives who have been generous with their hospitality, time, and companionship. My old friend Frank Thorn invited me to stay with him while I was doing research at the John F. Kennedy Institute in Berlin. With Ilse Bergmann, I found the most hilarious and bighearted landlady one can have inside the Beltway. Martin Klimke gave me shelter on route to New York, and I am indebted to my sister-in-law Irina for sharing her Chicago apartment with me twice. My uncle and aunt Leander and Ulla were always there to cheer me up and remind me that life has more to offer than scholastic rigor (yes, occasionally this was necessary). My father, who departed too soon, would have done the same, perhaps even with a nod of appreciation. Last but not least, I am extremely thankful for the southern geniality I enjoyed in the company of my good friend and fellow historian Hunt Boulware. May our paths cross again in the near future.

Finally, this work would never have crossed the finish line had it not been for the enduring support and patience of my beautiful wife. She is my loving consort, faithful friend, and prime inspiration. Elena, in ways too numerous to mention, I lovingly dedicate this book to you.

WE ARE THE REVOLUTIONISTS

INTRODUCTION

ON A COLD BUT PLEASANT DAY in December 1849, Professor Friedrich Wilhelm Carové returned to the University of Heidelberg with a momentous request. The author of an all-German proclamation demanding the worldwide abolition of slavery, Carové urged the theological faculty to confer an honorary doctorate of divinity on an American minister whom he had come to appreciate earlier that year at the World Peace Congress in Paris. James W. C. Pennington, the man Carové proposed for the honorary doctorate, was no ordinary candidate. A cherished member of the international peace and abolitionist movements, Pennington was also a Presbyterian pastor and, more sensational still, a fugitive slave who could boast astounding intellectual accomplishments since his escape from bondage. After becoming the first black man to attend classes at Yale, Pennington wrote a slave narrative and the first history of the African American people. Awarding the doctoral degree to this highly gifted black preacher, Carové emphasized, was one way for the faculty to pronounce "the universal brotherhood of humanity" and atone "for the sins Europe ha[d] committed against natural and human rights." His fellow professors concurred. Later that day, in a dignified ceremony, the degree "honor doctoris" was conferred on "Jacob Guil Carol Pennington." It was the first time that an African American had received this greatest of all academic honors from a European university.[1]

Pennington's journey from slavery in Maryland to the halls of German academia sheds fascinating light on a budding transatlantic dialogue about human equality that gained broader significance in the first half of the nineteenth century. The emergence of this transnational web of reform was made possible by a series of rapidly evolving developments in Europe and North America. Demographic growth, technological innovations, and economic expansion, as well as free and forced migration, caused profound shifts in the societies of the Old and the New World and undercut traditional assumptions about the value of the individual human being. In the wake of the eighteenth-century American and French revolutions, ideas of liberty and equality called into question various forms of human subordination. Burgeoning civil societies and expanding public spheres provided new outlets for challenging established class and power structures. In 1830 and more forceful still in 1848, popular uprisings struck at the foundations of Europe's hereditary systems of privilege, heralding to many the dawn of a new order. International reform ventures favoring temperance, socialism, pacifism, and women's rights were also on the rise.[2]

We Are the Revolutionists is located at the interface of the various democratic and revolutionary movements that swept through the Atlantic world from the events of 1848–49 to the end of the American Civil War, an era drenched in the language of nationality and freedom. Specifically, it probes how some of these movements intersected in the battle to abolish chattel slavery, which by then had been pushed in many minds beyond the bounds of accepted exploitation. Historians have sometimes noted the transnational currents that carried abolitionist ideas and activists across political and geographical boundaries but are only beginning to scrutinize them in greater detail. By 1849, the year Pennington received his honorary doctorate from Heidelberg, emancipation had been decreed in Great Britain, France, Denmark, and Sweden. Not so in Pennington's country of birth. Due to the growing global demand for cotton, American slavery seemed more firmly rooted than ever. Indeed, in 1858, South Carolina senator James Henry Hammond could smugly proclaim, "Cotton is king," and "no power on earth dares to make war upon it." But the characters highlighted in this book did.[3]

This book unravels the American drama of reform and emancipation from a transnational perspective. Like preceding works, it posits that the high tide of abolitionist protest in the United States cannot be fully grasped without charting the personal and ideological conduits linking concurrent democratic endeavors on both sides of the Atlantic. European critiques of American slavery have long been presented as an overwhelmingly British phenomenon. By the 1850s, the Anglo-American abolitionist network had been in place for more than a generation. Petitions, capital, lecturers, pamphlets, and fugitive slaves traversed the Anglophone Atlantic. This study looks beyond these patterns of communication between British and American abolitionists and shows that the political and social ties in the movement extended far into central Europe. In March 1855, Frederick Douglass roused the spirits of a sympathetic crowd in Rochester, New York, exclaiming, "England, France and Germany, the three great lights of modern civilization, are with us, and every American traveler learns to regret the existence of Slavery in his country." The travel experiences of Douglass, Pennington, and other antebellum activists helped cultivate bonds of solidarity between the various revolutionary movements of the age. Their transatlantic friendships, many of which were forged in the 1840s at international reform conventions in London, Paris, Brussels, and elsewhere, brought American abolitionists into fruitful exchange with a plethora of European democrats: Irish Repealers, English reformers, French socialists, and Italian, German, and Hungarian revolutionaries.[4]

The traffic of people and ideas across the Atlantic, however, went both ways. By the early 1850s, many representatives of the radical European factions whom American abolitionists had met on their trips abroad had been either silenced or driven out of their homelands. Especially in the aftermath of the abortive revolutions of 1848–49, participants were on the run from the aristocracies they had tried to oust. Not a few of them scrambled to North America for safety. This book focuses on the immigrant revolutionaries from German lands, the largest subgroup among Europe's political refugees. Numerically, these German-speaking "Forty-Eighters" represented merely a trickle in the tide of more than four million discontented Europeans who entered the United States between 1840 and 1860. Though tied together by what R. R. Palmer has called "a new feeling for a kind of equality, or at least a discomfort with older forms of social stratification," the exiles encompassed a spectrum of different political outlooks, regional backgrounds, and occupational orientations. Their ranks included lawyers, army officers, journalists, and craft workers. Some considered themselves liberal democrats. Others adhered to a traditional republicanism that held that civil society was perpetually threatened by corruption. Yet others identified with Charles Fourier's utopian socialism or Karl Marx's radical communism. Squabbles about the meaning of revolution, in both Germany and the United States, were ubiquitous. Founding various periodicals and associations to promote various goals such as workers' rights, women's rights, and free thought, Forty-Eighter democrats routinely bickered over the best way to create a secular paradise, which left them internally divided.[5]

Yet what piqued the curiosity of America's abolitionists most was that almost all Forty-Eighter radicals shared a profound aversion to the institution of slavery. With a ferocity rarely seen among immigrants, they attacked this system of bound labor that, in their view, grossly belied the founding ideals of their new country. They wrote fiery articles, authored poignant tales, defied proslavery laws, marched in the streets, and marshaled for war. Such activities were mainly local in scope and often confined to the printed page. Once under way, however, they came to enlarge the stream of abolitionist protest, the multiethnic currents of which are still vastly underexplored.

We Are the Revolutionists tells the story of the contacts and the exchanges, the coalitions and the disagreements, the quarrels and the friendships that evolved between German-speaking Forty-Eighters and American abolitionists. It is a book about the collaborative efforts of men and women of diverse origins propelled by the common goal to defeat chattel slavery. It traces the ways in which American reformers and German exiles challenged, reshaped, and occasionally, if only ephemerally, overcame ethnic and racial boundaries in their struggle for greater liberty. Whereas prior accounts have emphasized the separateness of these two groups, the present work examines their interconnectedness.[6]

These activists formed a community in the loosest of terms, a community anchored in personal relationships, mutual interests, and a network of print rather than tied to specific institutions or organizations. Conversations about how to build a slave-free society were fueled by a wide variety of concerns such as political economy, religion, and literature as well as work and gender relations. Abolitionism, after all, was one major thread in a grand, interwoven tapestry of democratic development where blacks and whites championed emancipation in a broader attempt to reform, educate, and elevate their fellow citizens. Too often the story of these connections has been left out when in fact many of these issues were discussed in concert. Appreciating the full scope of motivations that made German and American opponents of slavery react to and learn from one another, this book offers a fresh appraisal of American abolitionism after 1848: that of a forum in which interethnic partnerships were forged, partnerships that brought culturally distinct concepts of freedom, equality, and humanity into a prolific dialogue.

We Are the Revolutionists is also about the limits of interethnic cooperation in an age of heightened ethnic and racial sensibilities. Shared hostility to slavery did not automatically result in intercultural harmony. Aside from obvious language barriers, alliances between American abolitionists and German-born radicals were complicated by a set of disparate outlooks and conflicting agendas. Each group saw in freedom the great hope for humankind, yet each wrestled differently with the problem of achieving it. African Americans did not view abolition as an end in itself but conceived it as a first step toward implementing racial equality. The abolitionist campaign of most white native-born northerners was inseparably linked to the Protestant vision of a God-fearing America that rejected bondage, abhorred drinking, and respected Sunday worship. Except for their common hatred of slavery, little connected black activists and white reformers from New England and elsewhere to the Old World revolutionists who had mounted the barricades in 1848. The atheist leanings of some as well as the Lutheran, Catholic, and Jewish backgrounds of others contrasted vividly with the evangelical Protestant beliefs held by the former. Other controversial causes popular among immigrant radicals — revolutionary violence, socialism, antitemperance — tested the patience of northern abolitionists as well.

The fact that these relationships were often arduous, sometimes making individuals more conscious of their differences, can teach us a lot about emancipatory cultures in transit. They illuminate a kaleidoscope of ideas and ideals up for grabs in an Atlantic world thrown into flux by massive migration and revolutionary unrest. The migration-driven needs to reconceive kin connections and civic roles that Robert Wiebe has located in mid-nineteenth-century Western societies made themselves felt in the abolitionist movement as well. Wherever they had been born, people either living in or pouring into American territory were engaged in an ongoing, highly volatile "experiment in remaking identities." While some actors reacted to the turmoil convinced that the reality of social mixing made bridging man-made barriers necessary, others responded to the multiplying confrontations by embracing ever more-rigid conceptions of ethnic and national identity. The book's discussion of joint agitation among Forty-Eighters and abolitionists broadens our view of transatlantic abolitionism in the Civil War period. In doing so, it sensitizes us to the problems posed by an era of unprecedented geographic mobility and the ways in which the activists gave meaning to their uprooted lives in the ferment of revolution, exile, war, and emancipation. Instead of simply using the Atlantic world to better understand abolitionism, this study also argues that we can use abolitionism to better understand race, reform, and nation making in the mid-nineteenth-century Atlantic world.[7]

Liberty and Union: Atlantic Vistas

Comprehending the important correlation of protest and identity formation that resonated from the multiethnic chorus against slavery requires situating that chorus in the broader histories of democracy and nationalism. Nineteenth-century abolitionism can boast many midwives. Convinced that slavery was a crime against God and God's creation, radical Protestants in Europe and North America called on slaveholders to abandon their sinful behavior and free the slaves. Enlightenment humanists, stirred by the experience of revolution, demanded emancipation on the grounds that bondage violated the laws of nature and the "rights of man." Opposition to slavery gained further momentum through transformations set in motion by the transatlantic market and industrial revolutions. Although the slave-based cotton economy of the American South benefited immensely from an expanding global marketplace, northern commentators began to assert that it was impossible for the disparate work ethics of slave and free labor to coexist. Finally, blacks themselves contributed actively to their liberation. Prominent members of the African American community strove tirelessly to mobilize public opinion on both sides of the Atlantic against slavery and racial inequality.[8]

However, surprisingly little attention has been paid to the impact of germinating national identities on transatlantic discourses over slavery and abolition. Judged by today's standards born out of the experience of two horrific world wars, nationalism and abolitionism may seem strange bedfellows, but their affiliation should become clear once we excavate their common roots. Early nineteenth-century nationalism was inherently progressive and democratic. As older forms of authority eroded under the twin forces of economic and political modernization, the nation emerged as the principal nexus with the ability to bind together an imagined people across a given distance. Not only did it satisfy deep needs of community, which traditional systems could no longer fully uphold and modern class conflict threatened to undermine, but it also became the main vessel for peoples' aspirations for freedom and equality. Revolutionaries from Germany and England, from France and the United States, nurtured the tenet reverberating in the key texts of 1776 and 1789 that national sovereignty, individual rights, and civic equality were mutually reinforcing. Sixty years later, on the eve of the American Civil War, the Italian patriot Giuseppe Mazzini echoed this conviction when he asked, "What is a country . . . but the place in which our individual rights are most secure?"[9]

Early nineteenth-century nationalism was also homogenizing. Since liberal reformers everywhere believed that modern nations could be free only if they were united, it is easy to imagine the fear that the longevity of an institution such as chattel slavery struck in their hearts. In places where benighted forms of dependency lingered on, they reasoned, freedom could not reign supreme. Opposing slavery became more than a moral or economic imperative; national unity demanded it. "Liberty and Union," the ringing declaration of Massachusetts senator Daniel Webster, grew out of this strand as did Abraham Lincoln's famous observation that a country like his own "cannot endure, permanently half *slave* and half *free*." Nations were seen as elevating and unifying; absolutist rule, whether exercised by a monarch or a plantation master, was seen as oppressive and divisive. Americans and Europeans increasingly accepted this binary, associating freedom, equality, and progress with republican nations while connecting slavery, despotism, and backwardness with aristocracies. Charles Sumner, another Republican leader, made this point in 1856 when accusing southern planters of constituting a "Slave Oligarchy," thus putting the South's landed gentry in one league with the hereditary nobilities of the Old World. For the Forty-Eighters who fled to the United States, the battles against the

European aristocrats and the southern "slave barons" were likewise connected. "Opposition to the politics of slavery in America," mused the exiled German journalist Karl Heinzen, "is a battle against reaction in Europe."[10]

The promise of liberty and union, however, was a double-edged sword. Although Europeans and Americans tended to view national independence movements abroad sympathetically, they were also quick to bar from their communities those whom they came to look upon as detrimental to their ethnic and cultural identity. The question of who was "in" or "out" of the nation was among the most vigorously debated issues of the age. How much diversity was desirable? How much could be tolerated? To bring order to the confusion, theories defining nationality on the basis of race flourished. According to such theories, "Slavic" Poles could never become part of a "Teutonic" German nation, while "Celtic" Irish did not qualify as members of an "Anglo-Saxon" United States. From these beliefs, which found broad acceptance in the Atlantic world, it was only a small step for a settler society like the United States to embrace white supremacy. African Americans scored lowest on the racial scale of America's herrenvolk democracy, which derived the promise of equality for whites from the political exclusion of darker races. Most whites regarded blacks as a group lacking the prerequisites for republican citizenship, and long-standing associations of blackness with slavery provided compelling rationales for declaring them a pariah class unable to enjoy the fruits of freedom. Even antislavery politicians like Abraham Lincoln had strong doubts whether an American nation would ever be capable of accommodating whites and blacks. Colonization seemed a way out. The anti-immigrant nativists, meanwhile, took America's herrenvolk democracy to its logical extremes. To them, American democracy derived from the genius of their forefathers and was not to be shared with the non-Anglo-Saxon minorities streaming into their country.[11]

Radical abolitionists and Forty-Eighter exiles closed ranks to root out American slavery but also grappled with a kind of herrenvolk nationalism that applied the tenets of herrenvolk democracy to the forging and framing of nations everywhere. The supremacy of aggressive national rivalries that were cemented around 1900 was no foregone conclusion. Fifty years earlier societies were arguing, often passionately, whether their national fabrics should be ethnic or civic, racial or cosmopolitan. The book's protagonists reflect these ideological frictions very well. As people throughout the Atlantic world nationalized, interethnic contact provided salutary orientation. Some actors emerged from their dealings with strangers with a better understanding of what made them culturally unique, persuaded that a person's deepest attachments are inherited, not chosen. Predicting the national antagonisms of later generations, they would end up envisaging communities of common ancestry that were a given, an almost superhistorical fate to which individuals were inescapably tied. Straying from these supposedly naturally ordained connections, they feared, would only result in permanent exile and despair.

Nonetheless, interactions between abolitionist Americans and German émigrés also produced less narrowly defined — today we might say more tolerant — alternatives. Finding new sources of kinship in interethnic relationships, other radicals carved out the contours of a civic democratic ideology in which they learned to see the nation as a community of equal, rights-bearing citizens united in attachment to a set of political principles, among them emancipation, universal suffrage, equal opportunity, and the peaceful dialogue of different ways of life. For them, social belonging came to be a matter of choice rather than of descent. Against the vision of a racially exclusive nation, they pitted a cosmopolitan concept of nationality, one that conceives human diversity as a source of improvement, not discord. The fiery Boston abolitionist William Lloyd Garrison and his followers advocated disunion, favoring secession from the South and building a smaller American republic unsullied by the blemish of racial slavery. Radical German Americans like August Willich and Mathilde Anneke came to prefer the company of congenial English-speaking activists over that of their conservative countrymen. In their struggles for greater democracy, neither group wanted to see the blessings of citizenship confined to a particular class of people. Though accustomed to different local traditions and political cultures, they essentially agreed that the rights to life, liberty, and the pursuit of happiness, as proclaimed by the American Declaration of Independence, were not the privilege of a few but universally valid truths.[12]

This is not to say that feelings of ethnic rivalry or racial superiority were absent from transatlantic abolitionism. Racism and nationalism loomed everywhere, and black activists, native-born white agitators, and German-born radicals often found themselves estranged by distinctions of race, ethnicity, class, or religion. Yet the mere fact that emancipators of a different hue talked to one another about their experiences of oppression and expectations for freedom set them apart from people who did not even engage with persons stigmatized as racial or social outsiders. Among themselves, abolitionists and Forty-Eighters cultivated a rich dialogue about the meaning of freedom, equality, and nationality in an ever more intertwined Atlantic world. Even as their proclivity to condemn slavery in different ideological languages often heightened a sense of cultural otherness, individuals from both camps reached out to one another and started working together to guarantee civil rights regardless of skin color, national origin, class, and sometimes even of sex. In a society steeped in racist and nativist thought, such collaborations were nothing short of revolutionary.

Enter the Revolutionists

James M. McPherson popularized the notion that the Civil War was a "Second American Revolution," but he did not invent it. That concept was already ingrained in comments made immediately after the eruption of the sectional conflict. Karl Marx, Giuseppe Garibaldi, Jefferson Davis, and many of their contemporaries noted the war's revolutionary qualities. Expecting that it could only end with the liberation of four million slaves and "by annihilating that Oligarchy that formed and rule[d] the South," the abolitionist Wendell Phillips insisted that the Civil War was "primarily a social revolution." And when witnessing the April 1861 parade of the New York Twentieth United Rifles Regiment, a unit composed almost entirely of immigrant radicals, a veteran of the German Revolution jubilantly declared, "The spirit of 1848 has once more awakened."[13]

Who exactly were the revolutionists who crossed ethnic and racial lines to overthrow one of the United States' oldest institutions? Where did they meet, and under what circumstances? To avoid distorting generalizations, *We Are the Revolutionists* examines a distinct set of encounters between native-born abolitionists and German-speaking Forty-Eighters with the tools of microhistory and collective biography. This study is microhistorical in that it traces the interchange of ideas and identities within small-scale activist networks in particular communities. But it is also biographical in that it pays attention to the intersections of individual lives to lay bare the diverse roots, routes, and outcomes of interethnic abolitionism as well as its meaning for those directly involved. Specifically, the book centers around four cases of coalition building at four different sites, each covering a particular regional environment: central Texas, Cincinnati, Milwaukee, and Boston. Prominent Forty-Eighters cooperated with native-born agitators in all four localities, yet the way in which they did so hinged substantially on the distinct demographics and politics of these places. Regionally specific vagaries and personal dispositions shaped these interactions as much as the agreement that slavery was incompatible with democratic development.

Focusing on local conditions allows us to grasp important differences in how abolition, race, class, and ethnicity converged at the grassroots level, demonstrating that abolitionism was, in the words of George M. Fredrickson, a "decentralized enterprise, subject to local variation and internal factionalism." Moreover, this approach facilitates locating the characters presented here on abolitionism's complex ideological spectrum. Although antislavery and abolition were different reform movements, it is often hard to tell where abolition, which aimed at unconditional emancipation and usually envisioned civil rights for the freed slaves, began and antislavery, which desired the containment of slavery and opposed racial equality, ended. Slaveholders, for one, never bothered about such distinctions. The line was hardly less blurry once abolition became enmeshed in the broader stream of antisouthern agitation, even as radical abolitionists were careful to distinguish themselves from whites who worried about their own liberty but were indifferent to black freedom. Again region mattered. In slaveholding Texas, where hostility to slavery was potentially lethal, many activists were abolitionists at heart but in their public statements were hesitant to go further than adopting a moderate free-soil stance. Midwestern calls for ending slavery often emerged in conjunction with appeals for free homesteads in the territories regardless of race, even as these abolitionists met stiff resistance from local white supremacists. Meanwhile, in the intellectually progressive clime of urban New England, native- and foreign-born activists dared to assault slavery and racial discrimination in a much more spirited fashion.[14]

Chapter 1 maps political, social, and cultural developments in antebellum America at large and investigates the reciprocity between slavery, immigration, antislavery, and abolitionism, topics that have often been examined independently. In weaving them together, this book illuminates how the mass influx of Irish and German migrants beginning in the late 1840s magnified feelings of insecurity among native-born Americans and aggravated strident debates over race, nationality, and citizenship in the antebellum republic. It was against this backdrop that refugees of the 1848–49 revolutions launched their first critiques of chattel slavery, which earned them recognition from abolitionist circles but also marked them as troublemakers in the eyes of the more conservative Anglo-Saxon and immigrant populations.

Shifting away from the larger national panorama, chapter 2 revisits an almost forgotten episode of the antislavery struggle in the South, the Texas free-soil campaign, the heyday of which lasted from 1854 to 1856. A frontier state where slavery was predominantly viewed as a positive good, Texas was in many ways detrimental to antislavery and abolitionist enterprises. Undeterred by the odds, a band of German Americans and northern intellectuals joined forces to make a free state out of Texas. Several activists became friends due to shared highbrow sensibilities. Others bonded more tightly once they realized that their views on citizenship, social progress, and cultural uplift through education merged in crucial ways.

While the people active in the Texas free-soil movement overwhelmingly came from middle-class backgrounds, the situation differed in antebellum Cincinnati. Chapter 3 highlights interethnic alliances molded in the working-class districts of that city. In a city notorious for racial conflict and ethnic competition, a number of revolutionary exiles stunned Cincinnati's white conservatives by joining forces with local black and white abolitionists in the effort to build a democratic society without distinctions of race, class, and nationality. As a result of these collaborations, the persons involved rose above ethnocultural barriers, proving that ideological affinities in the abolitionist cause could at times spawn active solidarity in defiance of pervasive color lines.

Chapter 4 moves on to the shores of Lake Michigan, where two women writers, one German and the other New England bred, redefined notions of slavery, freedom, citizenship, and womanhood. The friendship of Mary Booth and Mathilde Anneke was uniquely transnational, a sisterhood that drove them to raise their voices against private and social injustices. In an intimate, ocean-spanning journey that led them from Milwaukee, Wisconsin, to the Swiss Alps and back, both women authored a collection of abolitionist stories in which they bound together their personal longings for women's emancipation with those of America's oppressed black population.

After covering locations in the South, the border-state region, and the Old Northwest, chapter 5 again employs a biographical lens to inspect a fourth and final abolitionist scenario that unfolded in Boston, the cradle of Garrisonian abolitionism. Although New England provided a fertile ground for a multitude of reform movements, including abolition, Garrison's followers constituted only a small minority in the Bay State. This did not change much even as Boston's black and white abolitionists were reinforced by a group of radical immigrants who organized around Karl Heinzen's German-language newspaper *Der Pionier*. In the whirlwind of war, Heinzen engaged in a lively dialogue with local black and white agitators, which gave him a greater appreciation of the democratic values of an evangelical culture he had so far eyed suspiciously.

Chapter 6 concludes with a postscript that sketches how several of these activists grappled with the legacy of their involvement in the abolitionist struggle through the difficult period of Reconstruction. Some continued the fight for a more egalitarian and racially tolerant United States beyond the legal deathblow to slavery, whereas many others seemed sufficiently content with emancipation and refocused their energy on new, supposedly more urgent projects. Under the impression of intensified nation building on both sides of the Atlantic, parts of the old Forty-Eighter intelligentsia turned conservative and began refashioning themselves as white citizens. These postwar divisions bring to mind the continuous, contingent, and erratic nature of the quest for democratic progress and intercultural understanding, of which the diverse but entangled revolutionists of the Civil War era gave a memorable example.

There is much to be gained by exploring the border-crossing companionships of individuals such as Adolf Douai and Frederick Law Olmsted in Texas, August Willich and Peter Clark in Cincinnati, Mathilde Anneke and Mary Booth in Milwaukee, and Karl Heinzen and Wendell Phillips in Boston. Doing so makes visible their interrelated critiques of the rapidly changing cultural and political worlds through which they moved. These men and women envisioned themselves as part of communities far smaller and far larger than the nation. Yet they raised questions about their society's developing mores that are startling in their intensity and far-sightedness. Returning to these characters, however, does not only elucidate their lives and ideas. It also demonstrates that two story lines that we, somewhat carelessly, have allowed to diverge — the struggle for emancipation and the activists' search for belonging — need to be reunited.

CHAPTER ONE

Entanglement Is Certain
1848 and the Challenge to American Slavery

The line between Freedom and Slavery, in this country, is tightly
drawn; and the combatants on either side are in earnest and fight
hand to hand. He who chances to be on one side or on the other,
if it be but in the estimation of a single hair, must fight, or die.
There is no neutral ground here for any man.
        —FREDERICK DOUGLASS to LAJOS KOSSUTH, February 26, 1852

Wander on the tracks of progress
Strive, in the name of truth,
To make future generations praise
What Turners seek today.
Man's Eden will return,
Slavery's yoke will break,
Once free people praise in songs
The Turners' noble deeds.
        —"The Song of the Turner"

WHEN FRENCH WORKERS CROWDED the streets of Paris in February 1848 to
demonstrate against rising food prices, few realized that this was merely the
overture to a greater revolutionary concert. The flames of popular unrest spread
quickly across the Continent, radically altering the political landscape of post-
Napoleonic Europe. The first crowned head to tumble was France's Louis
Philippe, whose abdication cleared the way for the Second French Republic.
Panic soon struck the ruling elites in Germany, Russia, and Austria-Hungary.
Klemens von Metternich, the old Austrian chancellor who had long denied national independence to different peoples inside and outside the empire — Poles,
Czechs, Hungarians, Italians — faltered and handed in his resignation on March
18. Meanwhile, the Prussian king Frederick William IV succumbed to public
pressure and bowed before the victims of the bloody March uprisings in Berlin.

Old World intellectuals overwhelmingly rejoiced at this apparent erosion of aristocratic power, interpreting it as a major step on the march toward national unity and democratic self-rule. Repeatedly they expressed their hopes for a better future by emphasizing the interrelatedness of the various revolutionary movements of the day as well as their kinship with those of the past. "Whatever happens in Paris, London, and St. Petersburg, happens in Europe," the French writer Victor Hugo astutely observed. Carl Schurz, then a rebellious student, wrote in hindsight that the French Revolution of 1789 "furnished to [them] models in plenty that mightily excited [their] imagination." At mass gatherings of German-speaking democratic workers, the Stars and Stripes was unfurled alongside the French *tricolore* and the revolutionary red flag. "Germany must become a free state like America" was a slogan widely used in pamphlets of that period, testifying that the legacies of 1776 and 1787 as well as 1789 served as a major source of inspiration for those directly involved.[1]

Such stirring invocations of the American Revolution did not escape American onlookers, who took a lively interest in the upheavals on the other side of the Atlantic. Echoing the sentiments of many of their compatriots, Boston citizens proclaimed on April 20, 1848, "As sons of those who rocked the cradle of American liberty, we exult over the birth of European liberty." Solidarity clubs were formed, and declarations of support were issued, indicating a broad ideological affinity for the European liberation struggles that extended to the highest levels of government. Dudley Mann, the United States consul in Bremen, noted with satisfaction that the German people had finally "unfolded the flag of right." No less heartfelt were the sympathies of Mann's superior, James Buchanan. Though advising caution, the secretary of state pledged that Americans would never "be indifferent spectators to the progress of liberty throughout the world."[2]

The warmest aspirations for the success of the republican movements in Europe emanated from the quarters of America's abolitionists. Many active in the movement enthusiastically hailed the upsurges of 1848, imagining a powerful nexus that linked their own fight for the underprivileged to others outside the United States. By equating persecuted European patriots to bondsmen, abolitionists found new arguments for freeing the slaves at home. "The cause of tyrants is one the world over, and the cause of resistance to tyranny is one also," boomed Wendell Phillips at an abolitionist congregation. Charles Sumner spoke in even more explicit terms about a flowering coalition between Old World revolutionaries and American abolitionists. As late as 1850, he contended, "Our movement here is part of the great liberal movement of Europe."[3]

This outlook also pervaded the resolutions passed at the annual meetings of the country's local and national abolitionist societies. While the various coups for national independence elicited general applause, abolitionists were specially rapt by European leaders doing away with the remnants of colonial slavery. At their 1848 convention in New York, Garrison and his followers promised to proudly remember "that one of the first acts of the French people, after the achievement of their own liberty, was to decree the immediate emancipation of [their] slaves." A few days earlier, on May 9, the American and Foreign Anti-Slavery Society had celebrated "the progress of emancipation in the colonies of Sweden, Denmark, and France" and expressed the hope "that the last spot on earth where slavery exist[ed would] not be the Republic that was first to proclaim the equality of man." Here were fellow emancipators, abolitionists thought, staunch partners in the cause of universal freedom. Little did they know that shiploads of these European revolutionaries would soon flee to America's shores, precipitating a close encounter that would show how deep the mutual sympathies of these two groups actually were.[4]

Colliding Cultures

Pro-European feelings in the United States cooled considerably once it became clear that the Old World liberation movements tilted toward disaster. All over the Continent, liberal and radical democrats fled their homelands to escape incarceration and possible execution. Americans who initially had been supportive of the popular insurgencies of 1848–49 did not hide their disappointment that the ancien régime had not collapsed but was alive and kicking. After Louis Napoleon had sealed his triumph over the French democrats, a disenchanted Edward Everett questioned whether Bonaparte's nephew would ever rise to be a French George Washington. That part, he lamented, "will prove, I fear, either beyond his strength or above his virtue." Harvard professor George Ticknor echoed Everett's skepticism. Ticknor gloomily stated, "[Republics] cannot grow on the soil of Europe. . . . There is no nourishment for them in the present conditions or past history of the nations there." More alarmed still, journalist George Sanders feared that the negative outcome of the revolutions might spill over and deepen already existing political divisions in his country. "Everywhere liberty is surrounded by secret or open enemies," Sanders surmised, declaring that the last thing Americans needed were fanatics adopting peculiar notions of reform that had run wild in Europe and had "assumed the responsibility of all the evils, real and imaginary, under the sun."[5]

Correlating with broader developments, such remarks furthered the belief

German lithograph, 1849, depicting the postrevolutionary crackdown on Europe's democratic movements (National Museum, Nuremberg). Switzerland, Great Britain, and the United States in particular became places of sanctuary for many expelled Forty-Eighters.

that the United States was an exceptional nation and that its own revolutionary tradition was superior. But they also betrayed a growing unease among white Americans about the throngs of European immigrants who had begun pouring into the country. Nativism, a mind-set best described as a collective suspicion of foreign-born people, became especially virulent in the second third of the nineteenth century. In an age that saw territorial expansion and the first signs of industrialization, immigrants came to provide large parts of the country's labor force. They built canals, laid tracks, constructed roads, erected buildings, and served as housemaids, assuming tasks traditionally confined to slaves in the South and to the urban and rural poor in the North. Prior to the 1840s, most Americans held that the multiplying Anglo-Saxons could easily absorb other European stock. This faith all but crumbled with the arrival of the Irish and the Germans. The prospect of social disruption through mass immigration heightened already prevalent anxieties stemming from the rapid social and economic changes of the 1830s and 1840s. In a climate of increased worries about the nation's future, many native-born whites found solace in a racial heritage that stretched back into a mythical past.[6]

By far the hardest hit by this resurgence of Anglo-Saxonism were the Irish, the largest European immigrant group of the time. Between 1845 and 1855, nearly 1.8 million people deserted the Emerald Isle as a consequence of the devastating potato famine. Americans ridiculed their rural-provincial background and voiced deep concerns over their religious proclivities. The Irish were a staunchly Catholic people, a fact that rekindled old scares about a looming Roman takeover. "How is it possible," marveled Samuel F. B. Morse in 1838, "that riot and ignorance in hundreds of thousands of priest-controlled machines, should suddenly be thrown into our society, and not produce here turbulence and excess?" Since the transplanted Hibernians used to be ruled by bishops, the nativist inventor contended, "they form a body of men [who] cannot and do not think for themselves." Among the Protestant clergy, no love was lost for the Irish either. In William Ellery Channing's opinion, their faith was blatantly un-American: it wrested from worshippers "the right to choose their own ministers, and the right of election [was] the very essence of [American] institutions."[7]

Routinely maligned for their Catholicism, the Irish immigrants were equally scorned for taking jobs that most native-born whites found beneath their dignity. Often it was plain destitution that drove the Irish into these low-wage positions, and the few skills they possessed left them with little bargaining power. For their American critics, this was as much a racial problem as it was one of class. Propertyless, lazy, and hopelessly benighted Irish, they argued, were by no means incorporable into a republic of small producers and independent landholders. At a time when debates over citizenship had become increasingly steeped in racist thinking, theories identifying Celtic people as biologically inferior were on the rise. Even their whiteness was called into question. "*Low-browed* and *savage*, *grovelling* and *bestial*, *lazy* and *wild*, *simian* and *sensual*," David Roediger reiterates, "were the adjectives used by many native-born Americans to describe the Catholic Irish 'race' in the years before the Civil War." The Irish American experience reflects the curious mixture of acceptance and apprehension that non-Anglo-Saxon antebellum immigrants had to brave—acceptance, because they helped satiate the country's soaring demand for labor; apprehension, because they reputedly fell short in numerous criteria for republican citizenship.[8]

To some extent this situation was also what the arrivals from Germany encountered, albeit in a less drastic manner. The one and a half million German-speaking people entering the United States between 1840 and 1860 differed conspicuously from one another not only in regional origin but also in their occupational backgrounds, religious beliefs, and political views. German American communities sprawled from the mid-Atlantic states all the way to the midwestern frontier. Regions largely avoided were New England and the plantation South. Often it was the lack of readily available homesteads, the unfamiliar climate, and the presence of chattel slavery that kept German settlers at bay. Warnings to avoid southern lands resounded from immigrant guidebooks and travel accounts. "There is little bustling life in these states," diagnosed historian Franz von Löher after a trip to the Carolinas. "The territory is onerously and depressingly enshrouded by the curse of slavery." Contrary to the Irish, the Germans were perceived as more desirable immigrants. Many of them brought some material resources into the country and skills that were badly needed in a rapidly expanding market economy. Germans also purportedly worked hard, thereby fulfilling the main requirement of free labor, which, as Abraham Lincoln prominently termed it, ought to open "the way for all — [and give] hope to all, and energy, and progress, and improvement of condition to all."[9]

Race is another factor that helps to explain why German immigrants tended to enjoy greater social mobility in the United States than the Irish. Ethnologists propagating notions of white superiority often spoke of a shared tribal lineage connecting peoples of Anglo-Saxon and Teutonic descent. In many of their accounts, the idea of the freedom-loving American was traced back to ancient Germanic clans resisting the onslaught of a voracious Roman Empire. "Our American liberty," Kentucky newspaperman James D. Nourse postulated, "had its origins in the German forests." A similar sense of racial kinship flew from the pen of George Perkins Marsh, who used the old term *Gothic* to show how much Americans were indebted to Germanic traditions. Believing that the Germans and the Anglo-Saxons represented two branches of the same family, most native-born whites figured that German immigrants would coalesce more easily with the Anglo-American majority.[10]

This is not to suggest that native-born Americans did not keep a wary eye on these newcomers. More than one-third of the German arrivals were Catholics, a fact that caused almost as many qualms among Protestant Americans as in the case of the Irish. The *Ohio Republican*, a nativist paper, complained that workers of German lineage were driving "white people" out of the labor market. In a similar fashion, Whig and later Republican politicians outdid one another in disparaging Irish and German American electorates as "voting cattle." That the bulk of the foreign-born had entered into a lasting marriage with the Democrats, who welcomed them as additional voters, seemed to them a product not of deliberation but of political ignorance.[11]

More often, though, anti-immigrant spokesmen clothed their critique of German Americans in moral rather than racial garments. Nativists stood close to several of the Protestant reform initiatives of the day. Eager to perfect the lives of their countrymen, these reformers were deeply troubled by the spread of

"A German Beer Garden on Sunday Evening," *Harper's Weekly*, October 15, 1858. Caricatures such as these suggested immorality and mirrored native-born reformers' concerns over the social mores of the recent German immigrant generation.

foreign cultural habits that, they held, undermined the effort to build a morally sound Christian America. Singing, drinking, and public outings were central parts of German American social life, especially on Sundays. Protestant reformers rarely discerned in these spectacles more than a profanation of the Sabbath. One of their organs, the protemperance *New York Independent*, lashed out at the "propensity to beer-guzzling" that characterized "the entire mass of [immigrant] German citizens." Another paper, the *Cleveland Express*, attacked German singing societies because they aided "in the perpetuation of foreign clannishness" and consisted primarily of "so-called 'German liberals,' the Socialists, the antireligious, property-dividing, law-hating emigrants from Germany."[12]

The refugee intellectuals of 1848 and their adherents received the harshest bashing from the nativist camp. One major complaint was that these exiled democrats started meddling in national politics with little respect for prevailing norms of government and political organization. "Ignorant and presumptuous," an anonymous writer seethed, these radical foreigners "are not satisfied to adopt American views or learn the tendency of American institutions; but they bring forward all the exploded European heresies, and endeavor to make them current here." Tennessee Whig John Bell, addressing the Senate in 1852, described Old World ideas of democracy as based "upon abstractions" that defied "American, home-bred ideas of liberty." The most sweeping condemnation of European radicalism came from Thomas R. Whitney, one of the instigators of the xenophobic Know-Nothing movement. He labeled the refugees from Germany and adjacent countries a dangerous "class of aliens" who had "acquired an almost instinctive hostility to all government," and whose extravagant notions of freedom and equality made them incompetent "to administer the affairs of a nation." For Whitney and his allies, the Forty-Eighters were grandchildren of 1789, not 1776; the cow from which they drew their milk, Know-Nothings insisted, was Jacobinism, to many antebellum Americans the watchword for revolutionary terror.[13]

The chasm between the radicals from overseas and their critics grew wider when some of the former began expressing views that were either highly resentful of established religion or avowedly atheist. Trained in the philosophies of Kant, Hegel, and Feuerbach, these freethinkers portrayed the church as a hierarchical, thought-stifling institution that had helped both throne and police state crush the revolution. Anticlerical papers such as Friedrich Hassaurek's *Hochwächter* or Christian Esselen's *Atlantis* were particularly unforgiving: they made no distinction between the European clergy and American revivalists, branding both as rank hypocrites.[14]

This generalization did not go unrefuted. Henry Ward Beecher, the influential abolitionist preacher, was anything but an inveterate foe of the immigrant. "We thank Europe for a great deal — for literature, ancient and modern," Beecher conceded, "but when the Socialists of Germany, and the Communists of France . . . come to America to teach us how to make commonwealths we think they are out of place, decidedly." Across the country, English-language periodicals of various orientations objected to the religious skepticism of the exiled revolutionists. The *North American Review* praised their diligence and erudition but feared that "the irreligious influence of thousands of German infidels must be felt . . . by the children who [came] after them," observing, "That is a grave subject of meditation for the Christian patriot." Congressman H. M. Fuller saw his land flooded with foreign radicals who, "taught at home to repudiate everything to be revered in human institutions," had "already raised the black standard of atheism, and declared a war of extermination against the faith which supported [native-born Americans'] ancestors."[15]

Exaggerated as these grievances may sound, it would be wrong to depict the German American revolutionists as innocent victims of nativism. Here was a group of immigrants who rarely dealt gently with the perceived shortcomings of their host society. And when criticized, they fought back, usually with a vigor and self-righteousness tantamount to that of their opponents. The Turners, the leading Forty-Eighter organization in the United States, are a case in point. Like their counterparts back home, the paramilitary *Turnvereine* never served simply as gymnastic societies; especially the newer ones advocated a variety of controversial causes including socialism and free thought. In 1851, a national Turner association made its continued devotion to the left-wing ideals of 1848 explicit by adopting the name Socialist Turner Confederation (Sozialistischer Turnerbund). Its charters declared temperance and Sabbath laws undemocratic and called on members to act as "nurseries of revolutionary ideas" in order "to achieve freedom, prosperity, and education for all."[16]

With their white uniforms, parades, and marching banners, the Turners quickly made headlines in the American press. One sharp-tongued report appeared in the September 20, 1853, edition of the *New York Daily Times*. Its author, though not entirely dismissive of the foreign democrats, could not fathom why anybody should feel so averse to praying and moneymaking. "Such radicalism," he asserted, "has no root. It will never bear the atmosphere of common sense any long time." The response came promptly. "Never would it occur to us to reply to some English-language article on European philosophy since, as the old saying goes, 'there are no weapons against stupidity,'" fumed the editor of the *Turn-Zeitung*. Nonetheless, to fend off the allegations made in the *Times*, he felt obliged to reaffirm a central strand of Turner ideology: "Anglo-Saxon civilization, which measures the value of a human being only on the basis of income, in which outer appearance is everything, truth and honor nothing, leads to moral servitude, material slavery, and antisocial barbarity; it destroys all bonds of society, consolidates the monarchical principle, wherever it exists, and undermines the republic."[17]

Naturally, such statements did little to close the gap between native-born Americans and the revolutionaries from overseas. They instead reveal a mounting immigrant disaffection with conditions in the New World. Although the early 1850s were a time of overall growth, not all Americans had an equal share in it. Forty-Eighters witnessing xenophobic outbursts, evangelical frenzy, the plight of urban workers, and the cementation of southern slavery began wondering whether American liberty was a limited blessing or a mirage altogether. A feeling grew that coming ashore here had not ended their pursuit of freedom; it had merely transplanted it.

Against this backdrop, it is easy to imagine that refugee intellectuals like Friedrich Hecker or Gustav Struve sought to bring American society into closer agreement with their ideals of human progress. Politically and economically, they admitted, its liberal constitution put the country ahead of all European nations; socially and culturally, however, it still seemed very much a wasteland. "I would feel more comfortable here if there were more paintings, better drama, and less religion!" the German émigré journalist Ottilie Assing exclaimed in 1853. "This disgusting garlic smell and the stench of religion permeate all of life." The fruits of the American Revolution had all but withered; what was needed to revitalize them, according to Assing, was not Protestant austerity but European Enlightenment culture. Gustav Struve shared this appraisal, brazenly proposing that the Germans had the "historic mission" to carry the torch of secular humanism into America's bible- and market-driven society. "The invigorating breeze of freedom" that Struve and his fellow revolutionaries brought with them would "more and more enable [them] to throw [their] whole weight on the side of freedom in the fight against the despotic prohibition laws, nativist arrogance, religious intolerance and monkish fallacies." Struve bragged, "We can give a prelude here of what a German republic will look like, and not even the most stubborn Yankee can object to that."[18]

Such colonization fantasies were in no way confined to Assing and Struve. They gave meaning to the diasporic existences of many Forty-Eighter exiles and helped them come to grips with the question of how ethnic identities might be retained in a country demanding nothing less than total assimilation. Julius Fröbel wrestled extensively with this problem in his book on German emigration, published in 1858. His travels across the United States and Central America led him to believe that all efforts toward creating insulated "New Germanies" would fail. Likening the American continent to a gigantic social laboratory where the descendants of various European peoples were vying for supremacy, Fröbel urged educated Germans to join forces with Americans of similar intellect and persuasion. Only then could cultural traits that were uniquely "German" be preserved in a maelstrom of ethnic rivalry. Fröbel's pluralistic vision and his ideas about interethnic cooperation were reiterated by other Forty-Eighters as well. Christian Esselen advocated a "crossing of the best in all nations," whereas Friedrich Kapp posited that only a fusion of "German idealism with American realism" permitted men like him to intervene effectively in U.S. politics.[19]

Waving the banner of German culture in the heydays of Know-Nothingism obviously raised some eyebrows on the American side. To their dismay, the newly arrived radical democrats had to acknowledge that opposition was brewing among their conservative countrymen too. Many of the older German Americans had little or no sympathy for the missionary zeal of the newcomers. All they did, one pre-1848 immigrant grumbled, "was flood our cities, beg, lament, criticize, and gloat in a revolting way," thereby inviting nativist attacks against their people. This estimation was seconded by ethnic leader Gustav Körner, a liberal émigré of the 1830s who became one of Abraham Lincoln's closest confidants. Körner ascribed the anti-German protests of the 1850s explicitly "to the arrogance, imperious and domineering conduct of the refugees." Milwaukee's conservative German-language daily, the *Wisconsin Banner*, hurled an even nastier tirade at the émigré intellectuals, castigating them as "radical and irretrievable egoists." Here in America, they want to "reform radically, but as in Germany they stupidly want to plant the new tree without first preparing suitable soil."[20]

Not long after entering the United States, most Forty-Eighters found their expectations of finding true civic equality thwarted. Social inequities, political divisions, internal strife — all seemed to have followed them across the Atlantic. A young Carl Schurz described this predicament in an archetypal fashion. "The democrat just arrived from Europe," he wrote, "who has so far lived in a world of ideas and has had no opportunity to see these ideas put into actual, sound practice will ask himself, hesitatingly, Is this, indeed, a free people? Is this a real democracy? Is this my ideal?" These were questions that would become even more pressing in a confrontation that still lay ahead — one that drew the German-born refugees into proximity with a group of native-born Americans who had long been formulating their own blueprints for revolutionary change.[21]

Casting a Moral Net

By the end of the 1840s, America's abolitionists were split into numerous suborganizations and deeply divided over party politics, women's participation, and the role of blacks. Ironically, the accursed Fugitive Slave Law of 1850 served to reunite them. Passed as part of the compromise between southern slaveholding and northern antislavery interests, the Fugitive Slave Law was a modification of an earlier act passed in 1793 and comprised harsher measures to assist white masters in the recapture of runaway slaves, including the much-hated provision that any white citizen could be enlisted in the hunt and arrest of suspected blacks. What congressional delegates vindicated as a paradigm of realpolitik represented an unparalleled affront to abolitionists of all ranks, who vowed eternal resistance to the law. More importantly, it made them aware that the North had forfeited its cordon sanitaire that purportedly had been keeping the crime of slavery off its estate for so long. "The last year has forced us all into politics," Ralph Waldo Emerson affirmed in 1851, indicating that the country was sliding into a new and more practical phase of abolitionist agitation.[22]

Meanwhile, the search for converts to the abolitionist cause churned on with undying devotion. For once, the momentum seemed to be on the side of the slave: The arrival of federal "kidnappers" in northern cities and the dragging away of fugitive blacks led to demonstrations of defiance and civil disobedience. Political splinter groups committed to halting slavery's spread into the new territories such as the Free Soilers and the Conscience Whigs gained in popularity, nurtured by rising outrage over the perceived weakness of the federal government to block the extension of southern interests. Antislavery sentiment also infiltrated the country's Protestant churches, which by the beginning of the 1850s had splintered along sectional lines. Last, the inflow of European immigrants spelled trouble for the "peculiar institution." If settlement patterns are indicative, few immigrants seemed keen on supporting a planter class that associated work with servility and bondage with law and order. Who, therefore, was to say that cries for universal emancipation might not swell to a mass chorus that would purge the land of a legacy of inhumanity?[23]

Abolitionist leaders had good reasons to assume that the immigrant poor would link their own misery to that of the black slaves. Both groups were often denigrated by native-born whites. Both did America's hard work, almost always without proper compensation; both had experienced oppression and had to leave behind a homeland. Because of these analogies, expectations were rather high that those who had fled the autocratic regimes of the Old World would not exonerate slaveholder tyranny in the New. In this very spirit, the members of the American Anti-Slavery Society noticed as early as 1840 "a general passion of the Germans for liberty" and were optimistic that translated speeches and tracts would further diffuse abolitionist principles among their "countrymen who use[d] the German language." No less trust was initially placed in the goodwill of the Irish. On a visit to the green island in 1845, Frederick Douglass rejoiced at what appeared to him "a total abstinence of prejudice against [him], on account of [his] color." Together with fellow abolitionists, he adored the intrepid rhetoric of the Irish freedom fighter Daniel O'Connell. Three years earlier, O'Connell had famously orchestrated a petition in Ireland that called on Irish immigrants in America to "cling by the abolitionists" to end not only slavery but racial discrimination as well.[24]

The exultation was premature. Before long, abolitionists had to realize that O'Connell's pleas had achieved nothing; the great majority of Irish Americans would not enlist in the struggle against slavery. They seemed relatively at ease with the "peculiar institution" and were sternly opposed to treating blacks as equals. Identifications of blackness with evil and racist defenses of slavery had been part of Irish Catholic culture for centuries. But it was the concern for their

own social and racial status in republican America that transformed these stereotypes into vicious enemy images and made the Irish despise the country's free
black population to an almost unrivaled extent. Competition for jobs was definitely a factor; the precarious position of the unskilled immigrant brought him
into direct conflict with the African American wage laborer. Added to this explosive issue were racially charged vilifications of Irish workers as "white slaves"
or performers of "nigger work"; their drudging alongside black competitors, it
was held, devalued free white labor and blurred the line between what it meant
to be a free citizen and a member of those races unworthy of that description.[25]

To "become white" and be recognized as full members of the republic, the
Irish desperately tried to distance themselves from their black neighbors and the
self-declared friends of the African race — the abolitionists — if necessary, with
brute force. In the face of vicious Irish-dominated antiblack riots, voices maintaining that it was useless to continue sending apostles of interracial solidarity
into ethnic neighborhoods multiplied. "It is a most deplorable circumstance,"
William Lloyd Garrison, the patriarch of immediate abolition, lamented in
1845, "that religiously and politically, almost the entire body of the Irishmen in
this country are disposed to go with the accursed South for every purpose and
to any extent. They are a mighty obstacle in the way of negro emancipation on
our soil." Equally dejected, the Unitarian radical Theodore Parker stated in 1855,
"Not an Irish newspaper is on the side of . . . freedom."[26]

Some of Garrison's allies, however, were not content with just regretting the
circumstances. Enraged over the mounting assaults of the Irish against his fellow
African Americans, Frederick Douglass adopted a more resolute standpoint. A
people riddled with ignorance and bigotry like the Irish, the black leader insisted, should not be enfranchised. "Pat, fresh from Emerald Isle, requiring two
sober men to keep him on his legs," is permitted to the polls, Douglass ranted,
while the "colored man, the native born American, receives nothing." Not only
did lawmakers treat foreigners better than African Americans, but even more
scandalous, large portions of the foreign-born used their privileges to bolster
this system of inequality. "Now I am far from finding fault with the Irish for
coming to this country," Douglass declared in April 1849, "but I met with an
Irishman a few weeks ago [who] told me that it was his deliberate opinion that
the coloured people in this country could never rise here, and ought to go to
Africa. What I have to say to Ireland is, — send no more such children here!"[27]

Douglass's searing rebuke of the Irish points to a nativist undercurrent in
abolitionist thought that has often been overlooked. But what about the second
principal immigrant group of the time, the Germans? Anti-German remarks are
virtually absent from the abolitionist record because immigrants of that nation-

ality were seen as more susceptible to messages of universal freedom. White abolitionists' affinity for German coworkers had clear Anglo-Saxonist dimensions. Unlike the Irish, who had "never much favored . . . individual liberty," Theodore Parker thundered in the racialist language of his time, the Germanic peoples were endowed with "the strongest ethnological instinct for personal freedom." In addition to subscribing to the popular stereotype of the "hard-working, honest, good-humored, solid" Teuton, New England reformers had grown up in an intellectual milieu cherishing German literature and philosophy. Ralph Waldo Emerson and his transcendentalist friends spoke admirably of Johann Wolfgang von Goethe, and the giants of the German Enlightenment, Kant, Fichte, and Hegel, were gaining prominence in the curricula of Harvard and Yale.[28]

Abolitionists respected these thinkers. The one they lionized, however, was the explorer and naturalist Alexander von Humboldt. An outspoken critic of all forms of human bondage, Humboldt acquired a passionate dislike of black slavery during his expedition to the New World from 1799 to 1804. Yet it was not until 1856 that the German scholar vaulted onto the American national stage. John Sidney Thrasher, a southerner lobbying for the annexation of Cuba, had just published a translation of Humboldt's essay *The Island of Cuba* that left out the author's abolitionist views. Humboldt's protest against the corruption of his work was widely circulated; so was an interview for the *New York Evening Post* in which the eighty-five-year-old Humboldt chided Americans for having made no progress on the slavery question. "You have gone backward, very far backward in every respect. . . . In Europe you will also find bad things. But I tell you, you will not find anything half as bad as your system of slavery, and I know what slavery is like in your country." In 1859, the *National Anti-Slavery Standard* honored Humboldt posthumously. It dedicated two issues to the German humanist, reprinting some of his strongest criticisms of the "peculiar institution."[29]

The revolutionaries who fled to the United States after the traumatic events of 1848–49 partook in the same Enlightenment tradition as Humboldt did. Yet there were also European freedom fighters who completely washed their hands of abolitionism. Few were more sensitive to the hazards of emancipation talk than Father Theobald Mathew, the Irish Catholic temperance advocate whose signature had embellished Daniel O'Connell's abolitionist petition in 1842. During his two-year lecture tour through the United States beginning in 1849, Mathew refused to jeopardize his antiliquor mission by speaking out against slavery. Abolitionists were outraged. Hardly had the fury over Mathew receded when another prominent visitor entered the scene. Lajos Kossuth, the exiled Hungarian revolutionary, arrived in New York harbor on December 4, 1851. Americans were immediately enamored of the flashy Magyar independence leader and extolled his cause in a series of parades and lavish banquets. Excitement for the Old World revolutions flared up one last time as Kossuth continued his voyage to New England, the South, and the Midwest. Hoping to gain political as well as financial aid for Hungary's freedom, Kossuth thanked the crowds cheering him onward but, with the courtesy of a diplomat, repeatedly declared that he would "not meddle with any domestic concerns of the United States." This, of course, included slavery.[30]

For abolitionists, such behavior was perfect treason. Here was an icon of European freedom who seemed indifferent about the progress of freedom in other parts of the globe. Unable to contain his anger, Edmund Quincy, editor of the *National Anti-Slavery Standard*, called Kossuth's visit a "fatal blunder." The Hungarian had "sold himself" to the slaveholding party and had "stooped to kiss the feet of American women-whippers . . . and slave-catchers," whose cruelties made those conducted by the Russian czar look soft. A group of Philadelphia blacks felt the same way; they pledged to "hold up to the scorn of the civilized world that hypocrisy which welcomes to our shores the refugees from Austrian tyranny, and at the same time would send the refugees from American slavery back to a doom, compared with which, Austrian tyranny is mercy." Kossuth's failure to identify with fugitives of a darker hue also stands at the center of Garrison's 1852 *Letter to Kossuth*. This 112-page pamphlet, the longest of its kind, marked the high point of the abolitionist polemic against the Magyar leader. "How . . . could you expect to find neutral ground? to please alike the traffickers of human flesh, and those who execrate that traffic? . . . to skulk behind the flimsy subterfuge of foreign non-intervention?" Garrison fretted. In a transnational union for liberty, he lectured, there was nothing "sublimely heroic" about loving one's own nation. All that counted was "to be true to the principles of justice and humanity, on both sides of the Atlantic, in every land."[31]

The Kossuth affair revealed to many abolitionists how fragile and fractious the bonds with Europe's revolutionists were. Whereas native-born emancipators rejected any vision of self-determination that did not address black bondage, chattel slavery at first seemed a matter of little personal import to the Forty-Eighter democrats. Most were still very much engrossed in their own struggle for nationality and freedom, in the quarrels that had driven them from their homelands and that affected them here as an immigrant people. Was abolitionism, as historian Timothy Mason Roberts suggests, a "transatlantic cause that did not gain momentum"? Frederick Douglass was sure that in the light of the mounting crisis this parochialism would not last. "Entanglement is certain" was his message to the refugees from overseas. "We allow no man to enter here without conflict. He must show his hand, try his strength, prove his metal; and there's no escape."[32]

Unworthy of a Republic

For the early nineteenth-century liberal German intelligentsia, chattel slavery was a moral and political anachronism, a flagrant contradiction of the founding principles of a country they actually admired. The Hamburg scholar Christoph Daniel Ebeling branded the institution "barbarous" and supported its abolition. Carl von Rotteck, the most pro-American of all German Enlightenment jurists, stated that slavery deviated shamefully from the natural rights doctrines promulgated by the Declaration of Independence. The poet Heinrich Heine, a fierce critic of Old World politics, gave classic expression to the rising indignation over black slavery in these circles. How painful it was, he lamented, to feel obliged to advise his countrymen to "go to America" when "everyone there [was] equal, with the exception, of course, of several millions who [had] black or brown skins and [were] treated like dogs."[33]

Heine's condemnation of a system evoking the specter of European feudalism resonated strongly with the dissenters who came to the United States in the first half of the nineteenth century. For Charles Follen, a German political refugee of the 1820s who became involved in the Massachusetts Anti-Slavery Society, the battles against the aristocrats of the Old World and the slaveholders of the New World were fought for the same ideals. Similar outlooks prevailed among the standard-bearers of Forty-Eighter democracy. "If the friends of freedom are ready to do their duty" in the fight against slavery in the New World, Karl Heinzen predicted, "it will be a turning point towards a better future . . . not only for America, but for Europe as well." The socialist Turners, at their 1855 national convention in Buffalo, denounced the whole institution of bondage "as unworthy of a republic and directly opposed to the principles of freedom." Carl Schurz likewise viewed black emancipation in a broader scope. On the eve of Lincoln's election to the presidency, he portrayed the southern planters as hopelessly isolated in a world set in motion by the machinery of civilization: "You hear of emancipation in Russia, and wish it fail. You hear of Italy rising, and fear the spirit of liberty may become contagious." But this was "the world of the nineteenth century," Schurz thundered, and if even the despots of Asia had to yield to the irresistible march of progress by beginning to abolish slavery and serfdom in their domains, then the days when American slaveholders could defend their customs at the bar of history were surely numbered.[34]

Hostility to slavery figured as one among many interrelated concerns of a more broadly focused group of immigrant radicals, many of whom cared equally about a plethora of other revolutionary goals. Most found their way into one of the principal manifestos of German American radicalism prior to the Civil War. Following Heinzen's invitation, a delegation of about thirty freethinkers and labor activists convened in Louisville, Kentucky, in February 1854 to discuss steps toward establishing a German reform party. Their deliberations resulted in what became known as the Louisville Platform, which spelled out several key demands from the radical democratic lexicon: in addition to attacking the clergy, championing the interests of labor, and petitioning for quicker procedures to acquire citizenship, the delegates, more boldly, went on to debate the abolition of the presidency and demand equal rights for women. Slavery, of course, did not escape the drafters' scorn. They termed it "a political and moral cancer, that [would] by and by undermine all republicanism" and supported its "gradual extermination" by prohibiting its expansion into new territories. Furthermore, the platform condemned discrimination against free blacks in the North, asserting that "skin color cannot justify a difference of legal status." Because of internal frictions among the drafters, the envisaged party never came to be. Their declarations, however, held special resonance for Forty-Eighter radicals across the country until after the Civil War.[35]

With their humanistic aspirations, the authors of the Louisville Platform represented only a small fragment of the recent immigrant generation and the German American populace at large. Liberal and conservative commentators repudiated the Louisville stipulations as impractical or recklessly irresponsible, fearing that they would enhance, rather than decrease, the nativist menace. Though few German Americans defended slavery as a positive good, not many actively campaigned against it. The overwhelming majority centered their attention on issues that affected their lives more immediately. Foremost in their list of requests were fair wages, protection from Sabbath and temperance laws, local self-rule, and free land for those seeking their fortune farther west — policies with which German immigrants initially tended to entrust the Democratic Party. Black slavery mattered little in this equation. Cruel as it seemed, it was widely regarded as a sectional and therefore remote problem, with virtually no practical relevance for immigrant self-advancement. Why complain about the southern way of life when there was plenty of land to be had in the West?

This collective apathy disappeared almost overnight when Illinois Democrat Stephen A. Douglas introduced his Kansas-Nebraska bill to the Senate on January 4, 1854. The measure was much needed. Settlers were anxious to stream westward into the unorganized region, and plans for a transcontinental railroad were waiting to be realized. For a speedy organization of the Kansas and

Nebraska territories, Douglas had to make concessions to southern senators, on whose assent he depended. The bill passed both houses in May but now carried two controversial stipulations: first, the application of popular sovereignty, which held that it was the right of each community to choose its own domestic institutions, to the problem of slavery; second, the explicit repeal of the Missouri Compromise of 1820, which banned slavery north of the 36° 30′ latitude line in what was then the Louisiana Territory. A provision that further aroused passions (but was killed later) was the Clayton amendment. It would have denied foreign-born residents the right to vote or hold public office in the new territories.[36]

As foretold by Douglas, the Kansas-Nebraska Act raised "a hell of a storm" in American party politics. The bill, opponents charged, opened large parts of the public domain to southern interests, conjuring up a scenario in which the North found itself in the stranglehold of the cotton barons and their system of unfree labor. To avert the worst, the abolitionist *National Era* issued a fervent statement, "Appeal of the Independent Democrats in Congress to the People of the United States," which was reprinted in various northern newspapers. Salmon Chase, Charles Sumner, and Gerrit Smith were among the authors. Branding the Douglas bill "a criminal betrayal of precious rights," the appeal called on the citizens of the free states to unleash a storm of "protest, earnestly and emphatically, by correspondence, through the press, by memorials, by resolutions of public meetings and legislative bodies." Last, the authors implored "the enlightened conductors of newspapers printed in the German and other foreign languages to direct the attention of their readers to this important matter."[37]

The avalanche set off by the appeal grew faster and bigger than expected. Across the North, scores of indignation meetings took place, resulting in the demand for nothing less than the immediate withdrawal of the Kansas-Nebraska bill. German immigrants conducted formidable anti-Nebraska rallies of their own in New York, Philadelphia, Cleveland, Cincinnati, Indianapolis, Chicago, and other northern cities. In early February, Pittsburgh's Forty-Eighter newspapermen jointly proclaimed, "We are enemies of slavery, and consider all extension of it treason to mankind." On March 3, 1854, Josef Hartmann, editor of the *New Yorker Demokrat*, and labor leader J. A. Försch presided over one of the largest German anti-Nebraska gatherings at New York's Washington Hall, with a crowd of at least two thousand in attendance. Resolutions were adopted that labeled Senator Douglas's popular-sovereignty rhetoric "an insulting untruth, intended to deceive and betray the people," and declared every defender of his bill a friend of "those who would steal away the rights of the free North." Similar motions were carried two weeks later, on March 16, in Chicago, where German

Americans had assembled to defy the Nebraska measure. As had been the case elsewhere, the protesters saw in it "an ominous prophecy of further attacks on Northern liberty" and immigrant rights and contended that it was "high time to make war" against all ventures aiming "to increase the preponderance of the slaveholding interests in the Union." Such comments prompted the *Cincinnati Gazette* to report "that [the city's] German population [were] almost to a man opposed to the bill" and duped Horace Greeley into claiming that the Germans "feel . . . more deeply" about slavery "than the native citizens."[38]

The truth, however, proved far less flattering to the German Americans. Despite a palpable discontent with Douglas's policy, many German immigrants were hesitant to leave the Democratic fold and try their luck in new and untested coalitions. The most acrimonious split occurred along sectional lines. In 1855, the Charleston, Savannah, Augusta, Mobile, and New Orleans branches of the national Turner confederation withdrew because they could no longer identify with the organization's avowed opposition to slavery. Differences of religion and class played a crucial role as well. Whereas urban German workingmen were most likely to wave the anti-Nebraska flag, wealthy entrepreneurs and immigrants living in rural areas, most of them Catholics, largely stayed away from these rallies. For them, the antislavery and abolitionist measures proposed by their revolutionary countrymen bore the stamp of the kind of radical democratic ideology that also ranted against the uneven distribution of property and vilified the churches as tools of the powerful. "Maintenance of the Union!—Democracy vs. Abolitionism!" were slogans with which the *New Yorker Staats-Zeitung*, the chief organ of German American conservatism, entered the fray. It thus linked anti-Nebraska German immigrants to the disunionism and evangelical fanaticism commonly associated with native-born abolitionists, for many older immigrants the harbingers of chaos.[39]

Were such ascriptions justified? A closer look reveals that even within the German American anti-Nebraska camp motivations could be quite diverse. The broad coalition they comprised was divided by important ideological differences. Of eighty-eight German-language newspapers in the United States, eighty opposed Douglas's bill, while only a handful of them advocated a sharper response. The most militant protests emerged from the radical plebeian milieu and the intellectuals associated with it. Their speeches and resolutions mocked attempts to pacify the "slave barons" and often declared solidarity with the slaves. A stronger, more mainstream current arose from the ranks of German American liberalism, led mainly by established middle-class immigrants who objected to the Nebraska bill but also hoped to restore the sectional peace of earlier decades. Reopening the slavery issue, they feared, could ignite the fuse to the powder keg that would blow the country apart. As partisan politics deepened, some German Americans returned to the Democratic Party, while others joined the Republicans.[40]

The small but strident group of Forty-Eighter democrats who harbored abolitionist beliefs and subscribed to the Louisville Platform usually framed their opposition to the Kansas-Nebraska Act around a strong enmity toward slavery as such. German left-wingers readily evoked their European past to warn against vacillators who believed in tempering northern attitudes toward slavery to appease their slaveholding countrymen. If the southern planters and their allies in the Democratic Party called to mind the European counterrevolution, then northern compromisers seemed like a reincarnation of Frankfurt's inept liberal majority. Seeing the signs of a gathering storm, as had been the case in 1848, German radicals fought hard to sharpen the nascent Republican Party's antislavery planks. Labor leaders Victor Pelz and Peter Rödel called for completing the work begun in 1776 and 1848, thereby turning this country into "a free democratic republic" where "slaveholders [would] brandish no whips" nor would they break up any more families on the auction block. Ottilie Assing favored total emancipation and considered it a shame that many Germans in the United States were "loyal Democrats who [were] outspoken in their support of slavery, and that others [took] a thoroughly passive attitude."[41]

What Assing referred to as "passive" was indeed the customary outlook of the greater portion of the German anti-Nebraska and Republican constituencies. Most voiced their indignation over Douglas's bill not out of a sudden urge to carry freedom southward but because they wanted to make sure that the West remained free from southern influence. Like the average northern protester, they adhered to the notion promulgated by the slaveholder Thomas Jefferson that white yeomen were the mainstay of a healthy republican society. The civic traits they embodied — honesty, industry, independence — dovetailed nicely with the popular idea that America was the place where every white man could escape permanent dependency by hard work. Slavery belied this free-labor ideal. Equating labor with servitude, it could not coexist with a society that regarded labor as the ticket to the economic autonomy of self-employed craftwork or free farming. The Kansas-Nebraska Act, its critics argued, ignored this basic insight. By theoretically sanctioning the introduction of slave labor into the two territories, it not only insulted the dignity of those toiling for their own improvement. Worse, it also moved the white laborer outrageously close to his black counterpart and the nightmare of chattel slavery for which he stood.[42]

Hence antislavery, free-soil, and antiblack sentiments conflated rather smoothly in the mass protests against the Nebraska bill. A racist system was fought with racist arguments, and German Americans proved no exception to this rule. Paramount to the dislike of slavery was the white farmer's fear that by tilling next to black slaves he might ultimately be mistaken for one. Consequently, most German American free-soilers found nothing hideous about homestead initiatives welcoming only "free white persons" to vacant public lands. Keeping slavery out of the territories, the *Baltimore Wecker* emphasized, was first and foremost about "white development." What really mattered, it affirmed, was not black emancipation but making sure "that the black race would not be allowed to expand further at the expense of the white race." Doing nothing to stop the influx of "ignorant, savage Africans" from the South, Friedrich Hecker augured, magnified the threat of a slave revolt that could turn out far bloodier than the fearsome Haitian revolution. Horrified by the prospect of racial assimilation, the *Mississippi Blätter* in St. Louis warned as late as 1859: "If the system of slavery and the black race with it spread even wider across the continent, then . . . this only works to speed up amalgamation and the demonstrated result of a mongrel race."[43]

Statements like these give an idea of the extent to which antislavery German immigrants had begun appropriating the languages of scientific racism and white supremacy, and how they used them for their own purposes. Rather than simply object to slavery's expansion, most German Americans presented their assessment of the institution in a way calculated to make them acceptable citizens in the eyes of native-born whites. In addition to respecting the Fugitive Slave Law, this meant subscribing to the tenets of white free-labor republicanism as well as learning to eschew those who challenged its racial boundaries. "We have nothing in common with the abolitionists," avowed the anti-Nebraska *Philadelphia Demokrat*, "but we stick fervently to Jeffersonian democracy and the Constitution of the United States."[44] The keenness of the moderate German Republicans to become part of the dominant Anglo-northern discourse on race made it harder for the radicals to persuade their countrymen to embrace a color-blind version of democracy. Cleveland Forty-Eighter Jacob Müller grudgingly acknowledged this. "Unfortunately," he recalled in his autobiography,

> there were more than a few among our more ill-educated German compatriots . . . who were of the barbaric conviction that Negroes were more closely related to the apes than to humans, that they even had remnants of an ape's tail. One of these German physiologues, Georg L. the cooper, a man who was otherwise splendid, gave drastic expression to this view in a German assembly in Nägele's Hall. August Thieme presented an excellent German address disproving the theory concerning Negroes and apes, which was shown to be the perfidious inven-

tion of pro-slavery politicians intended to mislead the ignorant. The speech made an overwhelming impact on the audience, but no sooner from the mouth of our master cooper, looming over the crowd: "*Niggers do too have tails.*" There was involuntary laughter — the impact of the speech was lost.[45]

Black Presences

That the abolitionist views of certain left-leaning German émigrés provided a striking counterpoint to those of the masses of native- and foreign-born whites did not go unappreciated in the African American community. As early as 1851, a society of free blacks in Cleveland showed their sympathies and offered "material aid" for the cause of German freedom, to which grateful Forty-Eighters in that city replied, "The German people, as soon as they shall have obtained the Democratic republic in the coming struggle, [will] use all means which are available to abolish slavery, an institution which is so wholly repugnant to the principles of true democracy."[46]

Support for the radical democratic refugees from Germany and elsewhere also arose from other black quarters. At their 1852 state convention, Ohio's African Americans passed a resolution stating, "Tyranny in Russia, Austria, and America is the same . . . and therefore the Russian serf, the Hungarian Peasant, the American slave and all other oppressed people, should unite against tyrants and despotism." Viewing the Forty-Eighter exiles as heaven-sent partners in their own pilgrimage to self-determination, black intellectuals developed a great interest in the newcomers. Among the most Germanophile African Americans was Frederick Douglass, who famously proclaimed, "A German has only to be a German to be utterly opposed to slavery." Douglass later qualified his statement, hailing "the many noble and high-minded men, most of whom, swept over by the tide of the revolution in 1849, [had] become [African Americans'] active allies in the struggle against oppression and prejudice." Physician James McCune Smith shared Douglass's enthusiasm for the recent German-immigrant generation. In one of his editorials, Smith portrayed them as a thrifty and law-abiding people and expressed the hope that, unlike the Irish, they would not "sleep on, nor lie dumb" to the sound of the slaveholder's lash. Apparently, Smith saw some encouraging signs, for in July 1861 he urged his black countrymen to learn the German language. "The German immigrants, are for the most part, a liberty-loving, caste-despising people," Smith asserted, "and they will trade and deal more readily with those who speak their own language."[47]

However, few German Americans were eager to have regular social intercourse with black people. Even inside the radical democratic milieu, only a handful of activists fraternized openly with African Americans or treated them as equals. Widely known is Ottilie Assing's romantic liaison with Frederick Douglass and the profound intercultural dialogue on slavery and freedom it engendered. Less known but no less astounding are instances of intermarriage that purportedly occurred between African Americans and German immigrants in antebellum Buffalo. Such relationships, however, were rather singular and represent an aberration in immigrant dealings with black Americans prior to the Civil War. Historian Hartmut Keil makes a similar point: even though German American intellectuals largely "condemned the principle of enslavement as inhuman," they "did not meet African Americans on an everyday matter-of-fact basis except in rare instances."[48]

Yet debates over the future of people of African descent on American soil proved difficult to sidestep if one hoped that slavery would eventually vanish. Deeply imbued in the Enlightenment optimism that history was moving to some better future, Forty-Eighter scholars essentially subscribed to the theory that disadvantaged races could realize their capacities under proper guardianship. What ignited controversy was the question whether blacks would one day reach a stage in their evolution that would allow them to stand on equal footing with whites. Julius Fröbel was decidedly negative on this point. Rejecting interpretations that cast Africans out of the family of human beings, he postulated nonetheless "that the negro race incontrovertibly [held] a position below that of the white race." To prove his point, Fröbel recited several fashionable racist arguments. That the black body carried less aesthetic value than the white one, he remarked, was evinced by the fact "that every negro or mulatto woman would feel honored if she had sexual intercourse with a white man, whereas the opposite never [held] true." Intellectually, blacks seemed just as subordinate for Fröbel, who claimed that people of color had yet to prove that they could ascend to the higher realms of culture. Finally, Fröbel took the political situation as evidence for black inferiority. "Had [the Africans] commanded greater intelligence and entrepreneurship," he contended, "they never would have been forced into slavery."[49]

Another major skeptic concerning the prospects of black development was the Forty-Eighter journalist Gustav Struve. His qualms, though, were not so much scientifically as politically motivated. Troubled by anti-immigrant writers claiming that not all whites were fit for civic participation, Struve replied that they were. Speaking in the racialized language of his opponents, he chided nativists for neglecting the European origins of the republic they sought to sustain. America had always been the project of a common "indocaucasian race," and Struve considered it a dangerous folly to lump the newly arrived immigrant and the ostracized black worker together in a universal outsider caste. Such a policy would not avert but rather hasten a deadly race war that the constant inflow of Europeans actually helped to prevent. Immigration, Struve emphasized, was the seminal question of the age; it would decide whether the country preferred "freedom or slavery, progress or stagnation, the Caucasian or the African element." Struve's fear of racial antagonisms elucidates that shared oppression did not automatically generate interracial solidarity. Rather than challenge white supremacist ideas, some émigrés came to reproduce them, conceiving them as an indispensable tool for promoting their interests in an increasingly race-conscious society.[50]

On the other hand, there were also German-born intellectuals whose democratic convictions did translate into sincere egalitarian attitudes. Christian Esselen regularly discussed in his *Atlantis* theories from the nascent field of ethnology, and more than once he grappled with scientists favoring a biologically fixed hierarchy of races. Even if there were racial differences, for Esselen they were always in flux and remained secondary to advancing human rights. Ottilie Assing, Germany's self-anointed "Negro expert," thought likewise. Entering America as a half-Jewish German woman, she soon discovered parallels between her own quest for self-assertion and the survival tactics employed by the northern free black community. With special empathy, Assing could write about African Americans as a downtrodden but decent people who, despite ongoing maltreatment, had not lost faith in a better tomorrow. "Almost without exception they are endowed with a kind and cheerful disposition, and the least Negro possesses a natural politeness and friendliness that is as far from servility as it is from importunity," she noted, trying to correct pervasive antiblack stereotypes among whites. Though Assing often resorted to typical nineteenth-century racial idioms in her journalism, her experience of belonging to an ostracized minority in Europe helped her espouse the cause of black Americans, sometimes with more ardor than native-born abolitionists.[51]

From Struve's negrophobia to Assing's will to assist, the tracts of the German American refugees of 1848 offer a broad spectrum of beliefs, ideas, and assessments on the subjects of race and African American uplift. Some held evolutionary beliefs; others clung to essentialist models of racial difference. The interest of these émigrés in slavery is palpable; yet their reluctance to approach the "negro problem" unambiguously shows that most Forty-Eighters were never fully able to divorce their democratic ideals from the larger social environment. As long as they felt secure in their self-styled role as heralds of revolutionary change, they could be truly roused by the plight of those kept in bondage. But as soon as they sensed competition, either from people openly challenging them or from those who seemed too alien, these same intellectuals could easily adopt an ethnocentrist position that left little room for the realms of cultural otherness inhabited by America's non-European peoples.

Given these limitations, one may wonder why black leaders like Frederick Douglass or James McCune Smith held the Old World democrats in such high esteem. Was it merely an opportunistic call for allies? Or did black intellectuals of the Douglass and Smith type compliment the expatriates not so much for what they were as for what they appeared to be in comparison to their racist white countrymen? African Americans who chanced to cross the Atlantic in the antebellum period often described their trips as liberating sojourns; the overall friendly reception and the absence of a strict color line in liberal European circles contrasted vividly with America's institutionalized racism. Experiences like these certainly bred expectations in the black community that the more enlightened segments of the immigrant populace might bring samples of this racial tolerance to America. Despite its obvious pitfalls, this "European dream" never died and lingered on in the black mind long after emancipation.[52]

Different groups pressed for the outlawing of slavery for different reasons and in different, sometimes conflicting ways. As factional and sectional strife intensified, some of these abolitionist agitators reached across the racial and cultural boundaries of their time and began cooperating for the most basic goal that held them together: ending slavery. In many cases, these collaborations persisted into the period of the Republican Party's rise to power and the outbreak of the Civil War. That the partners in this interethnic alliance came from different backgrounds and harbored different convictions, though, remained evident, both in the late 1850s and afterward.

CHAPTER TWO

A Firm Phalanx of Iron Souls

Free Men on Texas Soil

Ah, my dear Doctor, with how much greater cordiality and
satisfaction can I give the right hand of political fraternity to you
and hundreds of other foreign-born citizens of America who from
their own free choice, from love of Liberty and hatred of Slavery,
have become Americans than to those narrow-minded, bigoted,
slave-hearted, "poisoning" conspirators.

—FREDERICK LAW OLMSTED to ADOLF DOUAI, December 1, 1854

We came here with a firm determination to hold on to our
principles and to our contentions of right.

—FRIEDRICH KAPP, *New York Daily Times*, August 22, 1856

UNTIL THE WAR, most antislavery northerners never had any firsthand encounters
with the slaveholding South. Their critiques of the "peculiar institution" more
often stemmed from abstract beliefs than from concrete experience. Frederick
Law Olmsted, for one, was too much of an empiricist to rely on book learning alone. Born and raised as the son of a Connecticut merchant, Olmsted was
intimately familiar with the reform movements of his day and cultivated close
ties to New England's intellectual elite. Although sympathetic to many causes,
including emancipation, Olmsted was no zealot. Discussions with William
Lloyd Garrison and his lifelong friend Charles Loring Brace about the moral
imperative of immediate abolition had not convinced him in favor of abolition.
Olmsted, taken with the issue nevertheless, wanted to see for himself. In the
summer of 1852, he answered the call of Henry Raymond, chief editor of the
New York Daily Times, and traveled south to report on the ways and workings
of a slave society.[1]

The second of his three journeys through the South took Olmsted, who was
accompanied by his brother, John, as far as the outer rims of settlement in Texas.
Up to this point, Olmsted's portrayal of the country had been predominantly

one of utter dullness and desolation. The few grand mansions owned by affluent planters seemed worlds apart from the crowded slave quarters and shabby huts of the nonslaveholding white population. Shocked by this "unambitious, indolent, degraded, and illiterate" class of poor southern whites, Olmsted was all the more excited when he came across a different sort of nonslaveholding people during his Texas sojourn.[2]

"The country has a great deal of natural beauty," Olmsted wrote home in early 1854, "and we have fallen among a German population very agreeable to meet: free-thinking, cultivated, brave men." This is how Olmsted referred to a group of German-born immigrants who had settled in what is geographically central but was then called western Texas, in and around the towns of Sisterdale, Fredericksburg, and Neu Braunfels. German immigration to Texas began in the 1830s, but in 1842 it received a major boost. A faction of petty noblemen founded the Adelsverein, an organization that transported thousands of Germans, mostly peasants from Hesse, Nassau, Brunswick, southern Hannover, and western Thuringia, to the new land. The incentives for going to Texas were manifold, yet many of the first settlers were lured by the image of Texas as a land of plenty, a region of everlasting sunshine and abundant crops. Already in 1835, Hermann Achenbach, one of the first German pioneers, rejoiced at the vegetables of all kinds that could be reaped from the soil of this "new Canaan." Twenty years later — the state had won its independence from Mexico and joined the Union — hardly any traces of the aristocratic origins of German Texas were left. The Adelsverein had gone bankrupt, making room for an expanding and increasingly heterogeneous immigrant society that, after initial hardships, became well established.[3]

A Southern Counterculture

Historians, when debating the social configuration of the German Texans and their relationship to other ethnicities in the region, often pass lightly over the fact that there was no single German Texas. Rather than revolving around a center, German-speaking settlers spread out across different counties, clustering in scattered ethnic islands. The first waves brought various representatives of the middle classes to Texas: merchants, speculators, and university-educated professionals. As the numbers soared, the stream of migrants became more diverse, both socially and denominationally. Protestants found themselves living next door to Catholics and Jews, and the dialects spoken ranged from Saxon and Westphalian to Hessian and Alsatian. Most families tilled small plots of land, but there were also more prosperous landowners as well as artisans and shopkeepers who set up businesses in the nearby towns of San Antonio and Neu Braunfels. Generational and political differences played an important role too. Not many commonalities existed between the older, more conservative immigrant population and the few but highly politicized refugees who had chosen Texas as their exile after the failed revolutions of 1848–49.[4]

It was this last group that Olmsted spoke about so fondly. Well read and erudite, the revolutionaries from the Old World seemed like a pleasant diversion from the intellectual monotony that the Olmsteds had experienced thus far on their trip. One of their favorite discoveries was the small Forty-Eighter community near Sisterdale, where the Olmsted brothers spent a few days in the company of several exiled scholars and liberals, among them August Siemering, Ernst Kapp, and Eduard Degener. Olmsted's admiration for these men was enormous. Nowhere else, he wrote, could one "hear teamsters with their cattle staked around them on the prairie, humming airs from 'Don Giovanni,' or repeating passages from Dante and Schiller." Never before had the New Englander met a people "who earn their daily bread by splitting shingles" and with whom he could "engage in discussions of the deepest and most metaphysical subjects." Olmsted's voice rose to a crescendo as he reviewed their political biographies: "What have not these men lost — voluntarily resigned — that mean and depraved and wicked souls are most devout to gain. And for what? For the good of their fellow men — they had nothing else to gain by it. For their convictions of truth and justice. Under orders of their conscience. In faithfulness to their intellect. And they have failed in every earthly purpose, but are not cast down — are not unhappy. What shall we think of those from whom life was also taken — who as cheerfully and bravely gave their life also?"[5]

The romanticized image that Olmsted drew of these German-born farmer-intellectuals on the Texas frontier casts light on his social and political beliefs. Olmsted had been a Teutophile and intrigued by European liberalism ever since he and Brace had tramped up the Rhine in 1850. They passed through old townships, mingled with local peasants, beheld the ruins of medieval castles, and paid homage to Goethe's birthplace in Frankfurt. In expressing their enchantment with romantic Germany, Olmsted and his companion partook in a ritual of cultural and intellectual affirmation characteristic of nineteenth-century American overseas travel. Writing with sophistication about foreign lands was seen as a white — predominantly male — elite prerogative marking a person's entrance into the sphere of belles lettres and his admittance to the polite classes.[6]

But even more significant to Olmsted was the way in which the exiled revolutionaries who had wound up in central Texas intervened in the antebellum controversy over free and slave labor. Olmsted, while staying aloof from radical abolitionism, was convinced that free-labor capitalism was in every aspect supe-

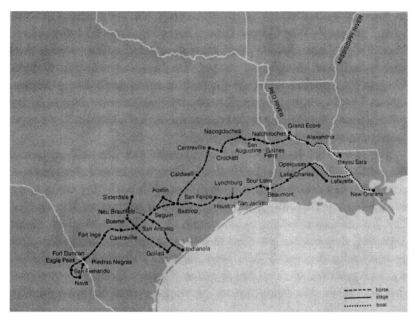

Olmsted's journey through Texas, 1854 (Beveridge et. al, eds., *Papers of Frederick Law Olmsted*, vol. 2: *Slavery and the South, 1852–1857*, 296; © 1981 The Johns Hopkins University Press. Reprinted with permission of The Johns Hopkins University Press). Most of the free-labor farmers whom Olmsted encountered during his Texas sojourn settled in the "German triangle," whose three points were Neu Braunfels, Sisterdale, and Boerne.

rior to an economy based on slave labor. His tours through North America and central Europe, where he observed the causes and effects of 1848, had broadened his identification with liberal reform and democratic nation building. The materials he gathered en route reinforced his belief that free-labor societies were not only more profitable but also offered the basic ingredients of civilization — schools, libraries, lyceums, businesses — which the laboring classes of unfree Europe and the slaveholding South widely lacked.[7]

How, then, did the German Texans differ from the Anglo-southern mainstream? Like their English-speaking neighbors, they invested most of their resources in cotton growing and other agricultural pursuits. But while slave labor was a common sight on the Anglo-Texan estates, the Germans, Olmsted noted, tilled, sowed, and brought in the harvest with their own hands, and they seemed to do so with greater efficiency than the slaves. During his stay in Neu Braunfels, Olmsted "saw no other negroes in town" except one young domestic servant and concluded that he had located an antislavery enclave in the middle of slave country. Yet Olmsted's view that slavery was virtually nonexistent where the Germans had settled was not entirely accurate, and his narrative of freedom-loving, nonslaveholding German farmers has to be taken with a grain of salt. Most of these farmers lived in places where there were few slaves anyway. There were indeed some, though comparatively few, German-speaking slaveholders. German Texan public opinion was also far from united on the slavery question. Olmsted, on the contrary, repeatedly crossed the line between ethnography and political journalism, helping to disseminate the myth of a German Texan population unanimously opposed to slavery.[8]

On his way back north, Olmsted corresponded with Charles Riotte, one of the political refugees he had befriended in Texas. Riotte wrote about dramatic events that had come to pass since the Olmsteds had left. The source of the commotion was a meeting that took place in San Antonio on May 14, 1854. The Sisterdale Free Society, an association of freethinkers in which Riotte, Siemering, Degener, and the other exiles were active, convened to discuss aspects related to democratic life in Texas. Some 120 of them adopted a platform containing a direct assault on the institution of slavery. Though fully aware that they were taking up a delicate matter, the delegates stated that slavery was "an evil, the abolition of which" was "a requirement of democratic principles." To couch their protest in constitutional language, they hastily added that the federal government should "abstain from all interference in the question of slavery," but "if a state resolve[d] upon the abolition of the evil, such state [might] claim the assistance of the federal government."[9]

This and the other resolutions propagating educational programs, workers' rights, and opposition to established religion were published in Adolf Douai's *San Antonio Zeitung*. Douai, like most attendants of the meeting, was a Forty-Eighter who had been forced to leave his homeland because of his radical views. At the time of his departure, Douai could already look back on a rich and erratic life. His work as a teacher had taken him from Thuringia, the land of his birth, to eastern Prussia and the Baltic region, where he tutored the children of Russian noblemen. Lobbying for a more democratic and socially progressive educational system, Douai joined the revolutionary movement and participated in a series of subversive activities in early 1848 that resulted in charges of high treason on at least five different occasions. Eventually he was jailed and driven into exile. Now radicalism was once more the charge brought against Douai and his fellow revolutionaries. To the ears of conservative German and Anglo-Texans, the San Antonio platform sounded inflammatory, and they condemned it as an attack on the existing social and political order. The outrage focused on Douai and his paper. Both remained at the center of the storm in the months ahead.[10]

The San Antonio convention was no isolated incident but the local expression of a larger movement that commenced with the founding of the national German American freethinkers' association, the Society of Freemen, in late 1853. It was the same organization whose delegates, on February 19, 1854, drafted the Louisville Platform, which proclaimed that slavery was an evil that ought to be abolished and demanded equal rights for free blacks. Printed in various left-leaning German American newspapers, the platform soon trickled into German Texan public consciousness. Its impact on the San Antonio resolutions becomes evident in August Siemering's statement that, though "the Louisville Platform had defects," it set an example worth following. "Let us unite in all our strength" was Ernst Kapp's and Siemering's call to action, "and then with our congenial American fellow-citizens about the principles which will be the basis of our next activity." Clearly, Siemering and Kapp hoped to fashion themselves as reliable partners for like-minded English-speaking activists. In the case of Adolf Douai and his newspaper, this fashioning became a matter of survival.[11]

The Olmsteds and Douai felt close to each other immediately. On the road from San Antonio to Sisterdale, they began exchanging views on various topics from history, philosophy, and literature. Each found pleasure in the other's erudition. "We listened to some details of a varied and stormy life," Olmsted recorded, "and were not long in falling into discussions that ran through deep water, and demanded all our skill in navigation." Olmsted, who knew some German, also had kind words to say about Douai's journalism. He thought that the *San Antonio Zeitung* was a superb newspaper, asserting that it "contained more news of matters of general interest than all the American Texan papers [he] had come across." The paper's progressive stance — Douai subtitled it a "social-democratic paper for the Germans in Western Texas" — appealed to the New Englander. Olmsted, who proudly applied to himself the label "Socialist Democrat," drew from his observations of European and American working populations the belief that society had a responsibility to uplift the lower classes. Much of this ideology resounded in the *San Antonio Zeitung*, whose editor seemed to have forfeited nothing of the commitment to social improvement that had guided his actions in revolutionary Germany. "I never saw a man more cheerful," Olmsted said of Douai, "and full of boundless hopes and aspirations for the elevation of all mankind (including Africans)."[12]

Aid from the North

The pressure on Douai mounted considerably during the summer of 1854. A boycott against the *San Antonio Zeitung* headed by conservative settlers was gaining momentum: subscriptions declined and merchants withdrew their advertisements. Unsettled by these developments, the stockholders of the *Zeitung* split and decided to sell the paper. Initially it was not the proslavery Anglo-Texans but the older immigrant establishment that was most vocal in the outcry against Douai. Not long after the San Antonio convention, some of them distanced themselves in public meetings from the abolitionist rhetoric coming from the Society of Freemen. Trying to appease wary southerners, they declared that the bulk of the German population in Texas had absolutely no intention of challenging the institution of slavery. Most Germans living in the Lone Star State, they pledged, were law-abiding citizens and wanted good relations with their English-speaking neighbors; they did not want to upset them like the "very few active fanatics" who had drafted the San Antonio platform.[13]

These and other accusations, however, seemed to have little effect on Douai. Despite financial setbacks and even threats to lynch him, he held on to his editorship. Friends eventually assisted him in buying the *San Antonio Zeitung* so that he could continue to bring his views on slavery and democracy before the public. One of these friends was Frederick Law Olmsted.

Apparently, Olmsted had been toying for some time with the idea of joining the efforts of the German Texan democrats; in an early letter to Riotte, he offered his service to the cause. Douai replied on September 4, informing the Olmsted brothers more fully of his situation. Moreover, Douai used the occasion to lay out some of his ideas on how to establish a free-soil state in Texas. While Riotte and Degener suggested bringing more European and northern antislavery settlers to the region so as to ultimately outvote the proslavery party, Douai stressed the importance of public education. Even though the Anglo-southerners were superior in numbers, Douai argued, the nonslaveholding majority, if properly instructed, might soon "find out how different . . . their interests [were] from those of the slaveholders." For this purpose, the *San Antonio Zeitung* had to be sustained and transformed into a bilingual organ that could win over English speakers as well.[14]

Olmsted's reaction was swift and decisive. To provide financial aid, he went on a fundraising tour that brought in a considerable part of the money Douai needed to purchase the *Zeitung*. Among those contributing to the cause, as either donors or subscribers, were Henry Ward Beecher, Theodore Parker, Ralph Waldo Emerson, and Charles Loring Brace. In a second step, the Olmsted brothers, approving of Douai's plan to publish some pieces in English, assisted him in getting English type for his newspaper. Finally, Olmsted also acted on Riotte's advice. In the winter of 1854/55, he penned a series of articles for the *New York Times* and inspired others for the *New York Tribune* and the *Hartford*

Courant highlighting the free-labor achievements of the German Texans and recommending Texas as a place for settlement.[15]

Before long, word of the ongoing struggle in Texas reached the abolitionist community in the North. The *Anti-Slavery Bugle* in Salem, Ohio, applauded the *San Antonio Zeitung* for its journalistic courage and denounced the Anglo-southern press for trying to silence it. Three weeks later, the same newspaper speculated that the days of slavery in Texas were numbered thanks to the steady influx of liberal foreigners. The *National Anti-Slavery Standard* shared this hope as well as the conviction that the "European settlers in North-western Texas [were], to a man . . . opposed to slavery." Expressions of solidarity also came from the 1855 convention of the Radical Political Abolitionists, who regarded "the German settlers in Texas . . . who [were] cultivating the soil by their own free labor as especially deserving [their] approbation."[16]

Two individuals, however, took more than just a general interest in the developments in Texas. Charles Loring Brace, Olmsted's old schoolmate, who was an Episcopalian reformer and an abolitionist of the more passionate sort, closely followed his friend's observations down South. Stimulated by their correspondence as well as the *New York Times* articles, he submitted a piece of his own about free-labor farming among the German Texans to the *National Anti-Slavery Standard*, thereby helping to bring the issue before a larger abolitionist public. Brace was widely known as an expert on contemporary Germany, Austria, and Hungary; he had earned this reputation while traveling these countries in the early 1850s, an experience that included a brief term in a Hungarian prison for alleged connections to revolutionary circles. Brace wrote two books on his European sojourn, *Hungary in 1851* and *Home-Life in Germany*. In the latter, he gives a favorable account of the social customs of the Germans, characterizing them as a warmhearted and genial people. Evidently it was this same geniality that Brace rediscovered in Olmsted's reports from central Texas, and which, together with his abolitionist convictions, induced him to take an active part in the emerging free-soil operation.[17]

Another protagonist in the campaign was Ernst Kapp's nephew, Friedrich Kapp, a trained lawyer and political refugee who had relocated to New York, where he became one of the most prolific German American writers. His main field was history, and slavery was one of his preferred subjects. Kapp had witnessed the proceedings of Germany's first elected national assembly at the Frankfurt Paulskirche as a young and combative journalist. Aligning himself with the democratic Left, he was appointed secretary of its parliamentary faction. After the reactionaries had regained control, Kapp fled to Brussels and Paris. In 1850, disenchanted by the outcome of the European insurgencies, he reached the United States, the final destination of his odyssey into exile. Kapp joined the antislavery efforts of Olmsted, Douai, and Brace in January 1855. He had just published a book-length treatment of the history of slavery in the United States, which Olmsted reviewed favorably for an American readership. Olmsted was also present at a lecture on the history of the German Texans that Kapp gave and heard his statement that with their free-labor agriculture the Germans had been quietly laying the foundations for a free state in Texas. Kapp had visited the German settlements on the southwestern frontier in 1852, and like Olmsted he was delighted to find a significant number of his more educated countrymen — a stronghold of revolutionary freethinkers. Responding to nativist qualms, Kapp told the American reform community that it need not fear the newcomers. Slavery, he argued, could be prevented from expanding further with, but never without, those immigrants "fighting in the front ranks in common with those who, in this country, [were] defending the most liberal principles and highest interests."[18]

Free Tillers of Their Own Soil

The formation of a transregional coalition of German American and native-born intellectuals under the banner of free labor indicates that the activities of the German Texan refugees eclipsed the stage of local affairs. For northern observers, but increasingly for southern ones as well, Texas became another battleground in the greater national standoff between two different systems of labor. In this ideological contest, moral and pragmatic arguments often blended into each other. As Eric Foner notes in his seminal study on free labor, this ideology was especially strong in the dynamic, expansive, and capitalist society of the antebellum North. Rather than define what came to be known as the industrial working class, wage labor was seen as a temporary state for the individual striving to rise beyond the burdens of the moment. Lighting the way to material success and social importance, this ideology appealed to a diverse constituency of white lower- and middle-class Americans. To these groups, free labor held out the promise of escaping one's original social position, and because of that they viewed the United States as fundamentally better than the rest of the world.[19]

From the standpoint of a free-labor advocate, nothing was more unsettling than the quasi-feudalist configuration of southern society. Underneath a small ruling caste of wealthy planters and landowners, the majority of nonslaveholding whites appeared to be without incentive for improving their own situation and thus their low standard of workmanship. As a class, they seemed indolent and produced only what was necessary to survive. The reason for this collective lethargy, according to Olmsted, was the "peculiar institution" itself. In the presence of slaves, all labor came with "an implied degradation," clouding the notion that labor was actually supposed to elevate the individual and his environment. The golden rule of the southern gentry was not to work at all, to be able to live without working. Measured against the principles of free labor, most southerners, Olmsted argued, were out of touch with national development, violating the ethics of self-advancement and social improvement.[20]

In search of a remedy, some proponents of free labor turned to the European immigrants who were arriving on America's shores in record numbers. Many native-born Americans, particularly those untainted by antiforeign feelings, hoped that the idea of free labor would facilitate assimilation and eventually "Americanize" the newcomers. Being an American, the *New York Tribune* maintained, had to do less with nationality than with adhering to a specific social and political creed: "The man who is imbued with a genuine democracy . . . is in his very heart's core American, though he first landed from an emigrant ship this morning; while the aristocrat, the tyrant, the filibustering slaveholder, the demagogue plotter against the liberties of the people is an alien and a foreigner, though native American blood has flown in his veins since the first Pilgrim child was born in the colony of Plymouth."[21]

Since the combination of *free* and *labor* sounded so appealing and was yet so undefined, there is little wonder that it was used as a rallying call by both American- and foreign-born antislavery activists. "Is there not a cheer in the very sound of FREE LABOUR COTTON?" Brace emphatically asked his readers. "The many handed, industrious free labour of German families is found cheaper, and of course far cleaner and more thorough than slave labour." Kapp argued likewise, maintaining that fortune favored only those who, like the German Texans, relied "on themselves and their workmanship." Douai insisted that democrats had to be "free tillers of their own soil," and he agreed with Olmsted "that slavery must not be attacked by philanthropical and humanistical reasons, but by economic . . . ones."[22]

Although the Texas free-soilers and their northern allies indulged in the rhetoric of free labor and free enterprise, they had a far less conciliatory view of capitalism than many other promoters of the market revolution. This is especially true of some of the activists coming out of the German revolutionary tradition. Many Forty-Eighter exiles were profoundly troubled after finding that the social realities around them hardly matched the highly idealized version of a bill-of-rights republic that they had envisioned. Often it was only a matter of weeks until first experiences prompted them to temper their enthusiasm and develop a more ambivalent response. One of the aspects of American life subjected to the most severe criticism was the utilitarian world of business and profiteering. Echoing the sentiments of his fellow exiles, Kapp could not understand why so many of his new neighbors seemed to be driven by no other desire than to get rich. He concluded that if Americans preferred the money of today over the ideas of the Founding Fathers, the history of the United States would have to be presented as a chronicle of declension, not progress.[23]

The prospect of a democratic citizenry submitting to the reign of the dollar raised considerable misgivings on the American side as well. Olmsted and Brace, while less harsh in their assessment of the situation, were equally concerned that pecuniary self-interest, if left unchecked, could become too powerful in American society. Eastern cities like New York, according to Brace, had already mutated into an "endless whirl of money-getting," showing no signs of that "healthy cheerfulness" and "the more tender and kindly expressions of affection" indispensable to a republican community. European societies, Brace observed, although failing in their political quests for greater liberty, had preserved traditions of sociability while many Americans in the industrialized North drifted into poverty and isolation or engaged in criminal activity. Could a people who tolerated this kind of social disparity in their midst lecture another on their social disparities? Laissez-faire capitalism, Brace reasoned, might furnish the economic but not the moral and political weapons to win the battle against slavery.[24]

Olmsted too was well aware that the Achilles' heel of northern society was people toiling with little hope of ever climbing up the social ladder. In discussions with slaveholders, he had to grapple with the contention that black slaves were better off than poor white wage earners. Their slaves, these slaveholders argued, were treated more humanely and given the kind of shelter and protection that northern "wage slaves" did not receive from their employers. Confronted with the charge of wage slavery, Olmsted told Brace that self-government had to mean more than governing for one's own sake: "We need institutions that shall more directly assist the poor and degraded to elevate themselves. . . . The poor & wicked need more than to be let alone." Emphasizing hard work and virtue, antebellum reformers were optimistic about the ability of the individual to reconcile the demands of market capitalism with the higher ends of a republican moral economy. Yet Olmsted believed that one could not inculcate in the lower classes a sense of civic duty by merely aiding them materially or teaching them practical skills. The concept of education that he advocated was both political and aesthetic, ranging from the private household to the town hall, aiming at nothing less than to introduce all levels of society "to refinement and taste and the mental & moral capital of gentlemen."[25]

Assuming the role of civilizer and public educator, Olmsted was sure to get the attention of the liberal refugees who had their own ideas about improving the economic and intellectual lot of the common man. The nineteenth-century German equivalent to Olmsted's middle-class concept of education was *Bildung*, a creative, self-reflective notion of identity development through which the individual, and by extension society as a whole, could ascend to the highest level of humanity. Douai set up the *San Antonio Zeitung* as an organ in which all aspects relevant to social and political progress, including the slavery issue, were open to scrutiny. Along these lines, Douai editorialized that, while he did not support "the violent removal" of slavery, he was certain that "much could be gained [in this matter] through unimpassioned discussion."²⁶

Proslavery southerners were highly suspicious of Douai's plan to establish a forum for public debate in their own backyard, presuming that this was simply a strategy for camouflaging abolitionist intentions. The climate of fear and self-censorship created by antebellum southerners around the slavery issue ran counter to Douai's notion of free enlightened discourse. Moreover, it reminded him of the repressive Old World structures that he and his fellow emigrants had left behind. The harsh, occasionally even violent attacks of the proslavery majority smacked very much of the police states they had vehemently opposed in Germany. "You had rather be off or we shall make [you] go," infuriated southerners told the foreign-born agitators. In this situation, slavery had ceased to be an abstract ideological problem. Invoking the right to free speech and using slavery as a metaphor to illustrate his own condition, Douai responded, "We did not come to Texas to find ourselves reduced to slavery in any form whatsoever." The *San Antonio Zeitung*, he pledged, had come to stay. In the following two years, the paper continued to divide its readers, standing out as a mouthpiece of fanaticism for some and an agent of public enlightenment for others.²⁷

Building a Literary Republic

Though the Texas free-soil activists wrote extensively about the economic dimensions of slavery, it was their own intellectual enslavement they feared most. For them, slavery was morally and politically wrong, but it was also useful as a yardstick for measuring their own degree of freedom. Even before similar events in Kansas made national headlines, Olmsted, alarmed by the reports coming from his German Texan friends, concluded that the defenders of the "peculiar institution" had abandoned the field of rational-critical debate and resorted to violence instead. To him, the South had become increasingly despotic, not only toward slaves and free blacks. Preserving the southern masters' authority,

Olmsted complained, required control of white behavior too. A nineteenth-century version of mild totalitarianism, not unlike that of the aristocratic courts of Europe, had emerged that implemented discipline through random lynching of whites deemed hostile to slavery. In a gesture of solidarity with Douai, Olmsted vented his anger over the crimes of the proslavery regime. He lamented that in the world of the slaveholder the powerful, by spreading fear and intimidation, were able to "forbid freedom of discussion . . . to establish an irresponsible and illegal censorship of the press; and to subject [the] mails to humiliating surveillance."[28]

Post robbery and interceptions of private messages allegedly bearing seditious content occurred quite frequently in the South, and Olmsted was no stranger to these practices. Several letters he received from Texas arrived with broken seals, which suggests that southern authorities were using all channels to gather intelligence about what they viewed as a conspiracy of foreign radicals and northern abolitionists. For this alliance stretching from San Antonio to New York, letters were the primary mode of communication, the nucleus of an interethnic antislavery network, and it was vital for the participants to take precautions against those seeking to disrupt it.[29]

Through these letters, the activists exchanged information, coordinated their movements, and debated issues of mutual interest. Besides synchronizing financial and other forms of practical support, they used this avenue to promote an intercultural dialogue about how to build a slave-free society. The consensus was that such a society should provide room for German- and native-born white Americans, and that both groups should benefit from it. "Colonies, merely composed of Germans, do not thrive well in Texas, at least not well in comparison with colonies mixed up with American settlers," Douai remarked to Olmsted, assuming that social mixing would dampen intra-ethnic strife and protect the Germans more effectively from nativist aggression. Olmsted, in turn, believed that the industrious settlers from the Old World were invigorating the American experiment. For him, they were not the lawless intruders depicted in xenophobic literature but "an exceedingly important element in both the material and the moral and political prospects" of the country. "Undebilitated by mastership or slaveship . . . persevering in whatever they undertake," the German Texans, Olmsted argued, were fostering a culture of democratic entrepreneurialism in a region of the United States that lagged far behind in that respect.[30]

One of the largest obstacles this project had to overcome was to convince a fragmented and diversified public of its feasibility. Many audiences needed to be swayed — abolitionists, free-soilers, nonslaveholding southerners, European immigrants — and each called for a different approach. In New York, Olmsted,

Brace, and Kapp worked hard to draw attention to the plight of their Texan allies, which became increasingly difficult as public interest in the antislavery struggle shifted to the more heavily embattled fields of Kansas. In Texas, Douai, thrilled by the prospect of continued northern support and determined to purge "the Aug[ean] stable of public opinion," expanded his antislavery operations. Much to the dismay of his German and Anglo-Texan opponents, he began publishing more pieces in English, hoping to illuminate for Anglo-southern readers the social diseases caused by slavery.[31]

Again Olmsted provided valuable assistance. Not only did he proofread some of Douai's articles, which Anglo-Texan editors had ridiculed for their faulty English, but he also supplied a wide range of literary resources for the *San Antonio Zeitung*. The most prominent northern papers that Douai received were the *New York Tribune* and the *New York Times*, both of which he could access thanks to the samples that Olmsted sent. Other periodicals he acquired with Olmsted's help were mainly free-soil such as *Putnam's Monthly*, a literary magazine that Olmsted coedited. Yet Douai also digested more-radical sheets, including the nation's chief black abolitionist organ, the *Frederick Douglass' Paper*.[32]

For the German-born editor, still a novice in the field of antislavery journalism, this material was a gold mine. Before long, he emulated the editorial style of reform-oriented northern papers, acquainting his readers with perspectives on slavery branded as subversive in the South and thus banned from southern public discourse. In November 1854, Douai obtained a copy of a letter by Thomas Jefferson that could be construed as antislavery and reprinted it in the *San Antonio Zeitung*. A few months later, Douai quoted Connecticut philanthropist Elihu Burritt, whose journal *Citizen of the World* he praised for touting the superiority of free over slave labor. And in December 1854, he opened his columns to a northern friend who, hiding behind a pseudonym, was none other than Olmsted himself. Incensed over the way in which the German Texan free-soilers were bullied by proslavery Anglo-Texans, Olmsted used this opportunity to teach "misguided" southerners a lesson on what American citizenship really meant: "Were not the few Americans . . . in Texas thankful enough to have Irishmen, Germans, Englishmen or men of any birth unite with them ten years ago?" he asked, reminding nativists that foreign-born men had demonstrated their willingness to assimilate by joining Americans in their fight against Mexico. "I thank God," he continued, "that I know as countrymen, men who are Americans, not by accident of birth . . . but because they accept . . . the great truths of that Declaration of Independence on which this nationality of ours was founded."[33]

Just as surely as Olmsted shaped the antislavery discourse of the Texas free-soil campaign, he found himself substantially shaped by it. The information he received from Douai and Riotte about the geological and social composition of central Texas led him to promulgate in northern papers that free labor could succeed on the southwestern frontier. Olmsted relied heavily on German-language sources when he and his brother were preparing *A Journey through Texas* for publication. Kapp's works on Texas helped Olmsted grasp the history of German Texan colonization from its aristocratic beginnings to the more or less autonomous, nonslaveholding agrarianism of the early 1850s. Another source that Olmsted consulted was August Siemering's sociological survey for the *Atlantische Studien* about immigrant life and natural phenomena on the Texas frontier. Degener recommended this piece in a letter he addressed to John Hull Olmsted in early November 1854.[34]

The bonds between the activists from two worlds were to a large extent tightened by political expediency. Yet conviviality and friendship were as crucial to keeping the conversation flowing, promoting democracy, to paraphrase the cultural historian David Shields, less through rationality than "fellow feeling." Their German acquaintances allowed Olmsted and Brace to satisfy their appetite for learning more about European culture. For the German Texans, corresponding with northern intellectuals meant a chance to escape the monotony of frontier life. Newspapers and books such as Olmsted's first major publication, *Walks and Talks*, which Douai read with great delight, appeared like a gateway to a culturally and aesthetically more refined America. "When writing to you — I am fully conscious of my living in an exile or banishment," Douai told Olmsted in late 1854. In a frontier town like San Antonio with no glamorous cultural institutions, he felt "isolated in the most pitiful manner." By the same token, Degener complained that Texans had achieved little in terms of setting up an infrastructure supportive of scholarly activities. Nor did Texans seem to care much about imparting knowledge to future generations as the means for obtaining education, according to Degener, were "still wanting."[35]

While the Texan Forty-Eighters looked north to forget the provinciality of frontier life, separate ties were being knit in New York. Kapp's literary collaborations with Olmsted and Brace — Kapp had reviewed Brace's *Home-Life in Germany* for the *Atlantische Studien* and dedicated his second book on American slavery to Olmsted — transformed into genuine friendships. Over the entire time of his commitment to the free-soil cause in Texas, the German exile kept close contact with the two New England–bred reformers. Finding pleasure in each other's company, they met in New York's literary clubs and lecture halls, invited each other to their homes, and arranged dinner parties for their families.

Friedrich Kapp (right, Print Collection, Miriam and Ira D. Wallach Division of Art, Prints, and Photographs, The New York Public Library, Astor, Lenox, and Tilden Foundations) forged close personal ties with Frederick Law Olmsted (left, National Park Service, Frederick Law Olmsted National Historic Site) in the effort to establish a free-soil state in Texas, but their friendship owed as much to shared highbrow sensibilities and a belief in social uplift through education.

They agreed that slavery was harmful to democratic development but also discussed various other topics. Like Olmsted and Brace, Kapp took great interest in the intersecting histories of Europe and the United States; with Brace, he pondered questions regarding the role of religion in society. Having spent considerable time abroad, all three viewed themselves as travelers of two worlds, capable of representing the one and talking with authority about the other.[36]

Conflicting ethnic loyalties, however, repeatedly brought to light fundamental differences. A particularly thorny subject was religion and its meaning for social reform. Like most anticlerical Forty-Eighters, Douai and Kapp had little patience with people who maintained that there could be no progress without faith in a supreme being. A disciple of the German atheist Ludwig Feuerbach, Kapp dismissed American revivalism as a form of "superstition that [bred] perfect idiocy." He thought that evangelicals were "self-conceited" and "hypocritical" and mocked abolitionist ministers who preached emancipation from their pulpits but were reluctant to back those who were ready to take up arms for a just cause. In his view, the promises of divine justice and brotherly love were totally inadequate and counterproductive responses to a problem of such magnitude as slavery. They only nurtured submissiveness and moral complacency, two ills Kapp had already seen at work in the botched events of 1848–49.[37]

Douai was equally worried about the dominance of religious sentiments in American discourses of social reform. "I abhor the system of religion," he told Olmsted and maintained "that it would do less harm to the interests of humanity, could every form of religious ideas . . . at once be eradicated from human minds." Douai gave religiously inspired abolitionists credit for possessing a strong sense of right, but like Kapp he distanced himself from the spiritual platform they stood on. Simply waving the New Testament, Douai argued, had not liberated a single slave. He was convinced that much more could be gained if abolitionists renounced Christianity and started treating the oppressed from the vantage point of secular humanism, as sovereign persons endowed with the natural right to resist their oppressors.[38]

Douai's radical humanism is noteworthy in a twofold sense. First, it testifies to the persistence of a European revolutionary tradition in America that denounced religion as a disseminator of myths and an accomplice of the aristocratic world order. Second, it reveals the inability of those identifying with this tradition to conceive of an American religious experience as distinct from the European. Douai could not understand how American reformers could invoke biblical morality in the name of freedom and humanity as long as European Junkers and southern planters were legitimizing their power on the grounds of Christian religion:

> Yes, I am hating with fury any system dooming mankind to ignorance and humiliation. I prefer a thousand times entire Infidelity engrafted in the popular mind, to every form of religion as long as it furnishes the means of enslaving men. And it cannot be denied, that the last cause of slavery is religion. In the name and for the sake of "God" peoples are enslaved and oppressed, negro slavery is kept up. . . . The clergy in the South of the Union are just as much the friends and associates of slaveholders against slaves, as in Europe they are the foes of the popular movements and the counsel[o]rs of . . . tyrants.[39]

Having warned Douai not to overemphasize his "infidelity" in an overwhelmingly Protestant country, Olmsted was quite surprised to see his friend deliver such a harangue. Although he sympathized with parts of Douai's rationalism, he did not fall for the notion that there was a dark coalition of slavery and religion that had to be smashed. Too strong was his sense that religion in America was not the ultraconservative behemoth that Douai imagined but an amalgam of different faiths and creeds that had their own — oftentimes anti-institutional and utopian — agendas of reform. Olmsted and Brace were children of this post-Calvinist culture, a world that was increasingly obsessed with the authority of individual conscience and the doctrine of man's convertibility to moral action. Brace in particular became the perfect example of a God-inspired reformer who insisted that Christian ethics carried a blueprint for secular improvement, and that true faith meant acting on it.[40]

Given their diverging viewpoints on religion, it is hardly surprising that the recipes for change proposed by the Anglo- and German American activists were not the same. Whereas Douai and Kapp envisioned a postslavery Union in which rationality could expand unfettered by religious custom, Olmsted and Brace were unwilling to take religion out of their formula for democratic nation building. Like their Puritan ancestors, they believed that their society had the historic mission to be a city on the hill, a model for humanity to admire and emulate. The failure of Europe's democratic revolutions, which had promised to sweep away the last medieval "relics of barbarism," troubled the two New Englanders. But even more annoying to them was to hear Old World politicians question the capabilities of America's republican system and make it a target of derision before the civilized world for tolerating under its jurisdiction a system as inhuman as black bondage. Recollecting an argument with a Prussian diplomat during his German sojourn, Brace confessed that "the blood tingled to [his] cheeks with shame" when he was confronted with the allegation that American slavery made the wrongs of European feudalism seem trifling. Olmsted and Brace, however, partly as a result of such criticism from abroad, believed that it was the responsibility of American reformers to vindicate freedom over slavery and prove that their nation was the chosen place for this millennial endeavor. The rise and fall of America's republican prestige, in their view, hinged more than ever on slavery's demise.[41]

This self-instilled exceptionalism did not sit well with the German-born revolutionaries, who held tightly to their own self-image as a democratic avant-garde. Kapp, a shrewd observer of American political culture, was outraged by American commentators impertinent enough "to suggest that the Europeans who [had] been tossed hither ought to first learn what it means to be a free people." What he expected to find in the United States was students willing to learn from the European refugees and their revolutionary experiences. Europe, Kapp argued, was unmistakably "in the center of world-historical development," while America had to be content with playing a peripheral role "unless it wanted to forfeit the right to call itself a civilized nation." Would his American friends subscribe to this European counterexceptionalism?[42] In a letter to a German friend, Kapp expressed serious doubts:

> I am surrounded here by an educated and refined group of American friends and acquaintances (Olmsted, Brace, Curtis, Hurbbet, Bancroft); I have always been treated by them with the utmost respect and courtesy and cannot at all complain with regard to my personal connections. Yet there appears to be an irreconcilable difference in how we view the essential matters of life. These people here, without admitting or even being aware of it, are all imbued with a kind of parvenu pride; they all more or less think of themselves as God's chosen people, which is the result of a strand of Puritanism that goes back to the Old Testament. Nevertheless, I believe . . . that the Americans will rise to a much more eminent position as soon as they get rid of Christianity. The hypocrisy that comes with it corrupts them. . . . In their history there are only two categories: good or evil, angel or devil. The things that don't fit in they either ignore or slander.[43]

Citizenship and the Color Line

Kapp's statement elucidates that different groups joined the abolitionist and antislavery movements for political and moral reasons but also out of a strong sense of ethnic pride. This is especially true of the Old World revolutionaries who, unlike other immigrant groups, came to the United States as a defeated people. In this situation, fighting the slaveholders, who stirred bitter memories of the European aristocracy, allowed the revolutionaries to rid themselves of the stigma of defeat and reclaim their role as stewards of democratic progress. However, the Forty-Eighters' claims to political and intellectual leadership in antebellum America were anything but uncontested. Next to antagonizing the more conservative elements in a heterogeneous and rapidly growing immigrant population, they clashed straight on with the schemes of American nativists, who held that these newcomers should have no political influence at all.

Douai and his fellow refugees quickly realized what it meant to take on one of the oldest institutions in the United States from the standpoint of European liberalism. To speak out against slavery in the South was hazardous enough for the native born, but to do so if one was from another country was unpardonable. For the *Austin State Gazette*, the plans of the Texan Forty-Eighters "to improve [their] homely American institutions" carried "the likeness of the bloody and drunken dreams of French and German liberty." George Fitzhugh, the rabid proslavery theorist, warned that the "red republicanism" of the Douai type would meld with the "black republicanism" of the North to inaugurate an age of anarchy. Similarly disquieted, one southerner, signing an open letter with the Know-Nothing epithet "Americus," observed: "These refugees . . . evidently design attempting to engraft their Utopian theories upon this country, as substitutes for our long and well tried institutions. . . . The American people," Americus presumed, "do not wish . . . to be overrun [by] the paupers and outcasts of Europe."[44]

Nativist accusations were also flying freely in the North, although there it was not so much the immigrants' stance on slavery but their ethnocultural practices that bred discontent. In New York, Kapp witnessed firsthand that ethnic conflict over temperance laws and other contentious issues could easily erupt into violence. A year after his arrival, members of the local Turnverein, returning home from their annual May festival, were assaulted on the outskirts of Hoboken by a nativist mob; one reportedly died, and several were injured in the brawl. Rather than deter the newcomers, anti-immigrant propaganda and violence only made them more conscious of their ethnic identity. To enunciate more forcefully the right of their people to prosper in America, some Old World intellectuals began embracing a pretentious ethnic nationalism through which they hoped to mobilize the groups they represented and defend them against further harassment. Particularly committed to this end was Friedrich Kapp, who haughtily spoke of himself as "a consul of German culture in foreign lands." The sanitized Germanness he constructed in his writings signals unity and strength while obscuring intra-ethnic differences. Narrating the history of his people in America as one of daring individual feats and rising grandeur, Kapp sent out a clear message to the native-born white majority: whoever rails against the German element in the United States and belittles its various contributions also ignores that America has benefited immensely from it.[45]

The literary effort to secure a place for the German Americans within the larger framework of the American republic raises another important question. Did the fear of being marginalized and "enslaved" by a hostile Anglo-Saxon majority in any way heighten Kapp's and Douai's awareness of other victimized Americans, specifically of those who had never been anything but slaves? Both Forty-Eighters defy easy categorization when it comes to describing their attitude toward African Americans. Neither one of them had close relationships with a black person. Most of their antislavery texts deal primarily with the effects of slavery on white men, leaving little room for issues related to the slaves themselves. Following Olmsted's example, Douai wrote extensively about the miserable living conditions of nonslaveholding southerners, labeling them a "white proletariat that is even more depraved than the one in the big cities and factories of Europe." References to black suffering are equally rare in Kapp's books. They give clear priority to an interpretation that places the slavery controversy in a broader historical context and treats it as one particular episode in a worldwide struggle against feudalism.[46]

In spite of this general inclination to refer to slavery in the abstract, the German exiles recognized that African Americans were an integral part of American life. Blacks labored in the fields and in the homes of wealthy Texas planters and were a familiar presence on the streets of New York. While Kapp did not wrestle extensively with antiblack discrimination, he developed a few thoughts on the future of the black people in the United States. He supported abolition and granting African American slaves full civil rights, but only in a gradual manner. He believed that the slaves, whom he compared to the medieval peasant classes of Europe, first needed to acquire through training rudimentary political and economic skills that would help them to survive in a free society. The task might be an arduous one, but Kapp was confident that African Americans possessed sufficient capacities for intellectual growth. The respect he had for black leaders such as Frederick Douglass suggests that he did not think that the African race was doomed to degradation.[47]

Douai was similarly optimistic that African Americans, if liberated, would rise above their former status as bondsmen. Even though he did not openly advocate immediate abolition — something he knew would have been unwise in his beleaguered position — blacks nevertheless played an important strategic role in his plans to halt the expansion of slavery. To Olmsted, he confided that enticing Texan slaves to abandon their masters made little sense as long they could only head for wilderness; however, once a chain of free-labor settlements had been erected in the western part of the state, "a general start would follow" and "no negro [would] be kept back . . . from running away." Thus the slaveholders would have to withdraw as their property would no longer be secure. But in case proslavery Texans were out for retaliation, Douai pondered a more drastic measure still: arming the fugitive blacks and putting them under the command of a united force of German American and native-born free-soilers.[48]

In later years, Douai's faith in the African American ability to resist grew even stronger, a conviction doubtlessly furthered by his interest in abolitionist fiction. A diligent reader of Harriet Beecher Stowe's novels, Douai was fascinated by such manly black figures as George and Dred, who, unlike the docile Tom, were ready to seize their freedom at whatever cost in blood. Their courage testified that there was "revolutionary talent" in the black race, a talent Douai thought was badly needed in a region where slavery had stultified the moral sense of most nonslaveholding whites. Suffering from the resentment he had to endure in Texas, Douai doubted whether the movement to drive the slaveholders from power was ever going to emerge from this part of the southern population. On another social scale, however, he now saw a people with equal capacity for growth and full of hopes for a better future. The blacks, Douai speculated, only needed a heroic leader; then "twenty-thousand insurgent negroes in the Carolinas would do to crush the entire southern nobility." What Douai then projected was a genuine class struggle. The poor whites, stirred from their political slumber and detecting the bonds that connected them with the black revolutionists, would join the uprising and complete the South's transformation from a feudalist society to an egalitarian democracy.[49]

Olmsted and Brace paid little attention to such revolutionary fantasies. Although they anticipated the downfall of the planter class as eagerly as Douai, both agreed that the impulse to overhaul southern society had to come from the outside, from devoted white reformers and statesmen. For Brace, helping those who could not help themselves, regardless of race or class, was first and foremost a religious duty, a task all who called themselves Christian ought to join in. As Brace emphasized, "the strong are equally bound to be merciful to the weak: men are equally under obligations to follow the Law of Love, and Slavery is equally wicked and damnable, whether mankind have one parent or twenty parents." Olmsted, on the contrary, had a far less sentimental view of the subject. To him, the notion of a monumental slave insurrection was simply ludicrous. "The niggers can't combine — therefore *can't 'rise'*," he stated after returning from his expeditions to the Old South. Yet Olmsted was not indifferent about what should be done with the slaves. He stressed an obligation to aid the enslaved blacks and prepare them for a life in freedom, not because it was the requirement of a particular faith, but because free-labor capitalism demanded it.[50]

To be sure, when Olmsted spoke about "letting the negro have a fair chance to prove his own case, to prove himself a man," he was not necessarily thinking about elevating blacks to the rank of citizens. Like many of his contemporaries, he had strong reservations about African Americans ever being able to compete with white people. For blacks who had spent their entire lives in servitude, he proposed social segregation and enacting a separate set of laws. But the question of racial equality or inequality was never Olmsted's main point. What he wanted to show was that there was a viable social alternative to chattel slavery. If one could demonstrate that blacks were able to master the first lesson of liberal society, the ability to enjoy the fruits of one's labor, then chattel slavery would lose its most important theoretical leg, the "supposed inherent inability of the negro to take care of himself." Then all the critics of the northern way of life, southern slaveholders and European aristocrats, would have to acknowledge the notion that Olmsted had been propagating all along: that there was nothing more just and more successful than a free-labor society.[51]

In this political equation, the black race was never an independent factor, nor was it given any value apart from its relationship to the white race. The main concern of Olmsted and Brace was the future of white America and the damage that slavery inflicted to its reputation as the beacon of Christian morality and republican progress. Taking up the cause of African American improvement was therefore not so much an end in itself but rather a means toward vindicating an experiment in democracy the success of which was uncertain at the time, on both sides of the Atlantic.

Compared to the paternalism of their American allies, the German exiles were even less sensitive of the African American dimensions of slavery. Entrenched in their Eurocentric worldviews, they were all but unable to grasp the peculiarities of the South's "peculiar institution," the racial foundations of which were arguably the most important. When Douai refuted the polygenist theories of the naturalist Louis Agassiz, he did not do so because they were racist; more relevant to him was that they provided a rationale for all kinds of human bondage. American slavery was not wrong because it victimized black Americans on grounds of their alleged inferiority; the actual outrage was that it seemed interrelated with recent European chronicles of oppression. Kapp attacked southern slaveholders in racialist terms, linking them to the "Romanic principle" of aristocracy and the abolitionists to the "Germanic principle" of freedom. Yet he had little to say about bondage's negative effects on blacks. Hence Kapp's stunning conclusion: "The slavery issue is not a negro issue. It is the eternal conflict between the privileged few and the nonprivileged many, between aristocracy and democracy."[52]

The attempt to divorce slavery from race led to grave misconceptions. The most obvious one was Douai's assumption that under proper leadership black and white workers would unite against their common oppressor, the southern slaveholding elite. White southerners, however, felt far more comfortable emphasizing their whiteness than fraternizing with those who had been relegated to the lowest ranks of the country's social hierarchy. The activists from the Old World were also not entirely averse to categorizing people according to skin color. For Riotte, it was already an encouraging symptom to hear poor southern whites say that they did not "want any more of these damn'd niggers" to move into central Texas. Douai, when pondering the future of his people in the United States, occasionally forgot his Enlightenment beliefs and came out with surprisingly harsh remarks: Indian tribes who resisted the onward march of civilization, he told Olmsted, faced extermination. And African Americans, Douai speculated halfway through the Civil War, would abandon the northern hemisphere, for the climate suited Europeans only. Although Douai was devoted to educating supposedly inferior races with a German-inspired humanism, racial amalgamation was not among the ideas for which he was fighting.[53]

Notions like these cut deep into the egalitarian fabrics spun by the Texas free-soil movement. They illustrate that the cosmopolitanisms of the American reformers and the Forty-Eighter expatriates were in fact distinct democratic ideologies, closely tied to the ethnic and national communities from which they emerged and which they were above all bound to serve. This is not to say that the black other passed by unnoticed or that the activists denied him basic human rights; ultimately, however, he remained an outsider, a mere instrument for implementing one's own blueprint for civilization.

The Limits of Texas Radicalism

At the end of 1854, the small band of antislavery German Texans looked hopeful. Having withstood the strains and uncertainties of the last months, they were now enjoying a phase of relative stability. The *San Antonio Zeitung*, sustained by resources from the North and the determination of its editor, had not gone down as a result of the boycott and was beginning to win back investors and subscribers. Douai's efforts to persuade nonslaveholding Anglo-Texans to join the cause seemed to bear fruit as well: "They are reading my articles and talking about them more than I could have expected. Since I published Jefferson's letter, a degree of respect and approval seems to be aroused that astonishes me," Douai proudly proclaimed.[54]

There were also other encouraging developments. Together with his partner Martin Riedner, Douai started a lithography business in San Antonio that promised additional income. And with Olmsted's backing he was supervising the installation of a Spanish-language free-soil newspaper through which they hoped to get the Mexican Americans in the region on their side. Meanwhile, northerners were up in arms over the Kansas-Nebraska Act and the extension of slavery's sphere of influence that it sanctioned. It was hard to foresee all the ramifications of this outburst of antislavery sentiment, but who was to say that the Texas free-soil movement might not also profit from it?[55]

Still, there were reasons to stay vigilant. Neither the attacks from the local conservative press nor the perils of proslavery violence had abated. Riotte and Degener reported skirmishes between proslavery southerners and German Texans accused of harboring abolitionist convictions. Another incident that Douai vividly recounted for Olmsted involved the lynching of three German settlers by a gang of Anglo-southerners. Several black slaves had disappeared from nearby plantations, and their owners, linking these incidents to the anti-slavery propaganda coming out of the German Texan community, held some of their German-speaking neighbors accountable. Well aware of the dangers under which he and his Texan friends were agitating, Douai repeatedly stressed the need for caution. The "firm phalanx of iron souls" that would allow them to carry out their free-soil designs for Texas, he reminded Olmsted, had not yet materialized.[56]

Not everybody agreed with Douai's soft-spoken approach. The strongest disapproval came from Louisville, Kentucky, where Karl Heinzen was editing his radical paper, *Der Pionier.* In one of his characteristic bursts of arrogance, Heinzen scolded Douai that "only idiots, cowards, or villains betray the principles of freedom for practical considerations." For Heinzen, there was no negotiating with slaveholders; not even concerns about one's personal safety were an excuse. Perhaps Olmsted was also not entirely convinced that the anxieties of his German Texan friends were warranted because the press campaign he had launched up north removed the last veil from the fact that Douai and his men had more in mind than free public debate. The *New York Times* editorials that appeared in rapid succession in January 1855 and which were to lure antislavery settlers down south were "built on [his] timber," Olmsted smugly declared. And when the *New York Tribune* published Kapp's lecture in which he rhapsodized about German free-labor accomplishments on the southwestern frontier, secrecy was no longer of avail. On February 9, 1855, Douai grudgingly followed suit, printing what had been the movement's primary objective all along: to make a free state out of western Texas.[57]

This public confession gave new ammunition to Douai's opponents. Now that the German editor had laid bare the true intentions behind his free-speech rhetoric, the proslavery camp had the material they needed to brand him and the party he represented enemies of the state. "We are in favor of the liberty of the press," the *Texas State Times* affirmed after reviewing the latest editions of the *San Antonio Zeitung.* But "a foreigner has no more right to attack the institutions of America . . . than the commander of the Hessians would have had to dictate to Washington the plan of the campaigns of the American Revolution." Afraid that Douai's renegade journalism might cause further unrest, the *State Times* closed with an extreme recommendation: "The contiguity of the San Antonio River to the 'Zeitung office' would facilitate, we think, the suppression of that paper. Pitch in." With even greater fury, the *Austin State Gazette* demanded the introduction of the death penalty for all persons distributing subversive antislavery material. "This beautiful and lovely country, intended by its products of cotton to become the home of millions of our Southern sons," it editorialized, "is too precious a heritage to be despoiled at this time by Abolitionists, and that incendiary hand, too, to come from foreigners to whom we have tendered the rights of American citizens!" Calls to take out the antislavery German Texans sounded in other regions of the South as well. A Louisiana paper presaged that Texas would soon be overrun by free-labor immigrants unless loyal southerners took immediate action.[58]

The anti-abolitionist, antiforeign propaganda had the desired effect. Emotions were whipped up, triggering an unprecedented wave of aggression against Texans accused of siding with the antislavery party. Due to his position as chief editor of their organ, Douai had to bear the brunt. Several times he had to fend off proslavery locals who called him a "God-damned abolitionist" and threatened to run him out of town. While most withdrew after a barrage of insults, one of these encounters culminated in a fistfight. According to Douai's own account, he was one day interrupted at work by an unexpected guest: John S. Ford, editor of the *Texas State Times*, had come in the company of a witness to demand retraction of an article in which Douai had accused Ford of falsely stating that he was on the payroll of northern abolitionists. Infuriated by Douai's refusal to do so, the southerner decided to use force. To Ford's detriment, it was the German editor who got the upper hand and "quietly beat him up until he bled."[59]

There were also other instances when Douai had to fear for his life. As he recounted in his autobiography:

In the middle of 1855 a band of 12 pro-slavery rowdies rode to San Antonio and boasted that they would lynch me and throw my press in the river if the citizens of the town did not do it. Immediately 12 turners with loaded guns occupied the roof of the house which stood entirely isolated; my old father, whom I had a short time ago allowed to come from New York, . . . barricaded the entrance to the house and collected a small arsenal of weapons. As an old soldier he seemed to get young again. The rowdies stayed away when they reconnoitered the situation.[60]

Although Douai and his family emerged unscathed from these confrontations, the political and economic fallout proved far more difficult to handle. Alarmed by the late proslavery onslaught, the conservative German Texans stepped up their rhetoric as well. Mass meetings were held in Lockhart, Houston, and Neu Braunfels in which they pledged full allegiance to the laws of the state and urged their kinsmen in Texas to disassociate themselves from the agitators in their midst. Eager to show that they had nothing in common with the antislavery party, some of them proclaimed their loyalty to southern institutions in the Anglo-Texan press as well. There they denounced August Siemering, who contributed regularly to the *San Antonio Zeitung*, and vilified Douai's paper, stating that it was in no way "the organ of any respectable body of citizens" in the Lone Star State.[61]

The *San Antonio Zeitung* rapidly lost ground. Again readers canceled their subscriptions — some refused to pay for them — the proslavery postmaster stopped delivering some of the more contentious issues, and advertisers started to withdraw. For Douai, it was particularly disappointing to see that people whom he had considered trustworthy were beginning to abandon him. Among the first to go was Riedner, the coproprietor of the *Zeitung*. Unable to buy him out, Douai was sued and forced to make the payments under great sacrifices. In the meantime, Riedner spread the story that his former partner was on the verge of bankruptcy and had "sold to the Northern abolitionists." The allegations were not entirely unfounded. In August 1855, Douai informed Olmsted that his situation had become so desperate that selling the paper and giving up his editorship were about the only options left.[62]

"Our friend Douai is in a corner again," Olmsted wrote after receiving word of the emergency in Texas. The recipient of this message was the writer and clergyman Edward Everett Hale, one of the protagonists of the New England Emigrant Aid Company, which subsidized free-labor colonies in the western territories. With Hale, Olmsted had been collaborating in another free-soil enterprise that began to outgrow the Texas project: the contest between pro- and antislavery forces in Kansas. Olmsted's support of the armed struggle of the Kansas free-soil community — he famously donated a howitzer for the defense of the antislavery settlement of Lawrence — had brought him into close contact with a number of leading abolitionists. Now he asked some of the Kansas activists to help sustain Douai as well. Since the Emigrant Aid Company recognized the importance of European immigrants for establishing slave-free states in the West, not much persuasion was needed. Charles Kaiser and August Bondi, two Forty-Eighter emigrants who joined John Brown's guerilla band to fight proslavery settlers, deeply impressed Hale. Some funds were raised that allowed Douai to carry on, at least for a while.[63]

The relief came at a crucial point but was insufficient to turn the tide. The problem was that the free-soilers in central Texas were still vastly inferior in numbers to their proslavery opponents. Even though Douai could report that immigration poured into Texas as never before, he had to acknowledge "that the new comers [were] mostly slaveholders." The stream of immigrants from Europe and the North did not flow as steadily and far as the German Texan intellectuals and their native-born allies hoped it would. This became even more frustrating when they began realizing that most nonslaveholding southern whites were unimpressed by the vision of a slave-free Texas. Rather than make common cause with the foreign agitators, these native-born whites clung to the model of society to which they had grown accustomed, defending it with increasing vehemence against perceived dissent from the outside.[64]

One who lost faith that a lasting union between German- and English-speaking Texans could ever be achieved was Charles Riotte. Exasperated by the mounting hostility against his faction, he came to conclude that the kind of society he strove for had to be built in a place other than Texas. Riotte took up negotiations with the governor of the Mexican provinces of Nuevo León and Coahuila over a land grant of two million acres; the goal was to secure territory for the relocation of Mexican and German Texan farmers. He had reached an agreement by December 1855 and announced the following month that he intended to move to Monterrey, from whence he wanted to administer the colonization project. Olmsted strongly objected to this plan, arguing that leaving the country now would only embolden the slaveholders and further damage the morale of the free-soil party. For Riotte, however, the battle was already lost. "Do not induce any good man to settle here!" he told Olmsted in a downcast mood. "It is of no avail, and I am afraid too he would by and by turn himself slaveholder or abettor of them."[65] To account for this bleak outlook, Riotte not only pointed to the virulent proslavery and nativist ideologies; he also recognized a more essential problem, a fundamental difference in political culture separating Germans and native-born Americans:

> We are judged from the standpoint of an American — indeed a very strange people! We look upon a political society or state as a *congregation* of men; whose aim it is to elevate the wellbeing of the aggregate by the combined exertion, and if required, sacrifice of the individuals, and thus to benefit all. Americans look first upon themselves as *private individuals*, entitled to ask for all rights and benefits of an organized community even to the detriment of the whole. . . . To us, the State is a ideal being, whose welfare must be our pride . . . to the Americans it is the *formal* guarantee of certain (inalienable) rights in a loose conglomeration of human beings to secure an internal "bellum intra omnes et contra omnes"; — to us honor of the state is that of each citizen, — to you (don't take that personally) the honor of the state has its foundation in the greatness of some men, — we idealize the community — you the individual! How is it possible that we ever should amalgamate? If you follow the difference of our starting points up through all phases of political and social life you will, I believe, arrive to the same conclusion I came to, that is, a decided: Never![66]

This was not the only discouraging note that Olmsted received from his German Texan correspondents in these gloomy days. Eduard Degener, who had hosted the Olmsted brothers at his Sisterdale farm in 1854, was in equal despair. Unlike Riotte, however, Degener did not believe that their project was crumbling because of an unbridgeable ethnic divide. Far more relevant, according to Degener, was the political split that existed within the German Texan community, between the democratic newcomers and the older immigrants who showed little interest in changing the status quo. His main adversaries were the conservative German settlers whom he accused of backstabbing the free-soilers by inciting public opinion against them. Degener could have endured the pressure from the Anglo-Texan camp, but what broke his heart was that most of his German-speaking neighbors had been disinclined to follow him. Hence his candid confession: "I feel rather ashamed of my countrymen." If the movement to make a free state out of western Texas was to have a chance still, the spark had to come from native-born white Americans, and it had to come fast.[67]

Exodus

The lights went out for Douai and his *San Antonio Zeitung* in the first months of 1856. After Riedner's departure, Douai had been toiling to the point of mental and physical exhaustion. Together with his old father, he spent up to fourteen hours per day at work, doing all the editing, typesetting, and printing of his own paper and the Spanish-language organ he had helped set up himself. "Half the city knows how poorly we live . . . that we never have fun and money, and live worse than other people in the city," Douai lamented in one of the last issues. When his income had sunk to a level where he could no longer support his family, he explained to Olmsted's brother, John, that it was pointless to go on: "There is, still, every reason to hope that Texas may, at some future time, become a free state. . . . But this much is undeniable: I am in no [way] the man for this task. I cannot do much in favor of this project; in spite of my peaceable character I am almost hated by everyone hereabout."[68]

The final issue of the *San Antonio Zeitung* appeared on March 29. To pay his debts, Douai was forced to sell the paper along with the press to Gustav Schleicher, a conservative businessman. Thus the paper ultimately fell into the hands of his political opponents, who, attempting to break with the radical policies of the past, changed its name to *Staats-Zeitung*. This outcome was bitter enough. Deprived of his editorial powers, Douai relived the very crisis he had faced five years earlier: succumb to a hostile establishment or leave the country. As in 1851, he chose exile. On May 14, 1856, John Hull Olmsted informed his brother, Frederick, then on another European sojourn, that Douai had sold out and was on his way to New York.[69]

Losing their sole public organ on Texas soil was a heavy blow for the Anglo- and German American intellectuals struggling to rid the southwestern frontier of slavery. Yet the story of their collaboration does not end here. With recommendations from his northern friends, Douai quickly adjusted to life in the free states and found new opportunities. His first major employment was working as a freelance journalist for Karl Heinzen's *Pionier*, a position he held until personal differences with Heinzen led to a split in 1860. Olmsted's reputation among northern reformers helped Douai acquire a second and a third rewarding job. After moving to Boston, he signed up with the educator and abolitionist Samuel Gridley Howe, who gave Douai a teaching post in his Institute for the Blind. Through Howe, Douai got in touch with protagonists of Massachusetts's free-soil movement, who now focused on defeating proslavery elements in Kansas. Simultaneously, he joined the staff of Charles A. Dana and George Ripley — both were looking for expert contributors for their *New American Cyclopedia*.[70]

Douai, now an antislavery celebrity, also became an active political speaker. During the presidential race of 1856, he appeared at several pro-Frémont rallies, the most memorable of which took place in the Broadway Tabernacle, where he shared the podium with Friedrich Kapp. It was during this campaign that Kapp implored his countrymen who were opposed to slavery's expansion to vote Republican. In a manner that mirrored his ambivalent relationship with Olmsted and Brace, he argued that "even supposing that the party of freedom in this country does not in every single question come up to what we consider the fullest extent of liberty and right . . . we are still bound to make common cause with this party against a common enemy." Although some members of the German American Left criticized the Republican Party because it accommodated nativists and failed to offer an alternative to free-market capitalism, almost all defended it as the lesser evil to the slavery-sustaining Democrats. To persuade his listeners, Kapp evoked an old immigrant dream. A Republican victory, he predicted, would arrest the further expansion of slavery and "open the lands of the West to emigration," saving "for [the immigrants] and [their] children free land and labor sufficient to prevent [their] being placed in want by each crisis." Four years later, Kapp and Douai again had a front seat when they were mobilizing votes for Lincoln. In Philadelphia and New York, they watched Republican Wide Awakes and German Turners march together in carefully arranged parades to muster support for the upcoming election. And at a mass meeting of New York's German American Republicans, Douai served on the committee as vice president, an honor that was also bestowed on Charles Loring Brace.[71]

Douai and his friends repeatedly tried to rekindle the Texas free-soil campaign during this turbulent period. Particularly helpful were Olmsted's connections to people inside the Emigrant Aid Company. Encouraged by Brace, who had heard more-zealous Kansas settlers talk of "taking Western Texas next," Olmsted called on Hale to help advertise his newly published book *A Journey through Texas*, through which he hoped to boost immigration of free-soilers to that region. Hale gladly stepped in and sent reading samples of the book to at least twenty-six New England editors. Another high-ranking member of the Emigrant Aid Company whom Olmsted was able to recruit was the Boston physician and humanitarian Samuel Cabot Jr. Together they conceived the Neosho project, a plan to connect the hitherto separated free-soil communities of Kansas and central Texas by inducing antislavery men to settle in the southeastern parts of what would later become Oklahoma. Since the bulk of immigrants for this project were to come from the German states, Kapp and Douai were also involved. Part of their mission was to distribute pamphlets among the newly arrived and find affordable land for those willing to populate the Neosho region.[72]

None of these plans came to fruition, however. As in previous years, the immigrant turnouts were too meager to make a difference. Moreover, reports from the southwestern frontier seemed to confirm that the German Texan antislavery party had virtually ceased to exist after Douai's withdrawal. And with no reinforcements in sight, even Olmsted began losing faith and gloomily predicted that "the German population [in Texas], dispirited and dispersed, [would] lose all its respectable qualities." One last effort to save the cause of a free Texas was undertaken in 1858. A meeting was held at the home of Amos Lawrence, president of the Emigrant Aid Company, during which, as Douai reported, it was decided to extract funds of at least nine hundred thousand dollars from investments in Kansas to build up a similar infrastructure in Texas. But because money was increasingly difficult to get once the panic of 1857 set in, this venture bore the mark of the utopian from the outset. The end came with John Brown's raid, when many wealthy abolitionist contributors, who were anxious to prove their innocence, thought it wiser to suspend all forms of financial aid.[73]

Politically, the Texas free-soil alliance was an utter failure. It took a war, not a newspaper campaign, to end slavery on the southwestern frontier. Douai, haunted by the Texas fiasco long after his departure, reckoned that events might have taken a different course if some of his partners had made greater sacrifices. Yet the real causes were more structural than personal. Outnumbered and outmuscled, the German and Anglo-American intellectuals fell short of garnering enough public support for their project. Too prevailing was the impression that Texas was firmly in the grip of slavery and thus barely suited as a destination for free labor. As a result, the intellectuals never had the kind of manpower at their disposal that they would have needed to create a second Kansas. This discrepancy was especially hard to stomach for some in the radical German American spectrum who took pride in "their" movement down South. Charges of nativism swiftly followed. As one German paper in New York protested, "If one hair is hurt on the head of an abolitionist in Kansas, the 'humane' press of the free states teems with lead articles, but when Germans and Irishmen are murdered by the dozens, one hears not a single word of criticism."[74]

Such observations often came from a distance and were prone to strong biases and exaggeration. The Texas free-soilers, after all, battled slavery on its own turf, remote from northern supply lines, and not where it intended to go. They had to put up with not only a hostile Anglo-southern majority but also a German Texan population that, for the most part, had no political ambitions except coexisting peacefully with its English-speaking neighbors. After Douai had moved north, the conservative *Neu-Braunfelser Zeitung* could finally proclaim victory. His people, the editor declared late in 1859, were loyal southerners; "we can truthfully assert that the mass of the Texan Germans are not opposed to slavery."[75]

The notion that nativism was especially virulent in the Texas free-soil campaign becomes even more untenable in view of the strong personal relationships that developed across ethnic boundaries. Most of these ties outlasted the situations in which they had been knit, providing conduits that the old allies continued to use for mutual advice and support. Olmsted and Kapp sustained their collaboration in areas ranging from joint newspaper ventures to proposals for the foundation of a gentlemen's club. It is also difficult to imagine that Douai would have accomplished his transition from life on the edge as an antislavery editor in Texas to one of relative social and economic stability without the patronage of his northern friends. Riotte, who did not stay in Mexico very long, received equal assistance when applying for a post in the Lincoln administration; it was Olmsted's intervention that secured his appointment in 1861 as United States minister to Costa Rica.[76]

But there were also those in the movement who met a less deserved fate. Eduard Degener, who refused to give up his newly found home in the Sisterdale mountains, eventually felt the wrath of the slaveholding party. A year after Texan secession, he stood before the Military Commission at Austin, where he was tried and incarcerated for disloyalty to the southern Confederacy. About sixty other Texan unionists, mostly German born, who feared similar charges headed for the relative safety of Mexico but were overwhelmed by a superior Confederate force near the Nueces River. Not a single refugee survived the assault, and according to what Kapp told Olmsted about the incident, it was there that Degener lost his two only sons.[77]

By and large, however, the activists managed to overcome and distract themselves from their political debacle in pre–Civil War Texas with the help of the social and intellectual bonds that connected them to one another. Although these bonds did not erase existing ethnocultural differences and at times made them more pronounced, they also generated an atmosphere of cordiality and friendship that gave some participants a greater appreciation of the democratic values of the ethnic other. Riotte, at first highly skeptical about the prospect of a multiethnic free-labor republic on American soil, conceded to Olmsted late in 1867: "You have reconciled me with America and the Americans . . . at a time when my experience in Texas had led me to believe, I, a republican by principle, had started in the wrong direction when going to the U.S." In the same year, another token of admiration was sent to Douai; yet the source it came from was a rather unexpected one. It was a newspaper, on the front page of which flashed the following statement: "This newspaper, the first to be founded in Texas by negroes, was printed on the same press which Dr. Adolf Douai founded in San Antonio in 1853 in order to combat slavery. It will be a great satisfaction to him that the freed slaves of Texas gratefully remember his dangerous and courageous agitation in their behalf."[78]

CHAPTER THREE

The Only Freedom-Loving People of This City

Exiles and Emancipators in Cincinnati

That class of Germans who are known as "Freemen" . . . are the worst kind of crazy visionaries ever thrown by circumstances upon our shores, and in the judgment of all reasonable men constitute by far the most dangerous element in our population. That they should unite with the negroes . . . is not surprising, in view of their antecedents.

—*Cincinnati Daily Enquirer*, December 6, 1859

The sympathy, the trust of the oppressed nationalities and races, we must not abuse it; we must not run from it like cowards, if we do not want to betray our own people, our own race.

—AUGUST WILLICH, *Cincinnati Republikaner*, December 27, 1859

WHAT HAPPENED IN NORTHERN VIRGINIA on October 18, 1859, was on the surface nothing more than a minor skirmish. Yet the news it generated led to a political earthquake. John Brown, veteran of the clashes between pro- and anti-slavery forces in Kansas, and eighteen of his followers—thirteen whites and five blacks—had seized the federal arsenal at Harpers Ferry, from whence they hoped to launch an insurrection among the slaves of Virginia. But the intervention of U.S. marines under the command of Robert E. Lee put an end to Brown's plans. Most of his party were either killed or captured. Brown, severely wounded and imprisoned, was sentenced to death for treason against the State of Virginia. On December 2, Brown was hanged in Charles Town. The death of the bearded abolitionist and the manner in which his execution was discussed reflect the inner tensions of a nation on the brink of civil war. To some, Brown was chaos and terror incarnate; others saw in him a martyr for freedom, or, to quote Ralph Waldo Emerson, the one who made "the gallows like the cross."[1]

Those siding with Emerson gave expression to the sentiment that John Brown was a God-inspired fighter in a series of public gatherings. In virtually every northern city, abolitionists of various degrees came together to honor a man who, in their eyes, had given his life for the cause of ending American slavery. From New England to Missouri, hymns and prayers resounded through the streets and church bells tolled in commemoration as friends and sympathizers mourned the deceased abolitionist warrior. One of the more remarkable John Brown meetings took place in Cincinnati's Over-the-Rhine district on Sunday, December 4. Over-the-Rhine was home to Cincinnati's German Americans. It was a bustling community: small shop owners, artisans, craftsmen, and ordinary laborers formed the backbone of a predominantly working-class culture. Many of these German-born workers were organized in freethinking and workingmen's societies, which gave public life in this plebeian milieu its distinctively radical features. August Willich, the socialist editor of the *Cincinnati Republikaner*, had announced the previous day that the city's Social Workingmen's Club was to hold a memorial meeting for John Brown.[2]

Around two o'clock in the afternoon, a formidable crowd filed solemnly into the hall of the German Institute. However, not all who attended the meeting were of German descent. As one bystander put it, there was "a motley crowd of both sexes, diversified by every hue common to the human species," including the "bronzed Frenchman, the pale-faced American, and the rubicund Teuton," who, to the observer's astonishment, sat on the same benches with "the copper-colored African and the greasy-skinned and odorous Ethiopian." This peculiar mix was also manifest in how the hall had been decorated for the occasion. To the rear of the podium, the Star-Spangled Banner was draped in mourning as were the portraits of Washington and Jefferson to its left. To the right of the podium, the black-red-golden flag of German republicanism stood unfolded. From the ceiling hung a large piece of drapery, ornamented in glaring letters with the words: "IN MEMORY OF JOHN BROWN." Shortly after the meeting had begun, a delegation of African Americans entered the hall, exhibiting a flag of their own, which they fastened to the ground alongside the others. Cheers and salutes followed and did not ebb until the African American standard-bearers took their seats.[3]

Among the main speakers was Moncure Daniel Conway, the Virginia-born Unitarian minister of Cincinnati's First Congregational Church. In his address, Conway portrayed Brown as a second Thomas Paine, as the one true heir to the humanist ideals that the English-born pamphleteer had disseminated through his writings. Then spoke Peter H. Clark, the black principal of the Western District Colored School. Clark proclaimed to those present that the events now transpiring "were more holy, more momentous to the well-being of man . . . than those of '76." He also thanked the multiethnic audience for doing justice to his race. By attending, Clark stressed, they bore testimony that they were "the only freedom-loving people of this city," willing to make common cause with men and women of a different color.[4]

Representing the German-speaking element, August Willich electrified the crowd with some words of his own. The labor leader delivered a fiery speech in which he denounced the ignorance of the Irish, depicted the evils of slavery, and told his hearers "to whet their sabers and nerve their arms for the day of retribution" when the institution and its supporters "would be crushed into a common grave." Anybody, Willich went on, who refused to confront those who favored the laws of slavery over the principles of freedom betrayed the founding ideals of the American republic. Adopting a policy of compromise would only result in the same kind of injustice and oppression under which the German people in Europe suffered to this day. The interracial crowd responded with thundering applause, evoking a unity that Willich later described as "the inner bond of humanity, [which] brought forth a harmonious melody sung by races and nationalities separated by nothing but outward appearance." As the sun set on this eventful day, Willich paid one last tribute to John Brown. Despite many threats, he headed a torchlight procession through downtown Cincinnati.[5]

Cosmopolitan but Divided

In a city infested with ethnic and racial conflict, Willich's plea for interracial solidarity largely fell on deaf ears. He knew the reasons why. For most Cincinnatians, the Over-the-Rhine gathering of black and white radicals was an appalling spectacle, a flagrant transgression of established social norms and customs. This is sufficiently reflected in the hostile coverage that the meeting received in the local press. In an exceptionally spiteful tone, the *Cincinnati Daily Enquirer* went after the German-born organizers of the meeting. "Their politics have ever been of the most degraded stamp, and of the most dangerous character to the peace and welfare of the nation." Startled by the foreign radicals' friendly conduct toward African Americans, the *Enquirer* wrote in disbelief: "They recognize no distinction of color in their social intercourse, and, if any thing, consider a negro a little better than a white man. They favor 'negro equality' with the whites in the most emphatic sense of the word." The *Cincinnati Volksfreund*, a conservative German-language paper, was equally indignant. It held that the only thing the Brown sympathizers had accomplished was to "discredit the great men of the Revolution," some of whom had owned slaves themselves.[6]

Over the first half of the nineteenth century, Cincinnati had turned into a hotbed of antiforeign and, to an even greater extent, antiblack sentiment. Strategically located on the Ohio River, the "Queen City of the West," as Cincinnati was affectionately called by nineteenth-century Americans, soon developed from a petty, late eighteenth-century frontier outpost into a bustling trading center that attracted an increasing number of merchants and settlers from the eastern states. The growth rate was breathtaking: in 1825, the United States census estimated 15,000 inhabitants; at midcentury, this number had skyrocketed to over 115,000, and kept rising. Cincinnati was not only among the fastest-growing places in the country. It also had one of the nation's most diverse populations, a fact that did not escape contemporary observers. Fredrika Bremer, the Swedish traveler who toured the United States from 1849 to 1851, thought that Cincinnati was a "pre-eminently cosmopolitan" city, endowed with "handsome churches, splendid hotels, academies, and institutions of all kinds."[7]

A large portion of Cincinnati's residents consisted of European immigrants from Ireland and the German states. By 1851, the Irish constituted nearly 12 percent of Cincinnati's entire population. Given their rural and provincial background, their chances to thrive in this city were limited. As the English traveler Isabella Lucy Bird reported during her 1854 stay in the Queen City, "[The] Irish are here, as everywhere, hewers of wood and drawers of water; they can do nothing but dig, and seldom rise in the social scale." The Germans left an even greater mark on Cincinnati's urban landscape. According to an 1859 estimate, they comprised about two-thirds of the city's foreign-born population. Stronger in numbers than the Irish, they were also socially more heterogeneous. From the very beginning, German immigrants stood at the forefront of Cincinnati's development. David Ziegler, a veteran of the Revolutionary War and a native of Heidelberg, became the city's first mayor in 1802. Among the earlier arrivals was also Martin Baum, a successful banker and entrepreneur who prospered in the nascent transportation industry. Jacob Kornblüth and Sebastian Meyer, both merchants of German descent, made a fortune in Cincinnati's booming textile factories.[8]

The insurgencies in Germany following the French Revolution of 1830 brought a new wave of German-speaking people to Ohio. Many of these newcomers were liberal academics who added a distinct flavor to public life in Cincinnati. These émigrés, who were called Dreissiger after leaving their homeland because of the political unrest of the early 1830s, deserve special mention because they provided the city with a dynamic intelligentsia that played an important role in local politics. The most influential member of this group was Johann Bernhard Stallo, who earned the respect of both English- and German-speaking citizens for his achievements as a scholar and a jurist. Next in significance were the immigrant politicians Charles Reemelin and Heinrich Rödter. Both were active in the founding of the *Cincinnati Volksblatt* in 1836, one of the oldest German-language dailies in the city. Serving on various municipal councils and in both houses of the state legislature, Rödter and Reemelin strongly identified with the principles of the Jacksonian democracy. Its emphasis on mass participation in politics and local autonomy appealed to these liberal refugees, and it was partly because of their activities that many immigrant voters aligned themselves with the Democrats.[9]

The Democratic constituency of the 1840s was diverse, linking together northern farmers, southern planters, Irish workers, and German Catholics, all of whom gathered under the umbrella notion of self-government. Then again, a community as multilayered as the Queen City Germans was not free of internal strife. Spending the winter of 1846/47 in southern Ohio, Franz von Löher deplored that his emigrated countrymen had "split into strong factions, religious and political, and in serried ranks continually menace[d] and attack[ed] each other." The immigrant generation that came to Cincinnati after the events of 1848 only widened this gap. As in previous years, the bulk of the newcomers were laborers, adding to the already impressive number of foreign-born workers who were crucial to Cincinnati's economic development.[10]

The new arrivals, however, had more to offer than strong hands and sturdy backs. Unlike other immigrant groups, many of them were not only hard working but also well organized and politically educated. Led by their intellectual spokesmen, they reshaped Cincinnati's German American community with new civic organizations, thereby hoping to sustain their homegrown ideals in an unfamiliar environment. This was the case when fourteen friends responded to the call of revolutionary legend Friedrich Hecker and established the Cincinnati Turnverein in 1848, the first of its kind on American soil. Other associations followed: radical workers founded the Workingmen's Club to combat unfair wages; freethinkers, faithful to their Enlightenment heritage, organized their own clubs to debate all kinds of literary, moral, and scientific issues. Although a minority, these revolutionaries and agnostics were shrill enough to unnerve their conservative kinsmen as well as many churchgoing Americans. This oppositional group of Germans, Bird noted, "are a thinking, sceptical, theorising people: in politics, Socialists — in religion, Atheists. . . . Skilled, educated, and intellectual," she concluded, they "constitute an influence of which the Americans themselves are afraid."[11]

By the mid-1850s, Know-Nothingism had become a major force in the region, and tensions between Cincinnati's immigrant population and local nativist bands were exacerbated by the Forty-Eighter democrats' activities. The most ferocious nativist onslaught in this decade was the election riot of 1855. After their candidate for mayor had been defeated, Know-Nothings went on a rampage against the Queen City's foreign-born residents. Cincinnati's German Americans, in order to defend themselves, barricaded the bridges leading into Over-the-Rhine and summoned their militia units. When attacking the foreign-born, nativists cared little about intra-ethnic distinctions. During Archbishop Bedini's visit in 1853, nativists and German freethinkers united against Catholic immigrants; both groups were up in arms over the Italian churchman who had become famous and feared for cracking down on liberals in his home country. Three years later, German-born radicals themselves became victims of nativist aggression. Marching back from a picnic near Covington, members of the Cincinnati Turnverein were assaulted by a mob of Ohioans and Kentuckians. Rocks were thrown and pistol shots exchanged, drawing blood on both sides.[12]

Anti-immigrant unrest was a sad reality, yet it barely exuded the intense racial contempt that native and foreign-born whites heaped upon America's oppressed black population. Bordering on slaveholding Kentucky, the Queen City was seen by numerous African Americans as a gateway to a better life. Virtually from Cincinnati's incorporation as a town, however, municipal authorities treated people of a darker hue as a caste inferior to all others. Even though Ohio's 1802 State Constitution disallowed slavery, it remained silent on the issue of civil rights for blacks. This provided sufficient leeway for the enactment of the Ohio Black Laws of 1804 and 1807, which barred African Americans living in the state from legal protection and political participation. The rationale behind these laws was to discourage further settlement of blacks, particularly fugitive slaves, in the region, but since these laws were never fully enforced, Ohio's black population continued to rise. In 1820, not more than four hundred African Americans resided in Cincinnati; thirty years later, the city had one of the North's largest free black communities: an estimated 3,300 people (roughly 3 percent of the city's overall population).[13]

Most blacks in Cincinnati found dwellings in the highly polluted quarters near the docks commonly referred to as "Bucktown" or "Little Africa." It was a struggling neighborhood: signs of privation and decay were everywhere. To nineteenth-century journalist Lafcadio Hearn, Bucktown conveyed the image of an early urban slum, a "congregation of dingy and dilapidated frames, hideous

Engraving of Cincinnati, *Harper's Weekly*, September 27, 1862. Affectionately called the "Queen City of the West," the polyglot river town was also a hotbed of racial conflict, ethnic rivalry, and European-inspired revolutionary activism.

huts, and shapeless dwellings." Residential segregation by race, however, was not a ubiquitous concept yet. Some African Americans, if they could afford higher rents, moved into adjacent white working-class districts. According to one statistic, the Irish were most likely to have black neighbors, but blacks could also be found living next door to German-speaking families. In 1850, for instance, 235 blacks were counted among the residents of Over-the-Rhine, Cincinnati's "Little Germany."[14]

Another major contact zone between blacks and whites was the workplace, which became a major breeding ground of racial antagonism. A vast number of Cincinnati's African Americans were manumitted or fugitive slaves who had acquired marketable skills during their time in bondage. But despite their ambitions and willingness to work, blacks were largely restricted to unskilled or semiskilled labor. Factors that denied blacks equal treatment were laws that made it illegal to hire African Americans who did not possess a certificate of freedom and the widespread refusal of white workers to work alongside a person of color. White resentment of black wage labor often exploded in violence as in the bloody riot of 1841, when Irish dock workers attacked their black colleagues, leaving many dead and wounded. To conclude that only economic rivalry relegated African Americans to the bottom rung of society would miss a crucial point. As David Roediger underscores, for native-born white workers but also for poor Irish and German immigrants, distancing oneself from those occupying the lowest rank in the country's social hierarchy was also a means of emphasizing one's whiteness, of asserting citizenship in a predominantly white republic. To be accepted as white meant not to be black, to be exempt from the burdens and inferiorities commonly associated with the black race.[15]

Abolitionists from the Other Shore

"Our Teutonic brethren are found guilty of the crime of loving liberty too well. Truly — a heinous crime in this age and country!" remarked the *Cincinnati Daily Commercial* with some irony at the peak of the slavery controversy. Republican papers like the *Commercial* were obviously pleased that numerous German Americans in and outside Ohio had placed themselves in the forward ranks of the anti-Nebraska movement and were also among the Queen City's most ardent foes of the "peculiar institution." But who exactly were the participants in Cincinnati's German American antislavery party, and which layers of urban society did they inhabit?[16]

To be sure, large parts of the German American population stayed aloof from this fervid display of antislavery and abolitionist sentiment. Prior to the high tide of the sectional controversy, slavery was not foremost on the minds of Cincinnati's German-speaking citizens. Catholics principally voted for the socially conservative Democrats, not because they regarded chattel slavery as a positive good, but because they had come to identify opposition to it with the extreme Protestantism of the evangelical abolitionists. The city's Dreissiger intellectuals generally disliked the institution. Illinois politician Gustav Körner called Heinrich Rödter one of Ohio's pioneers in the struggle against the spread of slavery. A closer look, however, reveals that until the 1850s none of these liberals seriously attempted to translate his privately held antislavery beliefs into political action. The 1843 statute of the German Democratic Society, the leading Dreissiger organization in antebellum Cincinnati, passed over the subject of slavery in silence. Similarly, Rödter's colleague Charles Reemelin, while in favor of blocking slavery's expansion, steered clear of abolitionism and professed to "care nothing" about the state's antiblack laws.[17]

In the first half of the 1850s, the mounting national polarization over slavery led to profound realignments in Cincinnati's German American community and eventually gave the upper hand to the antislavery party. The first anti-Nebraska meeting in the Queen City occurred on February 24, 1854, and was attended almost exclusively by German Turners. As Bruce Levine has shown, far more German Cincinnatians came out against the Nebraska bill than in favor of it. Moreover, the social makeup of these two groups diverged in conspicuous ways. Whereas craftsmen and workers formed the backbone of the city's moderate and radical anti-Nebraska forces, people with a white-collar background were more likely to side with the pro-Nebraska party. The crowd at Turner Hall, according to the *Cincinnati Gazette*, was "large and enthusiastic" and adopted a platform with remarkably sharp language. It called the Kansas-Nebraska bill "a disgrace to America and this age," and "solemnly protest[ed] against it in the name of humanity, liberty, and justice." The committee in charge included two notable immigrant radicals: Kaspar Gams, tailor and head of the local German American workingmen's society, and Wilhelm Renau, teacher and president of Cincinnati's German Debating Society.[18]

Gams and Renau were also present the following month at the state convention of Ohio's Forty-Eighter radicals, which took place just around the corner at Freemen's Hall. The delegates — representatives from various Turner, freethinking, and workingmen's societies — carved out a declaration of principles that went further than the propositions of most anti-Nebraska protesters. They not only condemned Whigs and Democrats for having "united around slaveholding, manhunting, and the Nebraska betrayal," but also called for the annulment of the Fugitive Slave Act as well as the eradication of slavery throughout the United States. More far-reaching still, they turned against interpretations of the free-soil doctrine favoring whites only. Free land in the West, the delegates insisted, should be handed out to all qualified applicants "irrespective of color." Little wonder that white supremacists saw disturbing commonalities between these foreign-born democrats and America's homegrown crusaders against slavery. The demand of Ohio's German-speaking radicals to ban slavery throughout the United States, the *Cincinnati Enquirer* spouted, was "an abolition one, of the most ultra character." Their declaration of "giving negroes a free homestead upon the public domain," the same paper stated, was another peculiarity that ran counter to the "true policy of this country," which was to "discourage free negroes from remaining in the Union."[19]

English-language American newspapers were not alone in pouring scorn on the declarations of Ohio's radical Forty-Eighters. The German editor of the Catholic *Wahrheitsfreund* belittled the efforts of his anticlerical countrymen as "foolish clamor" and "products of a tainted mind." For the *Cincinnati Volksfreund*, meddling with the color line was a "crime against the regulations of nature." Emancipation, the *Volksfreund* claimed, provoked miscegenation, which conservative German Americans feared as much as their native-born white counterparts. "It is merely an abstract truth that all men are created equal," the same paper held as late as 1859. "But if we erect states and create a social order, not all men have the same rights. In our opinion, the Almighty has made a difference between the white and the black race."[20]

Yet not all Cincinnatians responded negatively to the Freemen's Hall resolutions. To native-born emancipators, they signaled that abolitionist convictions also blossomed in quarters other than their own. Interestingly enough, the first English speakers in the region to salute the immigrant radicals were not white abolitionists but African Americans. As early as 1852, Ohio's blacks saw parallels between the recent European independence movements and their own struggle for liberty and expressed solidarity with "the oppressed Hungarians and German socialists in their efforts to throw off the yoke of despotism." They even encouraged teaching German in their schools, believing that this would "prove a great auxiliary to [their] cause." A few months earlier, the state's free black community had already shown its appreciation of the Old World radicals in a more substantial manner. On his fund-raising tour through the United States, the German revolutionary Gottfried Kinkel received donations from numerous people, including a group of Cleveland blacks. Their decision to support Kinkel's cause incensed many in the conservative Anglo- and German American camp, resulting in defamations of Kinkel as an abolitionist and "representative of unbelieving Germany."[21]

The local community of white abolitionists also took note of the democrats from overseas, but it was not until 1858 that they openly welcomed them as allies in a common struggle. In the early summer of that year, Cincinnati's immigrant radicals staged a major demonstration in support of William Connelly, a writer for the *Daily Commercial* who had been tried and incarcerated for hiding a couple of fugitive slaves. The Connelly trial lasted several days and was covered by every major newspaper in the city as well as the nationwide abolitionist press. In a crowded courtroom, prosecutor Stanley Matthews had to contend against a defense team put together by Levi Coffin including ex-governor Thomas Corwin and the Dreissiger émigré Johann Stallo, who had broken with the Democrats over the question of slavery's extension. By the time Connelly went to jail, he was an abolitionist hero. Unitarian and Methodist delegations flocked to his cell, hailing his efforts for the hapless fugitives.[22]

On June 11, 1858, the day Connelly's prison term expired, Cincinnati's German American enemies of slavery also paid tribute. Connelly's lawyer Stallo headed a large procession of Turners who honored the released prisoner with a torchlight parade. The rain poured down in torrents, but as the *Ohio State Journal* reported, this did not "dampen the enthusiasm of the multitude, which . . . must have numbered fully 3000." In the ensuing ceremony at Turner Hall, Connelly, who was sharing the speakers' platform with Stallo and the radical newspapermen August Becker and Friedrich Hassaurek, received loud ovations for his statement that he would not have rejected the blacks even "if [he] had been sure that the gallows would be [his] recompense." This display of interethnic fraternity made a deep impression on some of the older abolitionist organizations. Delighted by the performance of the Turners, the Salem, Ohio, *Anti-Slavery Bugle* commented: "Let us be of good cheer; the principles of freedom are not only extending themselves but are gathering strength in their development in new and unexpected sources." And the *Kansas Herald of Freedom* jubilated: "The German Turners are a heroic class of men. . . . God bless the men who thus stand by the sufferer and the oppressed!"[23]

Forging Bonds

That abolitionism had found a home in a small but energetic segment of Cincinnati's German Americans was less a surprise to another observer of the Connelly trial: the Unitarian minister Moncure Daniel Conway. Predestined to follow in the footsteps of his slaveholding family, the Virginia-born Conway had embarked on a spiritual career instead. His decision brought him into contact with a number of influential writers including Horace Greeley, Francis William Newman, and Ralph Waldo Emerson. Via Quakerism and transcendentalism, Conway came to recognize the value of independent thought and appreciate the liberal teachings of the New England–bred Unitarian Church. At Harvard Divinity School, he began wrestling with slavery and his southern heritage. This conflict came to a head in the summer of 1856 during his ministry in Washington, D.C. After denouncing slavery and the bloodshed in Kansas in a spectacular fashion, Conway was asked to resign. The militant tone of his sermon had alienated too many members of his congregation.[24]

Just two months later, Conway was on his way to Cincinnati; he had been called to the pulpit of the city's Unitarian First Congregational Church. For the gregarious young minister, the multiethnic river town was an intellectual revelation. The Queen City seemed to him "the most cultivated of the western cities," which he ascribed to the strong presence of German immigrants in the area. Conway was pleased to find in the city outlets of all kinds of reform movements, of "every new creed or social experiment." Most of his personal relationships evolved within his parish, but his appetite for new things also made him reach out to people of other beliefs. On one occasion, Conway sat down with disciples of the communitarians Georg Rapp and Robert Owen; on another, he talked to survivors of Fanny Wright's interracial community on the Tennessee frontier, listening with fascination to their stories of living together in a self-sustaining yet ultimately failed settlement of former slaves, free blacks, and whites. Cincinnati, Conway wrote in retrospect, offered "something of all America," and the minister was determined to make the best of this offer.[25]

Not long after his arrival, Conway became close friends with two leading exponents of the city's German American intelligentsia, Johann Stallo and August Willich. Stallo was by all accounts the first German Cincinnatian with whom

Conway interacted on a regular basis. A renowned academic skilled in both languages, the Dreissiger émigré was erudite enough to captivate the younger minister. Parallel to his career as a politician and a lawyer, Stallo published several pieces that propelled him into the upper ranks of contemporary American philosophy. But what impressed Conway most about the Dreissiger liberal was his advocacy of religious freedom. In a series of lectures as well as in speeches at court, he defended German-inspired free thought against Sabbath laws, Protestant Bible-reading, hymns, and prayers in public facilities.[26]

Stallo's assaults on the encroachments of institutionalized religion furthered his alienation from Catholicism. His break with the church of his ancestors left him free to explore denominations more congenial to his views. He started mingling with Cincinnati's Unitarians, whose liberal middle-class theology bore a certain appeal for the Dreissiger intellectual because it sought to harmonize religion with a rational humanism. Stallo was also glad that he found his dislike of slavery matched by the sentiments emanating from the Unitarian meetings. His sympathies for Unitarianism raised a few eyebrows among his German American friends, whom he exhorted to drop their fear of nativism and join hands with English-speaking enemies of slavery. But were not churchgoing Americans vilifying German-speaking immigrants as drunkards and infidels? An ardent opponent of Sabbath and temperance laws, Stallo was well aware of these attacks. Ethnic separatism, however, was no solution in his eyes. He underscored that the only way to secure peaceful relations between ethnically distinct but racially interrelated groups lay in mutual engagement. As he remarked at the 1856 singing festival in Cincinnati: "What we are witnessing here in this country . . . is not the unequal contest of two tribes separated by age and history. It is the encounter of interrelated people, all descendants of one and the same centuries, albeit with distinct upbringings and separate backgrounds. They do not meet as enemies. . . . The task at hand is not about ousting one another; it is about strengthening and assisting one another, each with the means available to him."[27]

From the mid-1850s onward, Stallo attended services in the First Congregational Church and reportedly spoke from its pulpit on several occasions. He also established ties to leading members of the community, above all to his fellow jurists and Republicans George Hoadly and Alphonso Taft, future president William Howard Taft's father. Yet nobody epitomized Stallo's ideal of a Christian emancipator who treats reason as his friend, not his rival, more perfectly than Moncure Daniel Conway. In the following years, Stallo emerged as one of the minister's closest advisors, accompanying him through many storms inside as well as outside the city's Unitarian congregation.[28]

Partly through Stallo's influence, Conway developed a fascination with German literature and the culture of German Cincinnati. With the permission of his church elders, he spent considerable time studying and reading books — several of them authored by Germans — through which he matured as a theologian and a writer. One such book was David Friedrich Strauss's *Life of Jesus*. By rejecting biblical miracles as myths and interpreting them as mere manifestations of human morality, Strauss reinforced Conway's own beliefs and helped him bridge the gulf between supernaturalism and reason. Conway's indebtedness to German thought also manifested itself in the magazine *The Dial*, formerly the organ of New England transcendentalism, which he resurrected for one year. Under his editorship, *The Dial* reemerged as a nonconfessional magazine, open to all who aspired to be "free in thought, doubt, utterance, knowledge, and love." Its pages teemed with references to scholars of the English-speaking world such as Emerson, William Ellery Channing, and Charles Darwin, but they also bore the imprints of ideas introduced by Hegel, Goethe, Humboldt, and Schiller.[29]

As Conway began preaching a radical transcendentalist theology mixed with the idealistic philosophy of the European Enlightenment, various factions of Cincinnati's heavily Germanized free-thought movement vied for his talents as a speaker. The Turners invited him twice. Another group to which Conway occasionally lectured were the Jews. The Unitarian minister enjoyed their company and felt especially drawn to the German-speaking Rabbi Isaac Wise, who seemed to him "a man of good great sense and energy." Finally, his actions also endeared him to the intellectual heads of the city's radical German American workingmen, among them August Willich, according to Conway one of "the most interesting citizens of Cincinnati."[30]

There was little at the outset of his life indicating that Willich would gain notoriety as a daring spokesman of radical democracy on both sides of the Atlantic. Born in 1810 as the descendant of an old Prussian Junker family, Willich first emulated his ancestors: he served in the army. But the hierarchical structures of the Prussian military soon collided with his Enlightenment beliefs. He resigned after embracing republicanism in an open letter to the king. When the Revolutions of 1848–49 broke out, Willich had become part of the Cologne circle around Marx and Engels and adopted a socialist outlook focusing on workers' rights and social improvement through education. At the side of Friedrich Hecker, Franz Sigel, and Mathilde and Fritz Anneke, Willich fought against the reactionary forces in the Palatinate and Baden. Beloved by his soldiers, he took no privileges and shared their hardships to the very end. After the revolution was put down, Willich fled to London, where he became a member of the Communist League. But political differences with Karl Marx soon generated personal friction. The factions split, and in 1853 Willich left London for good. He joined the Forty-Eighter exodus to the United States and moved to Brooklyn and from there to Washington, D.C. Working as a cartographer for the federal government, Willich made the acquaintance of Johann Stallo, then on a tour along the eastern seaboard. Stallo was impressed with Willich and persuaded him to relocate to Cincinnati. Willich arrived in that city in 1858, prepared to renew his fight for the underprivileged in a city reeling under the impact of race, class, and pre–Civil War party politics.[31]

A Republic of Labor and Intelligence

Willich's record as a revolutionary leader catapulted him to the forefront of Cincinnati's German American labor movement. What set him apart from most other local radicals were his communist leanings. "The Reddest of the Red," as he was nicknamed by both admirers and opponents, resumed his crusade for the rights of labor in America. Willich, as Conway writes, took over the *Cincinnati Republikaner* at Stallo's request and "made it a strong and radical paper." The *Republikaner* was the propaganda tool of the city's German American Social Workingmen's Club. Its mission was to educate the German-speaking working population and sensitize it to the social and economic injustices in a rapidly expanding capitalist society. In his inaugural statement as chief editor, Willich vowed to bring the socialist creed to life with a program combining mass education and political action. "We intend to support all those reforms that are supposed to make this republic a truth for everyone," Willich pledged, "to turn it into a community of free men that acknowledges only the authority of two interrelated powers: for a REPUBLIC OF LABOR AND INTELLIGENCE."[32]

At the time Willich penned these lines, the Queen City had already developed into a stronghold of antebellum labor activism. The downside effects of Cincinnati's dramatic growth were increasing job competition, seasonal unemployment, a stronger tendency toward mechanization and division of labor, and wage cuts in periods of recession. Willich, like most of his radical Forty-Eighter comrades, actively supported the laborers in their fight for higher wages and better working conditions. A dedicated socialist, he gave ample coverage to the plight of those who toiled without proper compensation. For Willich, the unequal distribution of wealth in a capitalist society was wrong not just because it condemned the working masses to poverty. More deplorably, it kept them ignorant, which the editor of the *Republikaner* perceived to be one of the biggest stumbling blocks on the road to human emancipation. "What can make us masters of this world," Willich printed, "are not material riches but the treasures of the mind." Without political and economic knowledge, the laborer could not see through the everyday inequities that consigned him to misery; without education, he remained "a stooge and a slave," not unlike his black counterpart down South, "incapable of gaining and defending his freedom despite all physical force invested to that end."[33]

Cincinnati's "Little Germany" offered fertile ground for the kind of intellectual socialism that Willich wanted to sow. By the middle of the decade, the city's Forty-Eighter plebeians had constructed a vibrant counterpublic: committed to preserving the tenets of radical democracy as they understood them, they subscribed to newspapers like the *Republikaner* or Hassaurek's *Hochwächter* and banded together in organizations such as the freethinking, workingmen's, and Turner societies. Apart from hosting political meetings of all kinds, these institutions served as important cultural and recreational centers. They staged dramatic and musical performances, conducted debating and lecture groups, and hosted clubs offering a range of spare-time activities from card playing to bowling and sharpshooting. Such events usually took place on the weekends, and native-born Americans strolling through Over-the-Rhine tended to look with amazement at these unfamiliar spectacles. Some found a certain charm in the social habits of the Germans, but conservatives snarled that "transforming the Sabbath into a day of Bacchanalian revel . . . should receive the condemnation of every one."[34]

Whenever time and weather permitted, German Cincinnatians took their ethnocultural traditions to the street. Public outings and parades were a recognized feature of German American communal life and were instrumental in shaping a collective ethnic identity that, among other things, helped moderate between competing factional identities in a diverse immigrant population. For Willich and his fellow revolutionists, however, the value of this festive culture lay not primarily in cultivating a shared Teutonic heritage. With even greater enthusiasm, they used it to keep alive the memory of 1848 and foster public interest in the ongoing European liberation movements. When the news reached Ohio that Felice Orsini had been put to death for his involvement in a plot to assassinate Louis Napoleon, members of Cincinnati's radical German societies marched to commemorate the political martyrdom of the Italian republican. And in the wake of Garibaldi's uprising in Sicily, German American Forty-Eighters — August Willich among them — joined a small band of Italian exiles and their American sympathizers in publicly calling for a unified Italy.[35]

Moncure Conway, a close follower of such rallies, greatly admired the intellectual vitality emanating from this democratic working-class milieu. He was especially fond of its contributions to the world of drama, which he vindicated against the traditional Protestant indictment of the public theater as a site of drunkenness and debauchery. Like his radical German-born friends, he believed that the stage could help form an aesthetically refined and well-informed democratic citizenry. Steadfast in his defense of the dramatic community, Conway partook in what was perhaps the most powerful demonstration of German American festivity before the Civil War: the 1859 centennial of Friedrich Schiller's birthday. In a two-day festival that spanned almost the entire city, thousands of Cincinnati's German immigrants as well as hundreds of English-speaking Americans turned out to celebrate the poet's one hundredth birthday. The main ceremonies began on the morning of November 11 with bonfires and cannon shots from the surrounding hills. Then a procession composed of several German societies and labor unions headed out amid singing and cheering on a parade through the city's core districts. The train of revelers came to a halt at selected locations, where they listened to speeches and recitals of some of Schiller's most popular verses. "All along the route, houses were gaily decorated with flags," the *Daily Cincinnati Gazette* observed, and in the windows of Over-the-Rhine, "there were pictures and busts, which showed the universal desire to do honor to Schiller." In the evening, the celebrations closed with plays and concerts: the German Institute performed *Wilhelm Tell*, and Wood's Theater delighted the audience with an English version of *The Robbers*.[36]

Conway stayed in the thick of the festivities most of the day. Sitting next to his friends Willich and Stallo at a banquet arranged by the Cecilia Singing Society, he raised his glass, praising Schiller as a prophet of freedom and human rights. In this situation, Schiller was no longer the cultural property of a particular nation. Those present at the banquet venerated and transformed him into an all-embracing "poet of humanity . . . the brother of the laborer and the poor; the brother, too, of the oppressed and captive." Schiller's legacy, in this interpretation, reminded European radicals and American abolitionists of their common obligation to fight social injustice and restore the dignity of the working masses, both free and slave, in an industrializing society. This theme resurfaced two days later in a sermon Conway delivered at his church. Still moved by the cosmopolitan spirit of the recent demonstration, he again ranked Schiller amid the noblest fighters for spiritual and political freedom. "Burns, and Shelley, and Schiller," the Unitarian reverend preached, "the masses do not read them with cold admiration — they love them, they meet together and speak with hearts all aglow of them."[37]

Such oratory made little impact on Conway's critics, who branded his views "obnoxious" and regarded his social behavior "frivolous." Unitarian gentlemen of property and standing began wondering whether a man who held dancing parties in the church basement and rubbed elbows with workers was fit to be their spiritual leader. "There was as much talk about his unclerical conduct," George Hoadly noted, "in going to the theaters and dancing, as about his doctrines." Conway, on the other hand, saw no point in changing his lifestyle. Modern times, he argued, required a different form of spirituality than the asceticism of his forebears. What, then, was the proper role of a minister? For Conway, the answer was clear: that of a mediator and a truth seeker. In an age witnessing the birth of technological innovations and scientific theories at every turn, truth could no longer be monopolized by a single creed, nation, or ideology. All were involved in a gigantic clash of opinions, a contest in which those ideas prevailed that were consistent with reason and open to dialogue. Anything else, Conway believed, would lead humankind back into the "dark ages." "Enlarge the place of thy tent" was his motto. In order to overcome the barriers separating nationalities, religions, and races, Conway insisted: "We must have more communion and cooperation. . . . We must bear witness to one another."[38]

In the fall of 1858, Conway began refuting from the pulpit the notion that the Bible was the word of God. It tore his congregation apart. Early signs of a cleavage had already become visible in January 1857, when members protested Conway's move to invite to their church Ralph Waldo Emerson, who was anything but a devout Christian. The minister's open rebellion against the accepted doctrines of his faith, however, caused a formidable uproar. Old-school Unitarians found it irritating that Christ's supernatural attributes were being called into question by somebody who sympathized with "the views of Strauss, the German rationalist, or infidel, or whatever you call[ed] him." After a series of verbal clashes that brought no settlement, Conway's opponents in the church played their last card: they petitioned for his removal.[39]

The whole affair ended in a pyrrhic victory for the reverend. Even though the pro-Conway faction was strong enough to deny the dissenters a voting majority, a schism became unavoidable. In April 1859, the conservatives left and founded their own Unitarian society, the Church of the Redeemer. Painful as this secession was, Conway and his followers, now informally referring to their church as the Free Church, recovered. Within weeks, the pews were being replenished with people who wanted to listen to this unconventional preacher who had promised to welcome anyone espousing uninhibited debate. And what they saw was truly without precedent in the religious history of Cincinnati. One of Conway's priorities following the split was to develop relations with the city's liberal Jewish community. More astonishing still, he allowed the visiting Hindu Brahmin Joguth C. Gangooly to speak before his congregation.[40]

Orthodox Protestants rubbed their eyes in disbelief as Stallo, Willich, and other German-born freethinkers rushed to Conway's defense. Prior to the inter-Unitarian feud, the minister's plans to broaden religion and make it more humanistic had already caught the attention of the *Cincinnati Republikaner*. Willich was confident that Conway spearheaded a project that "would lead to the same results among native-born Americans as it had among German Americans — to the religion of the free mind, the cult of art and science, and the realization of humanity." He concluded by wishing the movement "skilled captains and good wind for its sails." Twelve months later, Willich spoke in even more explicit terms about his growing intellectual affiliation with Conway. Informing his readers about the impending rebirth of *The Dial*, he lauded his friend as a person "fully and justly deserving the respect of all truth-loving free men."[41] The magazine itself, Willich rejoiced in a cosmopolitan fashion,

> will be a vanguard for progress in the realms of religion, science, art, and social life. It will be one of the few English-language organs qualified to fuse the pure German spirit with the Anglo-Saxon spirit — it will adopt a purely universal, purely humanist stance. We call upon our readers to attend to this forthcoming magazine as one that promises to make huge and important progress in that field of literature through which different nationalities shall be molded into one people, the people of all people, the people of humankind. We therefore happily welcome it as an ally worth an entire army in the fight against the black and hellish divisions of religious, political, and social crimes and prejudices.[42]

Willich had only a limited interest in Conway's spiritual biography. Far more meaningful to him was that he recognized in the Unitarian rebel a victim of established religion, a friend willing to adopt the Forty-Eighter tenets of free inquiry. The more heated the dispute between traditionalist and freethinking Unitarians grew, the more did Conway mirror Willich's own struggle for political and intellectual emancipation. Back in Europe, it had been the churches that, in concert with the ruling nobility, had stifled attempts to develop alternative ideas about the individual's place in society. Here in the United States, Willich encountered the same "dark spirit" again, now in the guise of Puritanism. For the red revolutionary, religion was false consciousness on many levels, and no segment of American society appeared free of its doctrines. They extended deep into the sphere of commerce and industry, where, according to Willich, honest work was being degraded by "money-makers and speculators" to a "mere tool of their machinery." They provided justification to southern slaveholders for the enslavement of millions of men and women. They steered the actions of the nativists, who thought of themselves as the rightful successors of "God's chosen people." Finally, they were discernible in the clamor of Protestant elites against intellectuals who were striking at the roots of time-honored religious and moral certainties.[43]

One such incident of conservative clamoring occurred in February 1860, during one of Emerson's visits to the Queen City. Emerson's stay was overshadowed by protests in the local press, which prompted Willich to assist Conway in defending the right of the Concord scholar to lecture in public. One month earlier, Willich had published a piece in honor of another of Conway's spiritual mentors, Theodore Parker, the religious iconoclast who was lying on his deathbed in Florence, Italy. It was the Bostonian Parker who had provided Conway with the model of a socially active and theologically courageous ministry. His friend Willich acknowledged this, telling his readers "that it [was] the duty of every German freeman" to stand up for these and other "American warrior[s] of the mind" so that they could continue to educate the public without fear.[44]

Flattered by such uplifting words, Conway moved even deeper into the world of German American rationalism. To his amazement, he discovered that the city's American agnostics and German-born atheists were conducting their own little discussion clubs in the backrooms of selected taverns. What piqued his curiosity most, however, was that these skeptics convened once every year to pay homage to Thomas Paine, the eighteenth-century champion of American independence whose public image had become that of a notorious infidel. "In early life I had heard Paine occasionally mentioned by preachers with abhorrence," Conway recorded, "but it was only in Cincinnati that . . . I became aware of the large mythology grown and growing around Thomas Paine." The freethinkers also converted the minister to the opinion that the English-born pamphleteer had been "the first to raise the standard of American independence; that it was he who had converted to that cause Washington, Franklin, John Adams, Jefferson, and other statesmen." Were Cincinnati's radicals right in claiming that the history of the American Revolution had to be rewritten? Conway wanted to know more.[45]

Public veneration of Thomas Paine had a well-known history in Cincinnati, dating back to the late 1830s. Two ceremonies, the 1859 and 1860 anniversaries of Paine's birthday, marked the zenith of this cult. On January 29, 1859, more than two hundred German American freethinkers and workers formed a procession and marched to Melodeon Hall, where they joined a gathering of American Paine admirers. Speeches were given in both languages and resolutions adopted, all with the intent of rescuing the Enlightenment radical from oblivion. Next year's celebration attracted an even larger crowd, an estimated one thousand people. The hall was packed as August Willich and the English-born agnostic Robert Treat delivered orations "of the most ultra-heretic character," in which they hailed Paine as an apostle of religious freedom. After that, emotions were further set ablaze by a catalog of resolutions that vindicated the "right to debate all opinions . . . and to assert difference" as the "inherent birthright of all mankind." Along these lines, one of the following resolutions venerated the teachings of Moncure Conway and like-minded clergymen: "*The Heretic Clergy* — Barker, Bellows, Conway, Martineau, Beecher, Parker, Chapin, and that swelling host of noble teachers are too numerous to particularize: Our hearts are stirred, not for the chiefs of sects, but for the champions of progress, of human brotherhood and universal freedom."[46]

Conway was not present to witness this outpouring of sympathy. He was busy preparing his own speech on Thomas Paine, which he gave later that evening in church. Drawing on Paine's ideas, Conway affirmed that religion, if it wanted to endure, had to concur with science and human morality and get beyond the petty orthodoxies of the day. The Unitarian minister had long ago crossed the threshold to nonconformity as he aligned himself with foreign-born radical workers and intellectuals, with whom he collaborated for the dual aim of public enlightenment and social progress. Although Conway steered clear of the militant atheism characteristic of many of his German American supporters, the ties of trust and companionship that bound the American minister and his immigrant friends together facilitated cooperation as they entered the most hazardous political arena of their day: the battle against slavery and its abettors.[47]

Race and Resistance

Peter H. Clark, the black teacher and activist, was surely elated over the rising interest among Cincinnati's freethinkers in Thomas Paine, a man of great symbolic importance to him as well. Clark was born in the Queen City in 1829, the son of a black barber and grandson of a Kentucky slave woman and her white master. He was given the best education available to an African American at that time — courses at private schools included Latin, history, and philosophy — but that did not shield him against discrimination. Prejudice, Clark recollected in 1873, "has hindered every step I have taken in life." During his apprenticeship in printing, he was fired by a new master who refused to train blacks. After taking over his father's barbershop, he became embroiled in a controversy with a white customer who was offended by Clark's policy of providing equal service to blacks and whites.[48]

The field in which Clark invested most of his energy was teaching. Convinced that education was the key to African American self-improvement, he followed his uncle John I. Gaines in the assertion that blacks would never earn the respect of the white majority without proper schooling: "We must be their equals in human knowledge, improvements, and inventions, and until we are, all schemes for equalizing the races upon the soil are nothing but cob webs." However, Clark's plans to elevate African Americans by educating them faced daunting difficulties. Although Ohio legislators allowed blacks to organize their own public schools, they left them direly underfunded. Clark's disputes with the Cincinnati school board led to his temporary dismissal from teaching in 1853. The charges raised against the fiery young educator were that he had his students question essential Protestant doctrines. "His views of God," a local newspaper reported, "were not those given by the revelations of the Scriptures, but from the book of nature." In this the article was not mistaken. Because white Christianity had in Clark's view come to bear the imprints of proslavery thought, he set out to explore a host of philosophical alternatives. Thomas Paine was one of the main guides on this intellectual journey, a quest that drew the black educator closer to Cincinnati's community of Anglo- and German American radicals.[49]

Clark appeared in the Unitarian record as early as 1852, but it was not until Conway took up his activist ministry that his passions were fully aroused. Unitarianism varied from most white denominations in that it generally accepted black members. Under Conway, this stance became even more pronounced, and it is easy to imagine Clark's respect for a man who fostered such interracial policies. And in case he needed additional evidence that Conway really cared about blacks, the 1857 Western Unitarian Conference provided it. Synods of this type were usually not prone to issuing political statements, but this time the situation was different. Weeks earlier, the United States Supreme Court had famously decreed in *Dred Scott v. Sanford* that African American slaves and their descendants were not protected by the Constitution and could never be citizens. Outraged over this ruling, the abolitionist Unitarians no longer held back their feelings. Fired up by Conway, the meeting denounced the Supreme Court's verdict as "one of a series of deliberate assaults on religious and civil freedom in America." In a second step, it declared it the "duty of Christians everywhere, in and out of the pulpit, to discuss freely and fully before the people this crime against man, and therefore against God."[50]

Conway preached on slavery only sporadically, yet his hatred of the institution was widely recognized. He had still been a student when Wendell Phillips ushered him to a platform outside Boston where he delivered his first abolitionist speech. A few hours earlier, Garrison had hypnotized the crowd with his legendary burning of a copy of the United States Constitution. Conway rejected this anarchic posture; still, his admiration for the leaders of the movement was unrivaled. The abolitionists, he stressed, were idealists of the highest order, crusaders for human rights with a concern for moral purity that made their cause a religious one. The democratic revolutions of the Old World, gallant as they were, had "generally been the struggle of proud races for political existence or nationality, the efforts of brave men for their own power or territory." Abolitionism, however, ranked higher than patriotism in Conway's esteem, for it stood for a "real 'idea,' namely the right of every man to himself, — an idea unconfined to [one] country in its importance . . . placed so high above any mere question of nationality." For Conway, being an abolitionist was not contingent on rank or origin. It was first and foremost a personal attitude, a test of conscience that every individual had to face.[51]

Intrinsically connected to abolitionism for Conway was the task of asserting the slave's humanity. Like most of his New England friends, the Unitarian minister was deeply troubled by the spread of race theories claiming that blacks constituted a distinct species, a mammalian subtype that was neither animal nor fully human. For Conway, the African American was very much a human being and an indispensable part of American society. Conway attacked polygenism not simply because it gave scientific legitimacy to black slavery; equally deplorable was its failure to appreciate the dormant potentials that lay in African American culture. The songs and hymns of blacks, Conway observed, "are the only original melodies we have," and in the artistic power of their language, African Americans were in no way inferior to whites. Blacks were an elegant people, and with their fertile, picturesque imagination, they would surely contribute more to the rise of a free and cultivated society than the depraved southern slaveholder. "In our practical, anxious, unimaginative country," Conway wrote, "we need an infusion of this fervid African element, so child-like, exuberant, and hopeful." Was it not better to nurture these qualities and channel them into the greater stream of a largely utilitarian society? Conway responded with a thundering yes. Although he retained a racialist conviction that different groups of people had unique traits, he believed that walling off blacks from whites would not strengthen but forever reduce the vitality of American democracy. Against the conventional wisdom of his age, Conway held "that the mixture of the blacks and whites is good; that the person so produced is, under ordinarily favourable circumstances, healthy, handsome, and intelligent." He argued, "Under the best circumstances, I believe that such a combination would evolve a more complete character than the unmitigated Anglo-Saxon. . . . Already we know that nations are great in proportion as they are of mixed races."[52]

To ensure the long-term survival of the republic, it would not suffice to rely on the cultural input of one people alone. What was needed was a powerful multiracial vision so that this democratic project could shine for all humankind:

> The evening star of the epoch of separate races is the morning-star of Human Unity. Men we have; but not yet Man. . . . We have not to build a Nationality on that continent; we have to rear a new race: to this we are bound by fate. We have already learned with some pains that the Negro is not a race that is to die out, or that can be crushed with impunity; and very near to this is the lesson that he is quite essential to the work that all races have to do on that continent, and which they cannot do until all unite as the fingers of One Great Hand.[53]

These were revolutionary words. But the one who wrote them had always preferred a silent revolution. Conway belonged to the abolitionist wing that sincerely believed in nonviolent protest and tried to persuade slaveholders with arguments rather than guns. Yet after years of peaceful agitation, even the most zealous pacifist had to admit that not much had been achieved. Toward the end of the 1850s, slavery seemed more firmly entrenched and more powerful than ever. Public opinion in the North had grown more hostile to slavery, but this was less the result of abolitionist propaganda than the perceived victories of the Slave Power: the Fugitive Slave Act, Kansas-Nebraska, and the Dred Scott decision. Tensions within the movement heightened. And when John Brown attacked Harpers Ferry, moral suasion seemed to have become all but a thing of the past.

Clark was of this opinion. He impatiently awaited the dawn of a color-blind America in which the "distinction of Irishmen, German, and African [might] be lost in the general appellation of American citizens." Unlike Conway, Clark felt that slavery could not be eradicated without bloodshed. The black educator, though a man of letters, acknowledged that from the vantage point of the oppressed, violence could not be ruled out as a last resort. Was that not the legacy enshrined in the Declaration of Independence, a document revered by black and white intellectuals alike? Natural rights, after all, included the right to resist — if necessary, with force. Although this line of reasoning gave Conway serious headaches, it was a crystal-clear affair for Clark. To his satisfaction, Clark found this same uncompromising position prevalent among Willich's plebeian revolutionaries.[54]

As editor of the *Cincinnati Republikaner*, Willich scanned the news of the day for evidence of an unfolding class struggle. According to his understanding, the great social conflict was between labor and capital, between the producing and the property-holding classes. Chattel slavery, he believed, represented this conflict in the most glaring manner. It had to be opposed not so much because it was a crime against the black race, but because it stood for a system of capitalist exploitation reigning on plantations and in factories alike. Willich told his readers that the situation of the white laborer was unlikely to improve unless he also confronted those who kept the black laborer in chains, unless he realized that "black and white slavery derive[d] from the same principle." As long as the white worker tolerated slavery, Willich maintained, he would "not even have set foot on the battlefield for the advancement of human rights."[55]

Since the socialist editor viewed American slavery primarily through the prism of class conflict, it is not surprising that he defined resistance to it on the basis of workers' rights. This position is reflected in the many commentaries on John Brown's raid printed in the *Republikaner*. In Willich's accounts, Brown swung an ax not merely at black slavery; he laid it deeper, striking at the root of the ancient division of humankind into masters and servants. Brown started out as a religious fanatic, but his death at the hands of a tyrannical state enshrined him in a pantheon of secular revolutionists alongside Robert Blum, Felice Orsini, and other European martyrs of freedom. The cycle of insurrection, imprisonment, and execution that the abolitionist endured resembled a ritual of political sacrifice in which the European radicals were perfectly conversant. As a figure on a universal democratic continuum, Brown came to epitomize moral principles that reached across nations and historical epochs. "Old Brown's deed . . . forces us to take sides — the way we judge Old Brown is the way we choose," Willich insisted in Manichean fashion. "On one side, the rights of man, equal to all — the principle of good. On the other, the laws that uphold power and bondage — the principle of evil."[56]

Willich and Clark praised Brown less for what he thought than for what he did. Then again, it was Brown's actions that made it difficult for Conway to fully embrace him. All three men were featured as main speakers at the John Brown ceremony on December 4, 1859, but the emotions underlying their adulatory rhetoric were not the same. Conway loathed warfare, and his approval of Brown's failed insurrection came only after some initial wavering. The fact that he was from Virginia further amplified his reservations about the morality of Brown's violent action. The people trembling in the wake of Brown's assault, after all, were not simply slaveholders but relatives and loved ones whom Conway had left behind.

On October 23, 1859, Conway had ascended the pulpit to address his congregation for the first time since the Harpers Ferry incident. John Brown had been the subject of the day. Moderates viewed Conway's discourse that day as a fair and balanced assessment; to his German-born allies, however, it was one big disappointment. Conway had labeled Brown a morbid monomaniac and, while admiring his idealism, had expressed the belief that all true abolitionists would "denounce the method" of Brown. After the sermon, Stallo had taken the Unitarian minister to his house, where, Conway recalled, "He argued earnestly against my view and my extreme peace principles." Stallo's objections had some effect, for in the following weeks Conway gradually succumbed to the overall enthusiasm for Brown in the abolitionist camp. Apart from sharing the podium with Willich and Clark on December 4, he mourned Brown's death in an additional memorial service at his church.[57]

But Conway's reflections did not stop there. His depiction of Brown as a heroic martyr had not erased his qualms about the use of force. In an attempt to come to terms with his mixed feelings, he wrote "Excalibur," a parable that lauded Brown's noble effort on behalf of slaves but hoped that no further violence would be necessary. Now that Brown had dealt slavery a "wound that [could] never be healed," the ground was prepared for those "who [knew] the power of the Sword of the Spirit, the LOVE which never faile[d]." A problem remained, however: by sanctioning one act of violence one could no longer condemn so easily subsequent acts inspired by the same ideals. What if slavery did not die from its supposedly lethal wound? What if further blows were needed to finish it off? Conway was well aware of this dilemma. It would continue to haunt him as the nation moved closer to war.[58]

Such dilemmas seemed fairly outlandish to Willich and Clark. The trauma of 1848 was still fresh, and if there was any lesson that the German refugee had drawn from it, it was that social change could at times not be attained without bloodletting. Clark echoed this conviction at the Over-the-Rhine meeting of black and white radicals, declaring to those present that they were "in the midst of a revolution that must be fought to the death." Too long had his people been trampled, too long had they been excluded from citizenship; now a war was being waged that "must be met by all the weapons of freemen." Willich was more than thrilled by Clark's performance. In front of him stood an audacious black leader who seemed to possess all the eloquence and determination required of a true revolutionist. His speech, Willich commented, "should have been witnessed by all defenders of the trade in human flesh. . . . How embarrassed, how mean would they have felt, had they listened to the stirring words of the black speaker whom they despise so much."[59]

The fact that Clark's abolitionism was impregnated with rationalism and revolutionary violence deepened Willich's respect for the black educator, which he reaffirmed only two weeks after the John Brown meeting. On December 18, 1859, a group of black men — Clark was allegedly one of them — attended a fair organized by the Cincinnati Turnverein but were sent away because their

The careers of August Willich (right, Library of Congress) and Peter H. Clark (left, Cincinnati Museum Center — Cincinnati Historical Society Library) intersected in late 1859, when both publicly defended John Brown. Willich praised the black educator's courage in the face of white supremacist aggression, while Clark admired the militant radicalism emanating from the speeches of the refugee socialist.

presence upset several white visitors. Although it turned out that Clark was not among the expelled men, the incident sparked a heated debate in the local German American press, and Willich wielded his pen fervently in defense of the black educator. Portraying Clark as a man "who, thanks to his superior social and academic skills, would hold an eminent position in any civilized society," Willich rebuked those who judged people on the basis of color instead of merit. He also published a declaration by the expelled blacks stating that they had left the Turner fair "with regret, especially since [they] had nourished great ideas of [the German Americans'] friendship for [their] race."[60]

Willich belonged to a radical minority that went further than merely protesting slavery's expansion or fighting the idea of bondage in the abstract. His egalitarianism did not include a color line that privileged certain races over others. Pushed to the lowest ranks of antebellum society, African Americans, according to Willich, were just as oppressed as the white proletariat in the slums of London and New York. They too had been suffering from the inequity of not receiving their due, which made them potential revolutionary agents. They too had a capacity for intellectual development and needed the leadership of courageous men like Clark who were able to incite it. They too partook in "the great family of human beings" and were thus entitled to solidarity with the white man. Such interpretations of the slavery conflict left many of Willich's white readers dumbfounded. Even though they might have disliked slavery, they did not intend to tear down the social wall that separated them from blacks. Willich thought otherwise, thereby inviting the scorn of the conservative press. The anti-abolitionist *Volksfreund* branded him a "German nigger worshipper" and accused him of promoting racial miscegenation.[61]

Far from being discouraged by this kind of slander, the editor of the *Republikaner* continued to brood over the racist incident at the Turner fair. He was particularly annoyed because the expulsion had occurred in his own social milieu and some of the perpetrators were German-born Turners. In his view, their behavior not only violated the tenets of Enlightenment humanism; more significant still, it dangerously tainted the public image of the Turners as vanguards of radical democracy. Antiblack discrimination was not a bagatelle for Willich; those who treated it as one either lacked proper education or were ideologically unfit to be members of a democratic organization.[62]

It is interesting to see how Willich tried to garner support for African Americans not only by invoking humanitarian ideals but also by appealing to ethnic honor. He believed that furthering democratic values regardless of race or nationality was the "manifest destiny" of the Germans in America, an idea that Willich had already spelled out as president of the Steuben Association in Washington, D.C. A people as highly cultured as the Germans, he argued, ought to abstain from the prejudices of other nationalities. From their tribal origins to the transatlantic migrations of the day, they had always served as exemplars of human brotherhood, either through knowledge transmission or the actual intermingling with other "races." This legacy, which bound the Germanic people to the abstract notion of human unity, made them champions of "all oppressed people," including blacks. Hence Willich implored, "We are only Germans and act as such if we implement the spirit of humanity. . . . The hate of the dominant nationalities and races, we must be proud of it, we must not elude it, we must be strong in order to break it. Only then are we faithful to our people, to our race." In this provocative narrative, which boldly identifies Germanness with the cosmopolitan advancement of human rights, race is not presented as a category of exclusion. Rather, Willich's clarion call was to rally his kinsmen around the banner of interracial solidarity, to redirect their attention to issues of class that he believed to be far more pressing.[63]

Willich knew that there was little hope of persuading his opponents to agree with him. But at least the Cincinnati Turnverein fell in line. On December 30, a majority of Turners adopted a resolution censuring discrimination on the basis of skin color and vowed to oppose the same under whatever circumstance. It was a vow they were going to be measured by in the turbulent years ahead.[64]

On Different Fronts

When Abraham Lincoln was voted into the White House, the rope between North and South was dangerously stretched. With the shelling of Fort Sumter half a year later, it violently snapped in two. South Carolinians, convinced that their vital interests would have been impinged had they remained in the Union, had been the first to secede; six states had followed by the end of March 1861: Mississippi, Alabama, Georgia, Florida, Louisiana, and Texas. Steadfast in his belief that secession was unconstitutional, Lincoln refused to negotiate with the departed slaveholding states. And when the Confederates started seizing federal property on their territory, the new administration responded with force. The war feared by some and desired by others had begun.

In the wake of Lincoln's call for volunteers, the Queen City glittered in red, white, and blue. Few had anticipated such patriotic fervor in a border town like Cincinnati, but in light of impending hostilities partisan squabbles receded before a common devotion to preserving the Union. From the big political associations down to the smallest ethnic group, Cincinnatians turned out in throngs to pledge allegiance to the flag. Among the first to join in were citizens of German and Irish descent. Conway's First Congregational Church sang "The Star-Spangled Banner" and listened to a sermon by their pastor titled "The Peril and the Hope of the Hour." On April 22, a band of Polish immigrants convened at Workingmen's Hall, testifying that they too felt obliged to defend their new homeland. By far the largest pro-Union meeting took place on April 15 at Catholic Union Hall. The podium was stacked with spokesmen from various segments of the city's white population, whose speeches evoked rapturous applause. So did Johann Stallo's remarks. He wished that the war would remove not only all party distinctions "but all distinctions between native and adopted citizens."[65]

Because regiments were first formed on a communal basis, young men usually signed up on the same muster rolls as their friends and neighbors. This facilitated the organization of ethnic units. Two such regiments were the Irish Montgomery brigade and the all-German Ninth Ohio Infantry, a unit composed almost entirely of Turners and craft workers. American-born Robert McCook, a lawyer with strong ties to the city's German element, became its colonel; August Willich was elected adjutant, later major. The Turners had begun preparing for war as early as December 1860. Every night they practiced military drill in Turners' Hall under the tutelage of the red revolutionary. Willich's engagement in this unit, however, was short-lived. In August 1861, he went to Indiana, where he assumed command of the state's German American Thirty-second Infantry, a task more befitting his military experience.[66]

For Willich, the war came as a relief. He had long waited to settle old scores with the people who had driven him out of his fatherland. This seemed possible now, for he perceived in the southern gentry an offshoot of the European aristocracy, believing that they imperiled freedom and democracy for all people. When he saw the huge turnout for his new regiment, he noted with satisfaction that "this [was] the patriotic answer of the Germans of Indiana to the call of their government to take up arms to protect its republican institutions." For strategic reasons, Willich did not explicitly mention emancipating the slaves as a motivation to enlist. The far greater motivation, he suspected, was to prove oneself a worthy citizen of the republic. By bearing arms in the defense of their adopted homeland, the German Americans, Willich reasoned, would show "that they [were] not foreigners"; they would provide indisputable evidence to nativist Americans that they rightfully belonged in this country.[67]

The history of the Thirty-second Indiana is amply documented. Its soldiers fought at Shiloh, bled at Chickamauga, and stormed the hills of Chattanooga. Willich never shrunk from the heat of battle; this made him extremely popular among his troops, who lovingly referred to him as "Papa Willich." In camp, they were kept from idleness with activities redolent of the intellectual socialism that their commander had espoused before the war. On one occasion, he regaled his troops with a speech about the causes of the present conflict that, as one bystander recorded, ended in "a lecture about astronomy, as well about other branches of human inquiry"; on another occasion, he delivered an agnostic eulogy apparently so stirring that it moved the soldiers to tears. Educating the masses, for Willich, was as imperative in war as it was in peace. The soldiers he cared for should return home one day as citizens of a republic untarnished by slavery and founded on true social equality. It was the hope of planting his European-bred ideas of human progress in American soil that towered above all others, that made life in the United States meaningful to a German revolutionary.[68] As Willich confessed in an 1862 letter to his old comrade Fritz Anneke,

> Working toward a solution of the social problem and calling attention to it is and
> will remain the only purpose of my life; this work alone not only makes life bearable but worth living in my eyes. . . . This is why I took over the "Republikaner,"
> this is why I engaged in trade unions and trade assemblies. This is how I reached

first results and arrived at a version of the social reform idea that was also com-
prehensible to the native-born American, and that influenced them so that they
began contributing in an active and powerful manner.[69]

In Conway's assessment, the war was no less imbued with historic significance. He too had to find his role in the present crisis. The most feasible options
for him were army chaplain or propagandist. Conway chose the latter. His inability to accept physical suffering was as much a factor in this decision as the
nightmare that he might have to confront somebody on the battlefield whom
he knew personally. Some accused him of cowardice, but Conway disclaimed
such charges by pointing to the fact that equally important work must be done
behind the lines. Literati like him, he believed, could aid the war effort best
with their pens. Now that the war was a reality, it had to be steered in the right
direction. Most northerners simply wanted to restore the Union as it had been;
Conway and his abolitionist brethren, on the other hand, increasingly saw the
war as a momentous chance to build a Union as it should be. Their mission was
to turn a quarrel about constitutional issues into a crusade against slavery.[70]

Conway was one of the first abolitionists to place the African American at
the center of the struggle. "We have the courage to slay and be slain, but not
enough to touch slavery," he admonished his countrymen. To argue for immediate emancipation as the only legitimate war aim, Conway crisscrossed the northern states, sounding the abolitionist trumpet before common people as well
as the political leadership in Washington and elsewhere. Southerners claimed
to be the true heirs of 1776, but Conway denied them that title. "Revolution
depends for its dignity and heroism purely upon the worth and justice of its
cause," he maintained. Rather, "the Revolution is on our side," and "as soon as
the nation feels that, and acts upon it, the strength of the South is gone . . . WE
ARE THE REVOLUTIONISTS." At home, Conway had Peter H. Clark step in
front of his parishioners and discuss the urgency of emancipation. The initial
results, however, were disheartening. On August 30, 1861, John C. Frémont,
the Union general in charge of the Western Department, single-handedly proclaimed martial law in Missouri and declared all slaves therein free. President
Lincoln, fearing that Frémont's move might cost him the few remaining slave
states in the Union, revoked the general's order and relieved him from command on November 2.[71]

Throughout the Union, telegraph wires ran hot with the news of Frémont's
dismissal. When it reached Cincinnati, the city's radical German Americans
fumed in anger. They had been enamored of Frémont, an outspoken friend of
the immigrant and the slave, ever since his bid for the presidency in 1856. Many

were also proud that German militia units had been instrumental in securing St. Louis for the Union in the early days of the war. An indignation meeting at Turners' Hall was scheduled for November 23. Stallo and Conway featured as principal speakers. Their addresses gave additional weight to the meeting's resolutions, which termed Frémont's removal "a sad blow to the Republic" and disastrous in its effects "upon the patriotism of the people."[72]

Such sentiments barely resonated outside the radical German American milieu. In New York, the pro-Democratic *Herald* was terrified by the prospect that radical "Germans and native Americans would unite to root out by violence whatever obstacle lay in the way of universal emancipation, liberty and equality to all, black and white." Most white Cincinnatians were also glad that Frémont's designs had been thwarted. To them, the war was never about freeing the slaves or boosting the welfare of the black man. In spite of being pledged to crushing a slaveholders' rebellion, they had not become more receptive to their black neighbors. After the fall of Fort Sumter, Cincinnati's African American men too wanted to elicit their patriotic feelings, hoping to prove themselves equally courageous and worthy of citizenship. But as Clark remembered, white authorities only scoffed at attempts to organize a black militia unit. They refused keys for a meetinghouse where the city's African Americans wanted to assemble and forced the blacks to take down an American flag hanging above the door of their recruiting station. "We want you damned niggers to keep out of this; this is a white man's war," city officials told a disenchanted black community. They moreover warned that "a mob was brewing" — enough to make a black person tremble at that time.[73]

Antiblack violence broke out eventually. As the war became more atrocious, people lost confidence in a speedy victory. The situation was further complicated by an economic recession that hit the Queen City in early 1862. The river trade sagged to a minimum, and hundreds of white workers found themselves replaced by black contrabands, escaped slaves who had come into the possession of the Union army and who were willing to work for lower wages. A visiting British correspondent was struck by the mounting "jealousy of the low Germans and Irish against the free negro," a resentment that was no doubt fueled by Cincinnati's conservative press. In July 1862, racial hatred erupted on a full scale: Irish- and German-born dockworkers launched a massive assault against newly hired blacks on the levee. The rioting quickly spread into Bucktown and "Little Dublin," wreaking havoc in both neighborhoods. An entire week passed before city authorities managed to quell the violence.[74]

Blacks were not the only ones targeted in this period. That much became obvious during Wendell Phillips's visit in March 1862. The announcement that he would speak at Opera Hall was a gross provocation in the eyes of local white supremacists. Hardly had the Boston abolitionist uttered his first words when he and his followers, among them Johann Stallo and a contingent of Turner bodyguards, were barraged with shouts and hisses, later eggs and stones. Attempts to pacify the mob failed, and when a fistfight ensued between Phillips's opponents and German-born supporters, the Bostonian had to be brought to safety. The incident made headlines in all major newspapers; for Peter Clark, who witnessed the commotion firsthand, it was just one more in a series of incidents proving that "the city of Cincinnati . . . still [was] pro-slavery."[75]

The treatment his fellow African Americans received in late August 1862 did little to change Clark's mind. A Confederate invasion into southern Ohio seemed imminent then, and Cincinnatians prepared for the worst. On August 26, a German American gathering at Turners' Hall demanded that "every citizen or non-citizen" should assist in organizing the city's defense. Mayor George Hatch echoed this request in a public notice on September 2: "Every man, of every age, be he citizen or alien, who lives under the protection of our laws, is expected to take part in the organization." As no black volunteers responded to the call, which is not surprising given the way they had been treated on previous occasions, Hatch decided to press them into service. A special military police was formed that dragged every healthy male they could find to a recruitment site across the river. These men became the Black Brigade, whose deeds were chronicled by Peter Clark. Assigned to digging trenches and similar menial labor, its members nevertheless developed great pride in their work. Hopes that it might earn them the gratitude of the whites, however, soon faded. The Black Brigade was mustered out of duty on September 20. Those who had served returned home with a feeling of having asserted their manhood, yet without having won any additional rights or privileges.[76]

Not quite four months after the Black Brigade had been disbanded, Lincoln's Emancipation Proclamation took effect. Clark greeted the event with a mixture of elation and sadness. Few of his old allies were around to celebrate this day with him; most had, in one way or the other, become casualties of the war. Willich, captured while riding back from a military briefing, sat behind bars in Libby Prison outside the Confederate capital of Richmond. There he languished another five months until he was released as part of a prisoner exchange. Before rejoining his troops, Willich briefly went home to Cincinnati, where friends and admirers gave him an enthusiastic reception. At that point, Conway was already out of the country. He had decided to promote the abolitionist cause abroad, starting in England. Conway left on April 11, 1863, and would not return to the United States for the next forty years. The reasons for Conway's departure are not entirely clear, but it seems that he could no longer bear the emotional horrors of this war, which he felt more profoundly than many other Americans.[77]

The Civil War tore apart friends and families. The alliance between Willich, Clark, Stallo, and Conway was also strained by the exigencies of armed conflict. But while the war separated them physically, it did not eradicate the concerns that had brought them together. Emancipating the slaves, they agreed, was a laudable first step; yet more was needed to arrive at the kind of social and intellectual democracy that these radicals envisioned, a sociopolitical order built on the tenets of free thought, racial tolerance, and class solidarity. Formal freedom alone did not help Clark to "forget the prejudices of the American people." Nor did it suffice to bridge the gap between workers and capitalists, which Willich strove to bridge all his life. "Certainly, this war is over, and one abnormality, slavery, has been enacted out of existence," the old warrior conceded in 1866. "But other intellectual, social, and moral abnormalities still exist in our midst, and their main reliance is brute force."[78]

Willich was in his fifties then, a battle-hardened veteran, still abounding in vigor for the causes for which he had put himself in harm's way. He was not the only one. The Civil War was a transforming experience, not just for the nation as a whole but for the microcosm of German, Anglo-, and African American intellectuals who in concert had openly defied the mainstream norms of antebellum Cincinnati. Even though they were never to reunite in this constellation, they had come to understand that their respective social projects intersected at crucial points. Willich, who saw a world stratified by class, learned to make common cause with people who considered race to be the main divide in American society. Stallo, once the war was over, vindicated giving African American men the right to vote. Clark detected in the socialist ideals of his immigrant friends another venue to hasten the advancement of black Americans. And in his self-chosen British exile, Conway foresaw the day when "the free progressive minds" of the Old and the New World might be bound "into one great fraternity." From their separate ethnic visions, these intellectuals had moved toward espousing a multiethnic vision of democracy promising equal opportunity to the Anglo-Saxon, the immigrant, and the freed slave.[79]

CHAPTER FOUR

Why Continue to Be the Humble Maid?

A Transnational Abolitionist Sisterhood

Men demarcate precisely the sphere within which women are
supposed to move; just like they do with colored persons. . . .
Both share the same lot. . . . Both are in an inferior position, are
the weaker; hence they are also the constrained, the oppressed.
—MATHILDE FRANZISKA ANNEKE, "Sturmgeiger," 1863

A woman's heart that breaks not though it bleeds
Is not so rare a thing as men may deem,
Believe me, we are not the broken reeds
That many times we seem.
—MARY H. C. BOOTH, "Awake," 1861

THE COUPLE THAT TOOK UP RESIDENCE in the Milwaukee home of Wisconsin
abolitionist Sherman M. Booth in December 1858 were no ordinary people.
Fritz and Mathilde Franziska Anneke had come a long way, and their journey
from the battlefields of revolutionary Baden to the distant melting pots of the
New World supplied them with a multitude of tales and stories. Mary Booth,
Sherman's young wife and a vivid storyteller herself, seemed particularly gripped
by the vignettes that her new female housemate had to share. One day her ten-
ant appeared as a modern-day "Joan of Arc," overflowing with memories of the
German uprisings of 1848–49; on another she impressed her American host with
excerpts from an oeuvre consisting of "fifty books, poetry, novels, and scientific,
and revolutionary works." Mary grew increasingly fond of the writer from overseas. "I find daily some new & admirable characteristics in Mad. Anneke — she
is more and more 'wonderful' continually," Mary penned to her mother. "Her
heart & soul are as great as her body — Her humanity is boundless. . . . It seems
as if every human thing wanted to nestle like a chicken under her wings."[1]

Sixteen years earlier, Mathilde's kindheartedness and piercing intellect had already spellbound a young artillery lieutenant in the Prussian army, Fritz Anneke. The affection blossomed, and Fritz and Mathilde married. Both were radical agitators, and when the revolution broke out, Fritz traveled south to serve as a colonel in the democratic militia. Mathilde, a self-reliant woman and editor of the feminist *Frauen-Zeitung*, stayed at her husband's side, even in the face of battle. Carl Schurz, then aide-de-camp in Anneke's regiment, acknowledged Mathilde's bravery, describing her as "a young woman of noble character, beauty, vivacity, and fiery patriotism." After the final defeat, the Annekes fled from persecution and took refuge in Switzerland. Their stay in the neighboring country, however, was not permanent. On October 8, 1849, Fritz and Mathilde boarded a steamer in the French port of Le Havre bound for the United States.[2]

The Annekes' first decade abroad was filled with professional setbacks and private tragedies. Firsthand knowledge of the events of 1848 was a marketable commodity, and Fritz and Mathilde, who spoke little English, found themselves in tough competition with many other émigrés selling their accounts as a means of economic survival. Personal calamities added to these feelings of insecurity. In Newark, where they published the radical *Newarker Zeitung*, the Annekes had to bury four of their six children. Two of them, Irla and Fritz Jr., fell prey to a smallpox epidemic, which might have been averted had Fritz agreed to an inoculation. The rift between the parents widened. Not only did Mathilde blame her husband for the loss of their two children; equally disheartening was his enduring failure to provide the family with a stable economic foundation. When the Annekes arrived in Milwaukee, their marriage was seriously frayed.[3]

By the late 1850s, Milwaukee had matured into a colorful frontier community, attracting settlers from the New and the Old World alike. The city's rapid expansion was primarily a result of its favorable location on the southwestern shore of Lake Michigan, western land speculation, and innovations in transportation technology. Milwaukee was incorporated by the territorial legislature in 1836; its population exceeded 10,000 by 1850 and surged to 45,246 in 1860. Many of its first inhabitants were pioneers from New England and upstate New York, but the arrival of immigrants from different parts of Europe soon gave the frontier town a distinctive multiethnic flavor. So heavy was the influx of foreign-born settlers that, around 1850, more than 60 percent of all Milwaukeeans had been born outside the United States. The Irish formed their own neighborhoods — so did the Polish and the few Scandinavians — yet none of these ethnic groups ever exerted an impact similar to that of the city's German-speaking element.[4]

Historically, the Germans were Milwaukee's dominant and most visible ethnic minority. Their settlement in southwestern Wisconsin followed roughly the same patterns as in other midwestern regions. In 1840, according to one chronicler, city officials reported a weekly average of 250 persons of German descent debarking at Milwaukee harbor. These numbers continued to swell until the mid-1850s, when pre–Civil War immigration from Germany into the United States reached an all-time high. At this point, Milwaukee's German-speaking residents were already well stratified along various regional, denominational, and occupational lines. The majority, more than 40 percent, were skilled workers and craftsmen, an estimated 13 percent belonged to the entrepreneurial classes, while 7 percent had a peasant background. Spatial cohesion was important for Milwaukee's Germans. The areas in the city where they agglomerated were wards 2, 6, 8, and 9.[5]

Visitors were quick to recognize the strong sense of ethnic kinship that had developed among Milwaukee's German-speaking population. By installing their own newspapers, parishes, taverns, and shops advertising goods in German, they managed to create a social ambience more congenial to their tastes and customs. As one traveler noted, "This genial atmosphere shines everywhere, lends the physiognomy of the city itself a friendly and comfortable air, and has even infected American society, whose stiff and icy tone has thawed to a limited extent under the influences of German customs." This urban facade apparently lasted more than one generation; at the turn of the century, one young woman still expressed amazement that many parts of Milwaukee "look[ed] like Germany; there were public buildings that might have stood in Strassburg or Nuremberg, ornate residences that were influenced by the German renaissances, and German faces, German signs, Teutonic speech."[6]

The German element's consolidation in antebellum Milwaukee was furthered by the emergence of a rich associational life. As early as the mid-1840s, the newcomers engaged and congregated in social domains ranging from the beer garden to informal music corps, marching bands, theater societies, and hunting clubs. The Forty-Eighters who relocated to the northwestern frontier intensified this process of ethnocultural organization. As in other places, they reconfigured the texture of Milwaukee's German American community with their desire to institutionalize their progressive social and political philosophies. Foremost in this purpose were the various Turner, freethinker, and labor movements, all of which established branches in what soon became known as the "German Athens" on Lake Michigan.[7]

Carl Schurz, Wisconsin's leading Forty-Eighter refugee, was certain that his fellow revolutionaries "brought something like a wave of spring sunshine" into German Milwaukee. They "awakened interests which a majority of the old population had hardly known," Schurz commented in retrospect, "but which now attracted general favor, and very largely bridged over the distance between the native American and the new-comer." Although Schurz's depiction of the exiled revolutionaries as intellectual and political vanguards has some validity, their impact should not be overrated. Before the Civil War, most German Milwaukeeans favored the Democrats, the party commonly associated with states' rights, local self-rule, and social conservatism. This voting behavior changed slightly in 1854 with the advent of the Republicans, whose antislavery platform appealed to the liberal and radical democratic end of the German American political spectrum. The greater portion of German immigrants, however, remained suspicious of the new party because of the bonds that traditionally connected them to the Democrats. Others opposed the Republicans because they allegedly welcomed in their ranks northern reformers of all types — abolitionists, nativists, and temperance and women's rights activists. It was this last concern that led the *Wisconsin Banner und Volksfreund*, Milwaukee's leading German-language daily, to put forth the following caveat: "As soon as the Germans desert the Democracy and go with the abolitionists, they will elevate to power and prestige a sect which thinks to turn the entire country into a 'Water-Cure,' . . . which seeks to prescribe the Bible . . . as the highest and only binding code of laws, . . . which wants to snatch the women away from their useful and influential sphere in the quiet domestic circle of the family, in order to draw them into the stormy seas of never-ending political agitation."[8]

For the Forty-Eighter intellectuals who wound up far west, the conservatism they encountered among the majority of Old World settlers was a disillusioning experience. The rank and file had not gone all the way to America to experiment with the unfamiliar; they simply wanted to live in peace inside the margins of a culture they knew and in which every individual was assigned a preordained place. The Annekes were not the last to learn that challenging the old immigrant leadership meant conflict, even in far-flung Milwaukee. When the city's German-born typesetters learned that Mathilde employed women in her newly established *Frauen-Zeitung* office, they immediately organized into a union barring female membership. Too eccentric seemed the idea to these men that women should compete with them for jobs — a woman's proper role, they held, was that of a loving wife and caring mother. Anything beyond that was not sanctioned by the dominant gender ideology of the time and considered unnatural. It was not the issue of women's rights, however, that fanned the flames of strife inside Milwaukee's German American community, but one that increasingly cast its shadow over the entire nation: the future of the South's "peculiar institution."[9]

Slave Catchers in Our Midst!

On March 10, 1854, federal authorities burst into a shanty located on the outskirts of Racine, Wisconsin. After a brief tussle, they managed to overpower and arrest the man they had come to apprehend. Joshua Glover, a runaway slave, had sought asylum in Racine, where abolitionists had helped disguise his true identity by giving him employment in a nearby mill. Not long afterward, his Missouri master discovered his whereabouts. He procured a court warrant and called on two deputy marshals to assist him in reclaiming his property. In line with the provisions of the Fugitive Slave Act, Glover was taken to a jail in Milwaukee, fifty miles north of Racine. There he awaited inquiry by a federal commissioner and would have been sent back into slavery if Wisconsin's abolitionists had not taken preemptive action. Learning that Glover was being detained in Milwaukee, hundreds of men marched to the jail and protested for the prisoner's release. Public excitement grew, and in the wake of an indignation meeting, an angry mob stormed the prison and liberated Glover. "In Wisconsin the Fugitive Slave Law is repealed!" a triumphant Sherman Booth told his readers. "PERISH ALL ENACTMENTS ESTABLISHING SLAVERY ON FREE SOIL."[10]

Milwaukee's immigrants did not stand idly by. Some of the recent Forty-Eighter arrivals were particularly livid that Wisconsin authorities seemed resolved to enforce the Fugitive Slave Act in a free state and convert the city jail into a slave pen. Most enjoyed good neighborhood relations with the few African Americans who had moved to Milwaukee. Fired up by reminiscences of the battle against European tyranny, immigrant leaders participated in the rescue with as much ardor as the American-born protesters. City clerk Henry Bielfeld and the journalists Moritz Schöffler and Friedrich Fratny directly involved themselves and served on committees formed to aid Glover. Rudolf Koss, chronicler of Milwaukee's antebellum Germans, noted that the jailbreakers were "composed of the most diverse national elements. People of all ranks and classes," Koss specified, "Americans, Germans, Irish, Dutch, Norwegians, blacks and whites, worked together, intermingling without significant disorder or mayhem."[11]

But it was Booth whom the Glover episode propelled into the national spotlight. As one of the ringleaders in the operation — Booth purportedly incited the mob to action with the rallying cry, "Freemen to the Rescue! Slave catchers are in our midst" — he had to face serious litigation himself. The widely publicized trials guaranteed him a place in the national press and molded his image as a defiant radical. Booth had come to his abolitionist vocation in the "burned-over" districts of New York, an area heavily exposed to revivalism and moral reform in the 1820s and 1830s. He became one of the figureheads of Connecticut's young Liberty Party, which argued that slavery could be attacked best within the existing political framework. Booth defended this third-party strategy against opposition from both the Garrisonian camp and the political establishment and carried this stance into the formation of the Free Soil Party in late 1848.[12]

Later that year, Booth, eager to raise the banner of party-based resistance to slavery on the western frontier, assumed the editorship of a radical free-soil paper in the nascent state of Wisconsin. Not long after settling in Milwaukee, he also experienced a turning point in his private life. His wife, Margaret, fell ill and died in 1849. Virtually at her deathbed, Booth made the acquaintance of Mary Humphrey Corss, a young and devout middle-class woman from Connecticut who gave him emotional comfort. Their wedding just months after the death of Booth's first wife met with much disapproval. Booth, however, dismissed these objections in the same moralizing posture that was characteristic of his public persona. The first years of the Booths' marriage seemed to justify him: despite having wed in defiance of social custom, the Booths ostensibly lived in marital harmony, and Mary gave birth to three girls, Mary Ella, Alice, and Lillian May.[13]

As editor of the *American Freemen* and later the *Wisconsin Free Democrat*, Booth tried to galvanize public opinion against any proslavery legislation coming out of Washington. He delivered blistering anathemas on the Fugitive Slave Law and was willing to shake hands with any person who adopted his radical stance. Though only a few diehard abolitionists had moved to Wisconsin, the overwhelming portion of that state's white population wanted to keep the western territories untouched by slavery. Booth campaigned hard to mobilize this free-soil sentiment and turn it into a political movement. Two almost simultaneous events, the Glover incident and the Kansas-Nebraska Act, revealed to Wisconsin's opponents of slavery the moral bankruptcy of their elected officials. On February 13, 1854, Booth supervised the state's first anti-Nebraska meeting in downtown Milwaukee, lighting a trail that ended six weeks later at a school house in Ripon hailed by some as the birthplace of the Republican Party.[14]

Every vote counted for the new antislavery party. Booth hoped that its message would resonate not only with American-born citizens. Immigrants had

generally been loyal Democrats, but now there were signs that the more liberal segments among the foreign-born were dissatisfied with the status quo and
searching for a new political abode. Recognizing this shift in party allegiance,
Booth urged his party friends to free themselves "from the taint of Know-
Nothingism." Nativists, temperance activists, and Republicans often made common cause in Wisconsin, which lessened the new party's appeal to the state's
sizable German American electorate. To counter this tendency, Booth set out to
establish ties with Carl Schurz, Bernhard Domschke, and other German-born
democrats in the area. Likely enough, the Annekes too were viewed by Booth
as potential partners in a common struggle. Yet the relationships that were to
evolve went far beyond political partnerships. They would move back and forth
between the public, the social, and the private, constantly testing the boundaries of all three spheres.[15]

Public Trials and Private Ordeals

Eighteen fifty-nine was a watershed year for the Anneke and Booth families.
The wounds struck by the loss of Fritz junior and Irla had never really healed,
slowly eating away at the conjugal bonds that had helped the Annekes weather
numerous personal and professional crises over the past decade. An additional
burden was Fritz's increasing discomfort with his American exile. His economic
misfortunes left him deeply frustrated, with the result that he began venting his
anger more directly at the conditions surrounding him. After learning that war
clouds were gathering over the Italian peninsula, Fritz saw a chance to revive
his revolutionary career alongside the democratic movements in Europe. When
several papers, among them Booth's *Free Democrat*, put him on their payroll as a
foreign correspondent, all obstacles seemed cleared. Fritz left for Switzerland in
May 1859, leaving Mathilde and the children behind with the Booths.[16]

Mary's relationship with Sherman was in even greater disarray. Booth's legal
warfare against the Fugitive Slave Law and the seemingly endless cycle of arrest,
applying for a writ of habeas corpus, release, and rearrest, made him a public
celebrity but also took a toll on his family life. In early April 1859, the police
once more knocked at Booth's door. This time they had not come because of
Sherman's involvement in the Glover affair. The prominent abolitionist was
now being charged with a far more scandalous felony: the seduction of Mary's
fourteen-year-old babysitter, a girl named Caroline Cook. The crime allegedly
took place on February 28, 1859, while Mary was out of town attending a wedding. Caroline later testified that she was unable to resist Booth's onslaught and
was "penetrated" three times. Booth pleaded innocent, but Mary did not be-

Sherman Booth (Wisconsin State Historical Society, WHi-9485). The jailbreak leading to fugitive slave Joshua Glover's freedom made Booth an abolitionist celebrity until the Caroline Cook seduction scandal cost him job and reputation.

lieve him. Obviously, this was not the first time that Sherman had let her down. Yet Mary was not left alone in her anguish. Viewing Fritz's departure as an act of betrayal, Mathilde could see herself in Mary's despair. Simultaneously, Mary constructed a link between her own and Mathilde's abandonment. Their relationship became more intimate. They began sharing household responsibilities and engaged in social pastimes such as reading, attending plays and concerts, and going for extended walks. And when Mary needed nursing because of her chronic lung problems, Mathilde watched over her. Clearly, Mathilde filled an emotional gap in Mary's life, and so did Mary in Mathilde's. "What I have I want to share with Mary. . . . I am her true friend; I never want to leave her, nor does she."[17]

Booth, meanwhile, was fighting for his political survival. Already his opponents were trying to cash in on the scandal, gleefully distributing news about the parties involved and ridiculing the abolitionist as a "long-haired seducer" and a "deceitful, bigoted hypocrite." Even among the Republicans, people disassociated themselves from Booth because identification with him had become a political liability. Carl Schurz, for one, was thoroughly repulsed by Booth's behavior. He suggested that it had done more harm to the Republican cause than any blow dealt by the proslavery side. To prove his innocence, Booth spent almost all his assets, including his share of the *Free Democrat*, on lawyers and detectives. Mary showed no pity nor did she give in to any of Sherman's concil-iatory gestures. Booth ascribed this to Mathilde's "bad influence"; Mary, he fig-ured, would not have been able to sustain such defiant behavior on her own.[18]

Wisconsin v. S. M. Booth commenced on July 25, 1859. Due to the notoriety of the defendant and the indecent nature of the case, the trial pulled hordes of curious onlookers into the courtroom. What they saw was a cunning perfor-mance by Booth's lawyers that ultimately split the jury in half. Instead of fend-ing off the prosecutor's attacks, they managed to sway the court into doubting the victim's integrity. Caroline, they argued, was not the innocent, well-bred girl next door but a flirtatious young woman with an unchaste character. The prosecution took the bait and for the rest of the trial focused on invalidating the allegations put forward by the defense. On August 8, Booth was acquitted and left the courtroom a free man.[19]

Mary, worn down by shame and her weak physical condition, was not pres-ent at the trial. Yet her mind was made up. She was looking for a way to leave Booth. Mathilde had been following the court procedures on her friend's be-half, and what she saw only hardened her resolve. A pioneer of the first interna-tional women's movement, Mathilde could not treat Booth's transgressions as a private and apolitical affair. Instead, they reevoked a fundamental dilemma in mid-nineteenth-century gender relations, one that Anneke had wrestled with extensively in her 1847 pamphlet *Woman in Conflict with Society*. Challenging the culturally prescribed separation of male and female spheres of influence in bourgeois society, Mathilde railed against the pitfalls of this system, which she saw as a great detriment to women. A society denying women political auton-omy, she contended, was unacceptable, for it left them dependent on fallible men. Worse, it degraded them into a position of dependency tantamount to slavery. Why, she asked, should women heed the laws that men had made "not for [women's] good, but for theirs" when women "have the same rights to the enjoyment of life as [their] oppressors"? Having suffered under this immoral system herself, Mathilde postulated that the individual's status in society should be determined by character and intelligence, not sex.[20]

The corresponding dictum in the United States to the German bourgeois model of a wife-mother was the "true woman." Similar to her German coun-terpart, the ideal American woman was perceived to be gentle, emotional, and sensitive. She was expected to concentrate her energies on household and chil-dren, thereby turning the home into a haven of tranquility for her husband, who was to provide for the family in the enterprising, calculating, and tempestuous worlds of business and politics. This separate-spheres ideology dovetailed neatly with the social realities of the time. Economically, men controlled nearly all the country's wealth; women had no right to vote or hold office; and in most cases, the right of women to own property or enjoy the wages they earned was either nonexistent or carelessly enforced.[21]

Mathilde Anneke did not see in the gender norms of white middle-class America the exciting alternative she had hoped to find. In her judgment, American women were not only "civilly dead," as Elizabeth Cady Stanton famously termed it, but were further hampered by blindly adhering to an illusive Christian faith. Reflecting her transformation from a devout Catholic to a radical freethinker and suffragist, many of Anneke's early feminist tracts conjure up the image of women living in a double cage. They suggest that in order to break out of the cage of male supremacy, women must first free themselves from the cage of Christian religion, a belief system that legitimized much of the antifemale gender bias of the time. Anneke's hostility to established religion was shared by many of her fellow radicals from overseas; at the same time, this stance set her apart from native-born feminists demanding equal rights not in spite but often because of their religious convictions.[22]

At first glance, Mathilde's friendship with Mary seemed unhampered by these differing outlooks. In the weeks following the trial, Mathilde practically took command of the Booth-Anneke commune. Sherman withdrew almost totally from his paternal duties — the seduction affair had cost him job and reputation — and left it to Mathilde to remedy the family budget crisis. Mary admired Mathilde's emancipationist traits but was reluctant to fully adopt them. The reasons for this were not just personal and generational — Mathilde was fourteen years older and far more experienced in political matters than Mary. There were also cultural forces at work. Mary was no revolutionary. In many ways, she epitomized the beau ideal of a "true woman." Purity, piety, domesticity, and submissiveness were the four cardinal virtues according to which she had been raised, and they remained inscribed in her self-definition as a woman in this turbulent period. Hence Mary was grateful that Mathilde had agreed to take over paternal responsibilities, a behavior that was more in line with her friend's radical notions of womanhood.[23]

Yet it would be wrong to say that her less activist model of female identity condemned Mary to passivity. With renewed vigor, she immersed herself in domestic activities such as housekeeping, churchgoing, and writing poetry, no doubt also to sooth her troubled mind. Mary's language was seldom militant in tone; it was tender, sensitive, and pious, indicating a reverence for the very classic feminine qualities that Mathilde had been striving to surpass. Interestingly enough, these two disparate conceptions of female self-mastery did not clash but entered into a fruitful symbiosis. Praising Mary's "character, her love, her innate sense of beauty, her compassion," Mathilde came to reassess her qualms about the evangelical cult of religious domesticity. By allowing Mary to expose her children to the "tender teachings" of the Bible, Mathilde acknowledged the importance of religion for educating the heart. Mary was not simply Mathilde's willing student. She was her companion, a source of moral strength and aesthetic inspiration, the sentimentalist pendant to Mathilde's rationalist approach to social reform. Theirs was a mutually enriching friendship that continued to bloom as they confronted American slavery, the most explosive issue of the time.[24]

The financial calamities in the Booth home persisted throughout 1859. Having lost nearly all his social prestige, Sherman began contemplating drastic alternatives. A diligent reader of Fritz Anneke's letters from Europe, Booth wondered whether he should follow in Fritz's footsteps. He knew that abolitionists had traveled to Europe before, some with considerable success. In January 1860, Mathilde told Fritz that Sherman had been rhapsodizing about going to England on an extended writing and lecture tour, and that he was hoping to win her husband as partner. "I think the plan I proposed . . . is a feasible one," Booth scribbled on the backside of Mathilde's letter, "& one that will pay."[25]

Fritz's European correspondence was enormously popular with Sherman's female housemates. His romantic portrayals of the Italian uprising and elaborate depictions of the Swiss landscape had a mesmerizing effect on Mary, and she was happy that Fritz had consented to embellishing his letters with the kind of flamboyant imagery she preferred. Together with Mathilde's tales and romances from the Old World, they implanted in her a longing for the faraway, a utopian counterworld where she could rid herself of all bodily and mental ailments, not to mention the dismal marriage from which she was struggling to break free. Coming to Switzerland, Fritz promised, would be like being born anew: "When you come to this most beautiful country on earth . . . to these wonders of nature . . . if you could only breathe that air, dear Maria, you never would be sick again." Little more was needed to convince Mary.[26]

Mathilde was at first skeptical about finding a sanctuary in the Swiss Alps but soon yielded to her friend's anticipation. In fact, she too was considering a reunion with Fritz because of ongoing financial difficulties. Also, she felt that a trip to Europe might further enrich her relationship with Mary. In spite of all the emotional intimacy, Mathilde still felt intellectually somewhat remote from her. "Deeper conversations that might enhance our knowledge and thinking are to some extent inconceivable," she complained. "The difference in our standpoints, and those of our languages, prevent so much." However, Mathilde believed that these differences were environmental, not personal. She was confident that they could be overcome by a change of location. Just as her stay in the United States had given her an inside perspective on American society, crossing the Atlantic in the opposite direction might enhance Mary's appreciation of her friend's radical European heritage. The proficiency she would then gain in these matters, Mathilde hoped, would broaden her intellectual horizon and make her a more valuable ally in the politics of social change.[27]

It was not in Switzerland, however, but in Milwaukee where both earned their first laurels as an activist tandem. The sectional crisis had deepened late in the decade, and after John Brown led his men into Harpers Ferry, a compromise on the slavery question seemed more distant than ever. The news of Brown's trial and execution sent shock waves throughout Wisconsin. On December 2, 1859, the day of Brown's hanging, there were two separate John Brown meetings in Milwaukee: the larger one took place at the local chamber of commerce and included most of the city's Republican leadership; a smaller, overwhelmingly German American band of Brown sympathizers, among them Mathilde Anneke and the Booths, flocked to Market Hall, where they expressed their grief and outrage over the impending death of the militant abolitionist.[28]

Tensions escalated further as another proslavery verdict was put into effect three months later, one that brought all travel preparations in the Booth home to a sudden halt. Booth, with the help of his lawyers, had so far repelled any effort by federal officials to make him serve his sentence for violating the Fugitive Slave Act. An impatient United States Supreme Court put an end to Booth's legal maneuvers on March 7, 1859. Robert B. Taney spoke for the court in reaffirming the constitutionality of the Fugitive Slave Law and overruling Wisconsin's highest judges, who up to this point had decreed in favor of the accused. Taney's proclamation hit the state like a bolt from the blue and impelled many to declare resistance to it, despite Booth's waning popularity. As late as December 1859, Booth still mocked authorities, telling them that they could find him "at any reasonable hour . . . ready to answer any attempt upon [his] liberty." This time, however, the federal authorities did not back down. They arrested Booth on March 1, 1860, and locked him up in the newly erected Milwaukee customhouse.[29]

Mathilde made no secret of her loathing of Booth as a husband and father; his public persona, however, she could not denounce that easily. Booth's steadfast convictions had always impressed her. Moreover, Booth welcomed the abolitionist energy coming from feminists, many of whom challenged slavery and racism in a broader effort to create new opportunities for their own self-expression. Once Mathilde fired off a diatribe against Milwaukee's Germans, censuring them for their poor "sense of justice," because she felt Booth received inadequate support from her countrymen in the crusade against bondage. Now that Booth had been imprisoned by a government Mathilde believed had turned into the extended arm of southern slaveholding interests, Milwaukee's men seemed to her as apathetic as ever. All they did, Mathilde protested, was pay lip service to democratic ideals that they did not truly uphold. What made her blood boil were antislavery politicians like her former comrade and Republican luminary Carl Schurz, who, in her eyes, indulged in a rhetoric of liberty and states' rights but failed to act on it. Fritz shared Mathilde's outrage, echoing her opinion that ideals mattered little in the opportunistic world of American party politics: "How they left their spearhead against the bestiality of slavery in the lurch ... to them a principle is nothing but a prayer for election, a promotion of one's own personal advantage, which they cast aside as soon as it is no longer effective, how they luxuriate in the most glaring and flowery phrases on whose realization they never reflect, people like Schurz, Domschke, and similar riffraff. And still, the disgraceful, tyrannical treatment of the prisoner on Wisconsin's 'free' soil! Compared to this, the current conditions in Prussia are much easier to endure."[30]

Even Mary, who might have felt tempted to gloat over her husband's incarceration, had no intention of leaving Sherman behind bars. The crime leading to his arrest, after all, was not sexual misconduct but aiding a fugitive slave, to her an act of Christian charity for which she had the highest regard. Parallel to finalizing their travel arrangements for Switzerland, Mathilde and Mary vowed to do everything in their power to help Sherman — in this situation more friend than foe — regain his freedom.[31]

In the remaining months, the women were Booth's major link to the outside world. Mathilde frequently visited Booth in his heavily guarded cell, intrepidly bringing news in and taking notes out. "The U.S. Marshall is in mortal dread of Franziska Maria," Mary noted gleefully. "He says she has the devil in her and might do any thing — that she could put her clothes on Mr. Booth — thus allow him to escape." Before a jailbreak could be risked, both women felt that the public needed to be swayed to condone such an act of insurgency. One strategy popular among Wisconsin abolitionists was to portray their state as an enclave of freedom under assault by an expanding slaveholding power. Starting in early April, Mathilde smuggled out several of Booth's letters to achieve just that effect. Published in papers in and outside the state, they rendered him a victim of a despotic, slavery-sustaining federal government that trampled on fundamental civil rights such as the right to assemble and speak freely. Booth, consciously invoking states' rights, provoked his fellow Wisconsinites: "Is there not virtue enough in the people to maintain their own honor and vindicate the decision of their own Courts?" Declarations of solidarity also came in from abroad. "The treatment you receive from the obedient tools of the nigger barons," Fritz Anneke seethed in an open letter to the *Milwaukee Sentinel*, "is unheard of even in the despotic States of this part of the world."[32]

The insurrection that Booth and Anneke had hoped to incite did not occur; nevertheless, by late June, Mathilde and Mary had recruited a band of about thirty men of American and German descent who were pledged to liberating Booth at all costs. With their house serving as the headquarters of this conspiracy, the women directed and were kept abreast of most of its activities. A committee was formed, a plot contrived: Booth should be freed on July 3 and triumphantly address the people on the following day, the symbolic fourth. The plan was never carried out. Several conspirators either came too late, came unarmed, or did not show up at the agreed-upon meeting point at all. Those who kept their word set up a small task force led by the Kansas veteran Edward Daniels but withdrew after learning that the customhouse guards had been alarmed and reinforced.[33]

One last attempt was undertaken on Independence Day. In the morning hours, Mathilde, Mary, and their remaining male assistants placarded large posters in Milwaukee's core districts bearing the caption

Freemen

to the Custom House,

At two o'clock,

To Prove our Day of Independence a Reality,

BOOTH

Will address the people

From his window.[34]

This was sufficient to attract a large crowd, but once again federal authorities had taken precautions. At the appointed time, they had Booth's prison window shut, making sure that he could not be heard. Far from conceding defeat, O. H. LaGrange, a young abolitionist from Ripon, jumped onto the roof of an adjacent storehouse and read out Booth's tirade against the Fugitive Slave Act, a copy of which Mary had given him and to which he added his own "revolutionary preamble." His demeanor was "spirited," the *Milwaukee Sentinel* commented, but evidently not spirited enough to stir the crowd to action. Sensing cowardice, Mathilde dejectedly remarked: "We had [tried] everything to obtain Booth's freedom prior to our departure. I had thought it to be a manageable task, and honestly, by my own life," she added with astounding militancy, "had I been permitted to be the leader of these people, he would be free now."[35]

On July 21, 1860, Mary and Mathilde, with their three children Percy, Hertha, and Lillian in tow, boarded a steamer in Milwaukee harbor. Traveling via Buffalo, New York, to New York City, from whence they sailed to Bremerhaven, Germany, they were scheduled to arrive in Zürich by late August. Mary departed for Switzerland with high expectations, hoping to restore her health and gain new impulses for her literary endeavors. Mathilde's feelings were more ambivalent. Although she wanted to give her marriage a second chance, she considered the move short term: "I can hardly imagine staying away from my second home for more than two years."[36] Mathilde, no doubt as a result of her stay with the Booths, had ceased viewing the United States as a temporary exile, and because of this she was all the more pained to see her new homeland mired in conflict. The seduction affair and Booth's incarceration had become symbols to her of all that was not right in this society, of the enduring discrepancy between America's democratic promise and the realities she discerned around her: the chasm between intellectual idealism and political practice, the divisions between men and women, the dichotomies of freedom and slavery. Leaving Milwaukee at this critical juncture had a bittersweet taste for Mathilde, one she came to terms with in a fictionalized essay titled "Erinnerungen vom Michigan-See" (Memories from Lake Michigan):

> We planned to say farewell to a friend, who, for his humane deed of rescuing a slave from the hands of his persecutors, was held prisoner behind iron doors in the cold marble fortress by the slavery-supporting government, and whom we had tried to free by force. . . . Our farewell was short, but double in sorrow that accompanies a usual separation. A handshake — a tear in which the hope of a quick release was mirrored, and a radiant glare in the eye, which declared thanks in the name of freedom — then a farewell, until we meet again! . . . From the window of this American Bastille, the prisoner could look out over the wide blue lake; it was a "tower on the beach" in which he pined and suffered, a victim of savagery and barbarism in the land of freedom and independence.[37]

An Asylum in the Alps

About four weeks later, on August 19, Mathilde and Mary landed safely in the German port of Bremerhaven. From there, they continued their voyage southward, stopping in Dortmund, Cologne, and Frankfurt, where Mathilde called at the homes of old friends and relatives, most of whom she had not seen for more than a decade. But these were only fleeting reunions. Not long afterward, the travelers crossed into Switzerland and reached their final destination, Zürich.

Warmly welcomed by Fritz, whose correspondences to American and European newspapers were beginning to give him some financial stability, Mathilde and Mary absorbed their new surroundings with great joy. The house where they were boarding was located on the city's western outskirts, providing the tenants with a breathtaking view of Lake Zürich and the adjoining mountains. Mary felt as if she were wandering through one of Grimm's fairy-tale worlds, and her letters home abound with picturesque descriptions of landscape and neighborhood. The climate was more than pleasant, gardens were adorned "with the most beautiful array of flowers," and out on the lake "little oar-boats [were] sailing continually" before their eyes. Fritz had not promised too much. All woes, bodily and mental, seemed to dissipate in this Old World idyll.[38]

The Swiss cantons, with their republican institutions and traditions of local self-rule, had attracted thousands of Forty-Eighter refugees from neighboring countries who sought shelter from the crowned heads they had tried to topple. The greater portion of these expatriates used Switzerland as a springboard to other places such as England or the United States; a minority, however, stayed for longer periods, some even permanently. Zürich, with an estimated thirty thousand inhabitants, received an appropriate share of the fugitive revolutionaries. Disquieted by the new cosmopolitan rage that blew through Zürich's streets, the Swiss poet Gottfried Keller confessed in 1855: "It is awful to see Zürich flooded with all these scholars and literati; and one hears more High German, French, and Italian nowadays than our old Swiss German." Even traditional festivities, Keller reported, had become subject to internationalization. "Fourteen days ago we had a great spring festival in our old town, during which all the nations of this earth, the wild and the civilized . . . were out on parade, either on horseback or on foot, in the most gaudy and delicate costumes."[39]

Unlike the provincial Keller, Mathilde and Mary were immensely grateful that Zürich left its gates ajar for artists and thinkers from across the Continent. The Annekes knew several of these uprooted intellectuals personally: the socialist Ferdinand Lassalle; Ottilie Assing's sister Ludmilla, editor of the diaries of Varnhagen von Ense; the physician Jacob Moleschott; the Countess Hatzfeldt; and Wilhelm Rüstow, a former officer in the Prussian army. Closest of all were their ties to the poet Georg Herwegh and his wife, Emma, whose house had become something of an international salon, an underground information agency for German and Italian revolutionaries. Francesco De Sanctis and Filippo De Boni, two followers of Garibaldi's militant nationalism, were frequent visitors, supplying the hosts and their guests with the latest news and gossip on the burgeoning Italian liberation movement.[40]

Fritz introduced Mathilde and Mary into this circle shortly after their arrival, and both were soon on familiar terms with Moleschott and the Herweghs. It was Mary's first encounter with Old World intellectuals on their own turf, and it is interesting to see how she managed to assert herself as coequal in the company of these widely admired literati. Not only did she tenaciously defend her religious beliefs in this agnostic milieu; she also participated in their discussions about art and politics. Herwegh, the celebrated bard of the Young Germany movement, fascinated her most. She regarded him "a fine looking man . . . with great geniality, & yet with Quaker like modesty" and thought his poems breathed "the very soul of melody." Instantly enchanted, she translated several of his pieces into her mother tongue. A few weeks later, Mary presented the first sketches of her work to the Herweghs. The revolutionary poet sparkled with delight, and Mary took his praising words as indication that her literary gifts deserved the ovations of a larger audience. "Seeing his songs in this foreign garment touched him, the poet who could be aroused so easily," Mathilde observed. Moments like these added to her conviction that Mary had enough genius to mature into a great poet and writer.[41]

Encouraged by the Herweghs and their associates, the two women threw themselves with enthusiasm into what would become one of the most productive literary collaborations of the era. Writing meant more than a pastime to them. They made it their profession. The *Wisconsin Banner und Volksfreund* and the *New Yorker Criminal-Zeitung* had hired Mathilde as correspondent when she was still in the United States; the *New York Independent*, the *Hartford Press*, and the *Home Journal* consented to publish Mary's poems and glimpses of Swiss life. In Switzerland, the list of periodicals willing to accept the women's literary and journalistic contributions expanded further. Benefiting from a growing appetite among German readers for news from the New World, Mathilde was able to sell her expertise in American affairs to numerous German and Swiss newspapers, including the *Allgemeine Augsburger Zeitung*, the most renowned German daily at that time.[42]

These arrangements promised to yield economic autonomy, which made Mary and Mathilde feel less dependent on their husbands for support. Booth, for his part, did little to win back his offended wife. Aside from inviting her to join the staff of the *Daily Life*, the paper he launched after being released from prison, he gradually cut back on his correspondence until he was exchanging information on only the most basic matters with her. His neglect obviously went so far that Mary accused him of denying their daughters a solid education. Booth had never been much of an entrepreneur, and in his handling of monetary matters he seemed as wantonly negligent as ever. By November 1861, Mary was at the end of her tether, labeling Booth a "blood sucker." Owing to her recent engagements with the press, however, Mary felt confident that by going about her work "earnestly and practically" she should "soon be able to earn something" for herself and her children.[43]

Mathilde was hardly surprised by Booth's behavior. The far greater disappointment was to realize that her marriage too was beyond repair. Whatever the emotions Fritz harbored inside (there was also some repugnance involved because Mathilde had grown overweight), he flatly stated that his priorities lay somewhere else than in the mending of marital ties. Fritz had gone to Switzerland to restore his battered self-confidence as a revolutionary intellectual, ready to switch the editor's pen for the officer's sword whenever he felt his talents were needed. Mathilde was aware of this, and although she certainly suffered from her husband's waning affection, she continued to praise his boundless fervor for promoting democracy and social equality. "We have to stay friends because of our intellectual bonds and our common struggle," she explained to her mother, "since love failed to hold us together."[44]

Fritz stood on the threshold of joining Garibaldi's army when in April 1861 dispatches announced that the United States had gone to war. From this moment on, the Risorgimento took a back seat in the Anneke household as everybody stared across the ocean in trepidation over the country's future. This was the hour of truth, the ordeal Fritz had been waiting for. Within days, he decided to sail back to the United States and offer his services in the battle against the southern rebellion. Short of money, Fritz had to postpone his departure until loans from his old Forty-Eighter comrades Gottfried Kinkel and Ludwig Blenker enabled him to pay for the trip. No less crucial was the backing Fritz received from his American friends. Once Booth had learned that the former Prussian artillery officer was on his way to Milwaukee, he extolled Anneke's military skills in his *Daily Life* and petitioned for Anneke's appointment as commander of one of Wisconsin's newly formed regiments. Booth's intervention was worthwhile. In October, Fritz was instated as colonel of the state's partly German Thirty-fourth Infantry. As far as these men were concerned, the fighting could begin.[45]

Defending the Union

"I wish this horrid war would stop but it will not, until slavery is given up, or a disgraceful compromise effected, which latter would be worse than war itself, & ruin the land in the eyes of other Nations." Mary Booth penned these lines only a few weeks after the Union army had suffered its first major defeat in the First Battle of Bull Run. And when Mathilde received word that Frémont had proclaimed slavery dead in Missouri, she rejoiced that "the people [had risen] in their awareness once again thanks to the spirited measures of the noble path-finder." Comments like these testify that Mary and Mathilde did not succumb to inertia once their men had deserted them. Miles away from the American drama that they were eying, they nevertheless tried to follow and comprehend it to the best of their abilities. More importantly, with little regard for conventional standards of female propriety, they publicly intervened in it at every stage, devouring all the information they could get and using all the tools at their disposal as writers and journalists to help define its meaning for others as well as themselves.[46]

Her revulsion of bloodshed notwithstanding, Mary embraced the war under the condition that it put slavery on the road to ultimate extinction. Being married to an abolitionist and having spent her childhood under the tutelage of reform-minded ministers, she had come to imbibe their vision of America as an egalitarian Christian republic. It was a nation in which faith rendered the distinction of master and slave impossible, in which the "slave mothers" and "the sons of Afric" enjoyed the same standing before God as their white owners. Mary believed that this color blindness demanded nothing less than a radical renewal of American society, even if that renewal could be brought about only by force. But it was a price she was willing to pay, and a just Creator would surely reward the sacrifice of those dying for the freedom of others. As Mary insinuated in one of her war poems, the fallen soldier need not fear death. Jesus Christ, John Brown, and the liberated slave would stand waiting at the gates of heaven and usher him into paradise.[47]

Mathilde shared her companion's hopes. Although her notions of progress lacked a religious superstructure, she too wished that the current conflict would democratize societal relations in America. Before returning to the United States, Mathilde's husband had completed "America's Second Fight for Freedom," a book-length appraisal of the sectional crisis that reflected Mathilde's views as well. Fritz labeled the Civil War a milestone event in the universal unfolding of liberty. What the world was witnessing, Fritz assessed, was "the greatest and most momentous fight for principles in the nineteenth century," which would decide whether the "great ideals" of 1776 were truly applicable to all human beings, including blacks. Fritz insisted that "civilized Europe" should monitor the developments overseas with utmost caution and supreme precision, hoping that they might inspire the Continent to move forward on its own path toward national self-rule. He was concerned to find in the German press a growing body of Americana, which he considered "very poor, very patchy, and not seldom very untrue." Some journals, he fumed, even sided with the "slaveholding aristocracy," thereby "slapping the face of justice, freedom, and humanity." A war of letters had erupted in Europe, one that seemed equal in relevance to the war of arms that had begun across the Atlantic.[48]

Mathilde's reports carry vivid traces of the belief that the United States was reenacting midcentury European upheavals and thus joining the family of democratic revolutions. The war's outcome, she sensed, would also influence events in other parts of the world. In her contributions to German and Swiss periodicals, she argued that the Civil War involved more than the quelling of a secessionist movement. Rather, she portrayed it as an epochal struggle between two principal but antithetical forces in world history, a millennial fight in which Liberty and Equality did battle against Throne and Altar. On one side, there were the southern planters, to her progenies of the European aristocracy; on the other, the free farmers and workers of the North, with whom Mathilde proudly identified. At times, she became so combative in her espousal of the abolitionist cause that her writing was even too much to bear for the German pro-Union press. "The *Allgemeine* has grown so timid on the slavery question that it discarded my well-crafted piece on American conditions," Mathilde protested in late 1861. In her view, the censorship regimes of the post-Napoleonic era had forfeited nothing of their ability to intimidate and suppress.[49]

Articles exulting over the feats of German Americans on the battlefields of North America sounded less seditious to German editors. In the Civil War accounts of immigrant journalists, sympathies for the Union frequently merged with an evolving ethnic nationalism — a tendency Mathilde tried to avoid. Her reports were rather unique in that they often went beyond the common soldier in their scope, putting the spotlight on various disenfranchised groups instead. In November 1862, she shifted her focus to the Indian tribes of Minnesota that had taken up arms against intruding white settlers. A few months later, after the Emancipation Proclamation had taken effect, an article was submitted to the *Ausland* that also carried Mathilde's handwriting. It dealt with the enduring problem of antiblack discrimination and contended that "the social status of free blacks in the free states [was] as vulnerable a spot" in the democratic fabric of the United States as chattel slavery itself.[50]

Mathilde, however, was not entirely immune to surges of ethnic pride. Occasionally she fell in line with the adulatory rhetoric of her fellow correspondents. At one point, she bragged that it was just a matter of time until "almost the entire German American population" would flock to the Republican Party and lead it to victory. Whether such remarks were meant to cater to the national vanities of a German readership is difficult to ascertain. Not so uncertain is that Mathilde impatiently waited for news picturing her husband in honorable pursuit of the enemy. If Fritz managed to distinguish himself in battle, it would boost a cause greater than himself. Specifically, it might earn him the revolutionary laurels that he had been chasing for years; and being the independent agitator she was, Mathilde would not have hesitated to claim what she regarded as her share of the glory.[51]

As the war dragged on, politics also figured more prominently in Mary's correspondence. Several letters show her as an expatriate who had grown extremely sensitive about her own nationality. Her European acquaintances, it seemed, took great delight in confronting Mary with everything they thought was wrong about the United States. Corrupt political elites, inept military leaders, and the failure of a republican government to act decisively against slavery were only three items out of a long list of grievances she had to grapple with. Mary was anything but unaware of these predicaments; often she hid her face in shame when people asked her to explain or defend the actions of her elected officials. "Your nation has been living a lie!" charged a traveling clergyman from England, who accosted her not long after Lincoln had revoked General Frémont's emancipation order in Missouri. "Tell them to abolish the SLAVERY CURSE, and then they can ask the blessing of God upon their land, without insulting Him with every prayer for peace, or belieing [*sic*] themselves with every boast of liberty."[52]

Then again, Mary was infuriated that people were bashing her country from the vantage point of a continent that she thought was far more burdened with a history of tyranny and repression. To prove her point, she reported that French authorities in Paris had prohibited the staging of a tragedy that Victor Hugo had written on John Brown. The play, she scoffed, was rated "incendiary." Similar incidents occurred in Germany and Italy, where Mary traveled in the summer of 1863 to interview Giuseppe Garibaldi. These experiences added to Mary's conviction that European criticisms of the United States tended to reveal more about the shortcomings of the Old World than about those of her native country. "Europeans are so much prejudiced against America," she complained, and it was this prejudice, she felt, that prevented them from appreciating her country's republican merits or, even worse, made some of them sympathize with the secessionists. Ferdinand Lassalle, the hotheaded German socialist, was anything but an apologist for the Confederacy; yet his denigrating remarks about the American antislavery movement precipitated a fiery response. "I had an awful fight with Lassalle about American affairs at the supper table this evening," Mary told Mathilde in August 1863. "He threw Daniel Webster in my face as a representation of the Northern Anti-Slavery Man — not willing to hear that he was cast out of his party for his selfish treachery & that he died of remorse

& shame. Loud as he screamed, I would talk, though, & did. . . . He thinks he knows everything & knows nothing—at last I told him he was an arrogant fool & that I would not talk with so ignorant an individual."[53]

Mary's quarrels with native Europeans point to a widening ideological rift between Europe and America, to a set of differing outlooks and self-ascriptions. Europeans still viewed their continent as the center of world development, whereas Mary believed that Europe was no longer entitled to this privileged position. The idea that the United States had a manifest destiny to spread its republican culture and serve as a beacon to other nations was deeply ingrained in her thinking. This exceptionalist vision met the stiff opposition of many Europeans, who liked to brag about their own achievements and readily placed themselves at the forefront of the civilizing process. A transatlantic culture war was under way in which the Civil War was used as testimony to verify the claims of either side. Fully absorbed by this contest, Mary urged her countrymen, "Abolish slavery, then swing the old stars and stripes in the face of Europe and of the whole world. Conquer yourselves, and you will have placed your Nation at the head of all the nations upon earth." Fired up by her nationalist rhetoric, Mary went on to assure her American readers: "To tell you the truth, Europe is jealous of you; deprive her of the right to throw the slavery question in your face, and she must, and will acknowledge your governmental superiority; it will not be agreeable to her at first, but she will do it by-and-by." Clearly, the prospect of America's political declension filled Mary with alarm, and her request was that her country address this unnatural state of things, shake off the stigma of slavery, and reclaim its role as the world's republican paragon.[54]

Imagining Emancipation

Abolitionist politics, ethnicity, gender, and practical economic concerns were tightly interwoven in the women's Civil War journalism. A major incentive for their writing was to elicit sympathy for the Union and abolitionist causes, yet they also wrote because they had to make a living. Money was sparse, and the fear that they might not be able to sustain their little commune runs like a thread through Mary's and Mathilde's letters. Their earnings as freelance journalists barely sufficed to cover rent, food, and clothing for themselves and their children. "I am obliged to write all the time, either on one thing or the other," Mary informed her mother about the hand-to-mouth existence that she and Mathilde were leading, "but where is the use in complaining." Mathilde attested to Mary's and her own industriousness, asserting, "Nobody displays more diligence and persistence in intellectual matters than the two of us."[55]

Whatever their efforts, the middle-class comforts that the two women strove for remained out of reach. Living on their own, they felt the strain of trying to be good mothers and professional writers at the same time. Publishing houses and newspaper agencies in Europe and America were mainly run by men who had little interest in granting equal payment to women. They often treated female writers unfairly, and the fact that women's access to activities outside the household was often constricted made it easy for them to get away with their behavior. Mary was no stranger to receiving late payments or none at all for some of her articles; neither was Mathilde, who kept a meticulous account of all her literary ventures. Only rarely did she succeed in compelling her publishers to meet outstanding bills as in December 1861, when she filed a protest to the *Augsburger Allgemeine Zeitung*. Most of the time, however, she was fighting an uphill battle. "If people would only pay me because I earn it, not because they have compassion," Mathilde lamented in a darker moment, realizing that she was not granted the same respect as her male colleagues.[56]

Health problems were another source of great anxiety. Mary's tuberculosis grew worse, while Mathilde suffered from hepatitis, which kept her in bed for weeks. In these difficult times, loans from acquaintances became the only means of survival. Among the first to help out were fellow writers in Zürich's refugee community, most of all the Herweghs. Then there was Gerrit Smith, an old friend of the Booths, who agreed to support Mary with a considerable sum. Mary's connections to the wealthy abolitionist and philanthropist dated back to the 1840s — Booth had been one of Smith's closest associates in the Liberty Party — and had never broken down entirely. Meanwhile, nothing of value came from their husbands: Fritz remained focused on his military career, and Sherman showed not the slightest inclination to give Mary more than the obligatory three dollars for each of her contributions to the *Daily Life*.[57]

Despite all social and physical setbacks, though, the two women fiercely clung to their vision of female self-advancement and improving their condition through literature. This also meant moving beyond the gendered spaces circumscribed by the ideology of separate spheres. Even Mary, formerly the epitome of a "true woman," was no longer uncritically wedded to that notion. She began constructing her own ideal of femininity, which had grown out of her private calamities as well as her friendship with the German-born feminist. Having adopted Mathilde's dictum that it "tastes sweet" to be "pecuniarily independent," she saw her writing in a new light. If her literary activities, as she confided to her sister, secured her a living and a good reputation, she could do very well without the "assistance one might expect from a masculine protector."[58]

It was at this pivotal moment that the two women began working on their most ambitious joint project: writing and putting together a compilation of abolitionist stories. The planned anthology, however, never went to press; only four pieces were published separately under Mathilde Anneke's name (although it is likely that more appeared anonymously in different German and American periodicals): the two short stories "The Slave Auction" and "Broken Chains," the novel fragment "Sturmgeiger," and, most notably, the short novel *Uhland in Texas*, which depicts the plights of a German immigrant family with abolitionists leanings on the southwestern frontier.[59]

These tales, which braid together the causes of female and black emancipation, served the dual purpose of propagating abolitionist ideas while ensuring their authors a decent income. Rather than cater to highbrow tastes, they appealed to a larger audience with popular fiction, written to meet the demands of a burgeoning literary market on both sides of the Atlantic. One of the most widely read genres of the time, especially in the United States, was domestic fiction, stories written chiefly by women for women and located in an intermediate sphere between the home and the outside world. Extremely popular for their moralizing plots and sensationalist techniques, they usually appeared first as serials in newspapers and magazines, which won them a mass audience.[60]

Gaining as many readers as possible was not the only facet that connected Mathilde's and Mary's stories to this larger trend. All of them deploy melodramatic imagery, often religious in content, in a way that strongly resembles the sentimentalist paradigm. This seems surprising if one considers Mathilde's earlier objections to religion in general and her dislike of sentimentalism in particular. Back in 1850, she had still warned that "tears and desires" in literature reduced women to "bland, sentimental creatures." Her exposure to the culture of American reform — not least of all her friendship with Mary — as well as her current financial troubles, however, made her abandon this dogmatic posture. By the time Mathilde moved in with the Booths, Harriet Beecher Stowe had already provided the model of an emotionally touching, socially explosive, and lucrative book with *Uncle Tom's Cabin*. And in the span of her relationship with Mary, Mathilde began conceiving that sentimentalism was not necessarily inimical to reform but could very well be used to that end.[61]

Mary's role in creating, writing, and editing these stories was essential. She agreed with Mathilde that publishing the tales in German rather than American journals would serve the abolitionist cause best because Continental Europeans were still largely uninformed on the subjects of slavery and antiblack discrimination in the United States. In a surprisingly ironic passage, Mary addressed this pseudo-ignorance and juxtaposed it with the beliefs of her racist countrymen:

"Europeans . . . have a general delusion . . . about colored individuals being possessed of a human nature, and manhood, and feelings — just the same as white folks! They think that there are immortal souls in black bodies, and they believe that in 'woolly heads' there are thinking brains, and they do not believe these powers of thinking lie dormant, either! Funny opinions, of course — but then people see differently over such a great expanse of water — the color isn't distinguishable — all seem to be alike MEN, and naturally enough — the children of a common father."[62]

Throughout the entire writing process, Mary was Mathilde's principal intellectual consort, her faithful critic and trusted resource. "She is more fortunate in conceiving the plot, not so much in organizing; this is what I do better," Mathilde told Fritz, acknowledging that much of her abolitionist fiction bore the stamp of her companion. This is especially true of "The Slave Auction," for which Mary not only provided the raw material but also assisted her friend in completing a first rough draft, a translation of which was published in Booth's *Daily Life*. For *Uhland in Texas*, Mathilde also relied heavily on Mary's input and coauthorship. As Mary revealed, "Madame Anneke and I am writing a romance together. I write & compose it. Then she translates & adds what she pleases, & I copy it a second time in English. This is to appear in a German paper, under our both names."[63]

Then again, what makes "The Slave Auction," "Broken Chains," and *Uhland in Texas* unique is not simply that they emerged from two different pens, but that they represent a fascinating synthesis of two different literary cultures. In the way they depict slave life and slaveholder barbarity, they seem rooted in the sentimentalist tradition of abolitionist fiction. The main characters of "The Slave Auction" and "Broken Chains," Isabella and Leila, are female slaves modeled after the good-hearted, obedient, and devout black slaves who populate Stowe's novels. Both live in constant danger of being sexually exploited by lascivious and brutal white men. Isabella, a "dark and beautiful mulatto," is to be sold on an auction block in Alexandria, Virginia, because her master was killed in a duel. Leila, the sixteen-year-old heroine in "Broken Chains," is the desired object in a quarrel over her dead mistress's inheritance. Lady Randall, the daughter, wants to humiliate Leila by sending her out to toil in the field; her brother Alan seeks to destroy her innocence by making her his lover.[64]

The female protagonists endure these and other mortifications in a stoical manner. Isabella finds comfort in her Christian faith. When told to sing by the auctioneer, she picks a religious tune with a German melody that moves the hearts of the more compassionate onlookers but also stirs the sexual fantasies

Studio portrait taken in Zürich of Mathilde Franziska Anneke, who is standing next to Mary Booth (Wisconsin State Historical Society, WHi-72188). Mathilde's friendship with Mary deepened during their stay in Switzerland, where they coauthored a series of abolitionist stories.

of the bidding slaveholders. Religion is an equally vital source of consolation for Leila and her enslaved brothers and sisters. Appeals to the Lord, references to a day of reckoning, and cries for the promised land resonate through the slave quarters after rumors have spread that many of them are to be sold farther south. The blacks, however, are not left in this state of anguish. In both stories, the female protagonists are saved from a terrible fate, not by a miraculous incident but through secular intervention. Redemption in the case of Leila and her friends comes through Lincoln's Emancipation Proclamation, whereas Isabella is eventually set free by Gerrit Smith's fictional alter ego, who arrives on the scene just in time to outbid his slaveholding competitors. Gerrit Smith's appearance in this story as a white deus ex machina is no accident. It was the authors' way of showing their deeply felt gratitude for the support they received from Smith and his family, which consisted not just of financial aid but of stacks of political speeches, treatises, and pamphlets that added depth to the women's abolitionist writing.[65]

Gerrit Smith's character in the fictional works of Mathilde and Mary is significant for another reason as well. His role as a charismatic and fearless agitator who helps blacks acquire their freedom signals a clear departure from the sentimentalist canon. Rather than having their figures undergo a process of moral-spiritual cleansing, the stories purport that social and political involvement are indispensable tools in the crusade to abolish slavery. This underlying message reveals that these texts partake in a second literary tradition whose program Mathilde had come to internalize ever since her first steps as a radical activist and female revolutionary. Her previous writings, her political tracts in particular, largely exhale the spirit of the German Vormärz, a protest movement in literature and politics with a strong emphasis on democratic propaganda, social criticism, and republican idealism. In the narrative solutions she devised for the slavery problem, Mathilde brought these very tenets to bear, even though she softened them with sentimentalist techniques. This combination was not so much aesthetically as politically motivated: by appealing to reason *and* feeling, by blending social criticism with emotional outrage, the authors hoped to achieve the maximum effect when depicting the horrors of slavery.

The cruelties displayed range from torture and the violent separation of families to the callous procedure of a slave auction and ghastly mercy killings of black babies by their desperate slave mothers. The most forceful indignation, however, involved lustful southern men targeting young female slaves. This double degradation of black women, on grounds of both race and gender, is a recurring theme in Mathilde's and Mary's abolitionist stories. The theme itself was not original — Stowe had already touched on it a decade earlier in *Uncle Tom's Cabin* — but in fusing it with her interest in women's emancipation, Mathilde managed to give it a new twist. Equating the plight of women with that of slaves was a tactic widely used in feminist circles, one that Mathilde was especially fond of wielding. "Why continue to be the humble maid 'who washes the feet of her lord,'" why continue to bleed "under the yoke of societal misery," she had asked female readers as early as 1847. "Ye women, who have become accustomed to a sort of 'happiness' for which you never really yearned within your youthful ardent breasts, understand: Your false and spurious happiness has turned you into smiling slaves; you have become numb toward others and your own kind because you no longer feel the scorpion which gnaws on your own heart and cheats you of your heart's best blood." Linked to such statements, the fates of Leila and Isabella become instrumental to Mathilde's promotion of women's rights. Laying bare the evils of southern slavery, both characters emerge as symbols of female oppression, not just of black women but of women all over the world.[66]

The figure of the European immigrant highlights another major theme in these tales, that of ethnic politics. In "The Slave Auction," the part of the newcomer is played by Carl van Rensellar, the descendant of an old Dutch family and a gentleman revolutionist. Rensellar enters the picture as a model abolitionist, whose humanist upbringing leaves him no other choice than to actively espouse the cause of black emancipation. This earns him the esteem of his American allies but also pits him against the slaveholding faction, some of whom draw him into a debate over the Kansas-Nebraska Act and the right of the foreign-born to free homesteads in the West. The discussion moves back and forth until Rensellar manages to silence his opponents with the following aphorism: "The man who comes to us from a distant shore, who says that he wants to live and work among us in peace and goodwill . . . has proven what no native-born can prove: that he has an American heart." Binding together issues of citizenship and antislavery, Rensellar echoes a core demand voiced by Mathilde Anneke and other Forty-Eighter intellectuals: fidelity to principles of democracy and free labor, rather than nationality, ought to be the touchstone of true Americanness.[67]

Immigration and abolitionism coalesce to an even greater degree in the short novel *Uhland in Texas*, which marked the high point of Mary's and Mathilde's work as a bicultural writing team. *Uhland in Texas* is rife with instances of Forty-Eighter heroism in the fight against slavery. The jovial atmosphere of the opening chapters evaporates when the two immigrant comrades Wallenstein and Gilmore and their families are cast into the torrents of the Civil War. Much of the ensuing narrative revolves around the efforts of these pro-Union expatriates to protect their little German American idyll on the southwestern frontier against Confederate attacks. After the older Gilmore is killed in an ambush, Wallenstein, a battle-hardened Forty-Eighter, takes over and transforms his newly acquired plantation, Uhland, into a desert fortress. Alongside his native-born American friends and a band of loyal blacks, he holds his ground until summoned by General Benjamin Butler to assume command of a black regiment. The marriage of Wallenstein's sons Adalbert and Engelbert with two of Gilmore's daughters makes the hero's triumph complete. At the end of the novel, he presides over a utopian rural community that, as the narrator prophesies, "will expand and blossom once the war winds have abated — in memory of the German poet, and in honor of the German name."[68]

With this tale of immigrant valor, Mathilde and Mary shift the German

American Civil War experience from the periphery to the center of this historic event. Both take great pains to portray the exiled republicans not as self-righteous troublemakers but as socially correct liberals whose political and cultural virtues refute nativist prejudice and endear them to likeminded native-born Americans. John Hamilton, a fictionalized incarnation of John Brown, is so impressed by Wallenstein's superior sense of civic duty that he considers dropping his religious doctrines in exchange for the German immigrant's secular humanism. Even southern slave owners find no stronger rebuke against their German foe than to sneer that "he stands on the platform of German humanity." Wallenstein's victory is meaningful in a twofold sense. First, it allows the authors to compensate for the setbacks in their own struggle for emancipation as well as for their inability to contribute militarily to the ongoing fight. Second, it legitimizes the presence of German immigrants in the New World and advocates a rapprochement between European liberalism and American abolitionism as the foundation for a postwar democratic order.[69]

It is against this backdrop of white conciliation that the authors present the relationship of Anglo- and German Americans to America's principal nonwhite ethnic group, African Americans. Strikingly enough, Mary's and Mathilde's abolitionist fiction shows few traces of independent black agency. The blacks in *Uhland in Texas* for the most part reside in a narrative substratum, a burlesque countersphere to the more serious realm of public affairs that the whites inhabit. This does not mean that they are presented as unfit for refinement — many of the blacks on Gilmore's plantation are intellectually superior to the slaves living on the surrounding Anglo-southern estates — but their development is ascribed exclusively to their exposure to European Enlightenment culture. The few instances when freed blacks seize arms to aid their white emancipators reveal a similar structural dependency. Rather than fight as autonomous individuals, they serve as barometers for the benevolence of their German- and native-born American protectors, who figure as the only agents truly capable of advancing civilization.[70]

If the women's humanitarianism maps the potential of their abolitionist discourse, racial paternalism demarcates its limits. Although their concern for the slave was heartfelt and sincere, it cannot be treated separately from their errand to position themselves and their ethnic groups in the forward ranks of an imagined multiethnic democracy. Abolitionist protest and ethnic self-fashioning were complementary and mutually reinforcing elements in Mary's and Mathilde's search for a new womanhood, in both fiction and fact. The following incident demonstrates this as well. In the morning hours of January 1, 1863, the two women gave a small Emancipation Day reception at their Zürich home. Suddenly there was "a rap," as Mary recalled, and an unexpected acquaintance entered, "a young mulatto of about twenty years of age, whose scholarly attainments and irreproachable character have won for him a distinguished position in the best social and literary circles of Zurich." Mary had a keen sense for the symbolic value of this visit. The outstanding erudition of this representative of the black race, his knowledge of "art, literature — modern and classic — as well as in the languages," she claimed, proved false all those clamoring that it was impossible to bestow upon these people the gifts of Euro-American civilization. Animated by a vision of human progress that was both radical and ethnocentric, Mary and Mathilde listened with satisfaction as their black guest honored them with a toast. "I came," he solemnly declared, "because, in this momentous moment, I wanted to speak with some sympathizing friends of the glorious prospects of my down-trodden brothers across the ocean — for to-night the slaves of America are free!"[71]

Final Vows

The four years that the two women spent together in Switzerland were the most intellectually enriching and emotionally fulfilling of their lives. Financial pressures and personal maladies weighed heavy on their communal bliss, yet they never fractured the bonds of comradeship that had grown stronger with every shared success and failure. They came to enjoy a salon for two — as literati, they found pleasure in the works of the other and could always, in a darker hour, draw hope and inspiration from this common well. The emotional ties binding Mary and Mathilde together were extraordinary, even in light of Victorian conventions of romantic female friendship. The love and devotion they had sought in their marriages was the love they gave to each other. The women exchanged passionate love letters, hugged and kissed each other, and slept in the same bed. Sexuality was implied but not necessarily involved. In an undated note, Mary reassured her companion, "You are the morning star of my soul . . . the saintly lily of my dreams — sweetening my life with your ethereal fragrance . . . dearest, you are the *reality* of my dreams, my life, my Love."[72]

Mathilde and Mary wanted to sustain their little commune far beyond Zürich. Reuniting with their husbands was not an option that they seriously pondered. Mary's separation from Sherman was final, and the emotional distance between Mathilde and Fritz had not diminished either. When Fritz had gone to war in 1861, Mathilde still held his public persona in high regard. His career in the Union army, however, ended in disaster, breaking even this last straw of affection. The low point came in the summer of 1863, when he was hauled before a military court and dishonorably discharged from the officer corps. Obviously, it was Fritz's condescending airs toward fellow officers that had brought him that far. Her husband's self-righteousness had always worried Mathilde. "Steer clear of these small personal wars. They give no honor and no fame," she had begged Fritz in September 1862. His inability to do so seemed to have initiated his downfall. For his wife, the shame was all but unbearable.[73]

Mathilde and Mary's plan was to earn enough public recognition as writers to become established in America's thriving literary community. "We shall probably settle in the East on our return. It is better for literary pursuits there," Mary informed her mother. Although the two women were content with life in Switzerland, they never viewed the mountain republic as a permanent home. Mary remained profoundly attached to her native country, a feeling that was further intensified by the fact that she had left behind many of her friends and relatives. The separation from her daughter Ella, who was staying with her grandmother in Connecticut, pained her most. Maternal anxieties were as much a reason for Mary to remain focused on America as the desire to stay connected to social and political developments overseas.[74]

Mary's idea of finding "an editorial engagement on some magazine or paper" on the eastern seaboard appealed to her German friend. The deeper Mathilde delved into European politics, the more candidly she voiced her opinion that this was not the continent to grow old on. Its leaders, she grumbled, had learned nothing from the follies of the past. Particularly alarming to her was the state of her own people. "Lagging behind in their nationalist fervor, they rather think of instating an emperor than giving themselves a republican constitution," she complained in the fall of 1862. Not quite two years later, she gloomily added: "I don't believe in a revolution in Germany. Michel just won't get tired of being kicked around. . . . Incredible how submissive people are here." The democratic surge of the Civil War, Mathilde concluded, had not spilled over into Europe. The truth could not have been more frustrating. Mathilde's vision of a postwar United States, on the other hand, stood in striking contrast to her bleak forecast regarding further developments in Europe. She strongly believed that her own and Mary's future lay on the other side of the Atlantic, in one of the cultural centers of a cosmopolitan American republic. "When the rebellion will be vanquished," she confidently predicted, "the United States will soar to unprecedented heights. In a few years, the South will be densely populated by soldiers and northern entrepreneurs and will be reconstructed with the help of these immigrants and the freed negroes. . . . We will intervene decisively in the politics of Europe and of the entire globe. We will propagate our ideas and support the revolution wherever it may rear its head."[75]

Nothing would have made Mathilde happier than to see this scenario of world revolution come true with Mary at her side. Their story, however, took a different turn. Despite the care and medication she received, Mary's lung condition worsened. By early 1864, breathing caused her so much pain — she had also begun spitting blood — that she had serious doubts whether she would ever recover. With near death on her mind, Mary uttered one last wish. She did not want to leave this life without reuniting with her family in Connecticut. In June 1864, Mathilde escorted Mary and her youngest daughter, Lillian, across the Swiss border, as far as the Alsatian town of Mühlhausen. From there, Mary continued her passage back to America alone. The two never met again.

Mary's departure left a deep void in Mathilde's life. She had not attempted to hold back her friend; knowing that Mary's health was failing, she did not want to stand between her last wish and her impending end. Still, after Mary's departure, grief almost overwhelmed Mathilde: "The dream is over, and fate, grim fate, has torn us out of it, not as soft as we hoped and believed it would." With Mary, Mathilde was not just losing a soul mate; she had to part from a woman who, having ascended from the depths of a male-dominated environment, had become a trusted ally in the quest for women's self-empowerment. To see her friend return to the United States at this juncture troubled her profoundly. Would Mary, in her weakened state, feel tempted to betray their common emancipationist legacy? The threat of falling back into old habits, Mathilde feared, lurked behind every corner, and without her patronage, Mary might not be able to resist "this poison."[76]

Ten months later, Mathilde's dark premonitions became reality. Mary Booth passed away in New York, nursed to the very last by friends and her family. Mathilde was devastated. The news reached her at a time when she was en route to America herself. Now that the southern rebellion had been crushed and a new Union promised to rise from its ashes, Mathilde did not want to stay away any longer from the country of her choice. Her reasons were not merely political. It was time to plant new roots: "For the good of the children, who ought not to suffer the curse of homelessness as their mother did, I take them with me back to their fatherland. I go back because it is there where I have my unforgettable loved ones, both in life and death."[77]

On July 31, 1865, Mathilde set foot on American soil for the second time. She was forty-eight years old. After brief interludes in Hartford; Peterboro, Connecticut (where she visited Mary's grave and stayed with the Corss and Smith families); and St. Louis, Mathilde once more settled on the shores of Lake Michigan. Milwaukee's liberal environment, she found, was ideally suited for her undertakings. In the remaining years of her life, Mathilde concentrated on passing on her democratic ideals to a new generation. Apart from maintaining a voluminous correspondence with male and female radicals of similar temperament, she participated actively in numerous reformist ventures in and outside Wisconsin. Her unflagging industry culminated in the founding of the Milwaukee-Töchter-Institut, the city's first women's academy, which Mathilde directed until her death on November 25, 1884. Its core values — social equality, solidarity with the weak, popular education — were the same ones that Mathilde had been propagating all her life in order to end what she regarded as the civic enslavement of women.[78]

Again she won the respect, and occasionally even the friendship, of many of her American comrades, most notably Elisabeth Cady Stanton and Susan B. Anthony. Yet none of these connections had the intimacy nor did they reenact the sweeping intercultural work that had been the hallmarks of Mathilde Anneke's relationship with Mary Booth. It had been through her eyes that Mathilde had gained a deeper understanding of many of the cultural strands running through the web of American abolitionism. Mary, in turn, became more defensive of America abroad but also learned to see her friend's secular radicalism in a more generous light. This then was the legacy of their transnational sisterhood, moving testimonies of which have survived in the texts they produced and the fictional characters they created, from the beautiful Leila and the innocent Isabella to the fearless John Hamilton and the chivalrous Wallenstein.

CHAPTER FIVE

Let Us Break Every Yoke

Boston's Radical Democracies

To conquer, we must reach all. Our object is not to make every
man a Christian or a philosopher, but to induce everyone to
aid in the abolition of slavery.

> —WENDELL PHILLIPS, *Philosophy of the Abolition Movement*,
> January 27, 1853

They take each other's hands in Uncle Tom's humble cabin but
are at each other's throats in the church of the Lord. What a
happy accident that this country is blessed with slavery; otherwise
there would be no common ground for the American and
German freemen to stand on. Our mediator, our only one, is
Sambo. Long live Sambo!

> —KARL HEINZEN, *Der Pionier*, January 29, 1859

THE FUNERAL SERVICE PROCEEDED as he had wished. In the early afternoon of
November 15, 1880, a column of Turners from Boston and surrounding towns
flocked to his house on Cedar Street. They were dressed in mourning, for the
man to whom they had come to pay homage was no more. Karl Heinzen, editor of the *Pionier* and one of the most adamant proponents of German-bred
radical democracy on American soil, had died three days ago of the late effects
of a stroke he had suffered the previous year. He was seventy-one years old. By
October, Heinzen had been certain that he would not get better. He summoned
the people closest to him to his bedside, demanded pen and paper, and sent a
final request to a friend to have his works published for the benefit of his wife.
Only one more time did his feeble hand wield a pen, to sign a petition for wom-
en's suffrage. A decided atheist until the very last, Heinzen refused any sort of
spiritual guidance that might have braced him for a possible afterlife. The value
of a human being, Heinzen had always preached, was determined not by faith
but by the content of his actions. This was his personal creed, and friends made
sure that it emerged prominently during the obsequies.

The casket in which Heinzen's earthly remains were laid was unpretentious, bearing some floral offerings and no insignia other than the simple caption "Rest." S. R. Köhler, the freethinking editor of the *American Art Review*, delivered the main address. He eulogized Heinzen's staunch belief in the perfectibility of humankind and stressed his "imperative endeavor for the universal." The next to say a few words was the feminist Edna D. Cheney, who paid special tribute to what Heinzen had done for the social elevation of women. After that, the speakers adjourned, and the coffin was quietly carried out. There were eight pallbearers, all German-born Turners, and as they took their places ahead of the mourners, a local German music society struck the first chord of Handel's "Dead March." The procession grew to about sixty persons, consisting of the band, members of the Boston Turnverein on foot, and relatives in carriages. At Forest Hill Cemetery, where Heinzen was to be interred, Turner president Carl Eberhard gave a brief last speech. It was a gray and chilly November day, but as the casket was lowered into the grave, the evening sun, for a fleeting moment, broke through the clouds.[1]

Heinzen's death moved people inside and outside the precincts of Boston. Letters of condolence were mailed to his widow from all corners of the country, along with resolutions of sympathy drafted at commemorative exercises of freethinker societies in Milwaukee, Cincinnati, Indianapolis, Buffalo, and elsewhere. The most elaborate memorial meeting, however, was organized by Boston's German American Turners. On February 22, 1881, Turner Hall was solemnly decorated with German and American flags and an oversized portrait of Heinzen. The stage was packed with speakers and musicians who honored the deceased with some tunes and feats of oratory. Then the chairman announced Wendell Phillips. Gray and fraught with age himself, the sixty-nine-year-old abolitionist had difficulties ascending the platform. Yet his rhetorical powers were unfailing, and he could still command them to captivate an entire audience. He spoke for about thirty minutes, recounting several instances that made him esteem Heinzen as a worthy ally and trusted friend. "I never met him on the streets without a feeling of the highest respect, and this respect I paid the rare almost unexpected courage of the man," Phillips recalled. "He stood with us," he added, "when men did nothing but jeer and insult the cause, when scholars affected to despise it, when mobs broke up our meetings and man's social and pecuniary life was ruined by being seen in them. He flung himself into our ranks . . . with his whole heart, taking on his shoulders the whole yoke, in all its heaviness and self-sacrifice." Unlike so many other immigrants, the senior abolitionist remarked, Heinzen had never betrayed the love of liberty for which he had been driven out of his homeland and had always insisted that freedom knew no confines of race, gender, or nationality. "Remember life is neither pain nor pleasure," Phillips quoted Tocqueville at the end of his speech. "It is serious business — to be entered upon with the courage — with the spirit of self-sacrifice. Surely if any life ever exemplified that ideal, it is the one we meet to remember, and as far as we can, to imitate — that of Karl Heinzen."[2]

Brahmins and Paupers

On January 6, 1859, the *Pionier*, whose office was located on Oak Street diagonally across from Boston's Turner Hall, went into its fifth year of existence. Its proprietor was in high spirits. Karl Heinzen had worked hard to find a social environment congenial to his revolutionary politics. Over the last fifteen years, he had led the life of a political vagabond, braving persecution, confiscation, and countless feuds with fellow journalists. Scrambling for safety after the fiasco of 1848, Heinzen applied his extreme views on race, gender, and religion to American society. He denounced slavery, promoted women's rights, and attacked the churches with stunning militancy, yet his disposition to pound his reforms in with a club deterred many potential sympathizers. Notorious for his personal polemics, Heinzen could always come out with a caustic phrase or two. To evade controversy and keep the *Pionier* alive, the debt-ridden Heinzen had to pack his bags repeatedly. Would Boston, America's "cradle of liberty," be the last station of his odyssey?[3]

Heinzen felt confident that his ideas would gain greater traction in a city that prided itself on being the country's intellectual epicenter, which harbored such dissenting voices as the agnostic *Investigator* and Garrison's *Liberator*. He fondly recalled that it was in this "Athens of America" that he had experienced one of his rare highlights as a public speaker: more than two years earlier, German- and native-born American Bostonians had applauded his lecture on the morality of radicalism. Here one could observe "the freest tendencies in religion and politics that have grown on American soil," Heinzen asserted, "as well as their most able and persistent spokesmen." Thus, if there was a place where his paper might thrive "as a mediator between German and American letters," it had to be on and around Beacon Hill.[4]

Founded in 1630 by Puritan settlers, Boston could look back on a rich intellectual history. Education spurred the city's growth into a major commercial stronghold. Goods from all over the world flowing in and out of Boston harbor expanded the economic sphere and created enormous prosperity for those directly involved. The foundation was laid for the emergence of a solid middle class — small traders, artisans, shopkeepers — on top of which resided a caste of wealthy merchant princes. Well bred and socially influential, these "Brahmins" brashly viewed themselves as pillars of a republican aristocracy. Bent on invigorating society with the newest trends and ideas from Europe, they were at the same time nationalists committed to making Boston the "city upon the hill" that their Puritan forebears had envisioned. Nobody expressed this ambition more candidly than the Brahmin poet Oliver Wendell Holmes Sr. He considered his hometown "the thinking centre of the continent, and therefore of the planet," and coined the maxim, "[The] Boston State-House is the hub of the solar system."[5]

The Brahmin world was replete with the spirit of self-determination and an unshakable faith in progress. Such enthusiasm for man's improvability could easily take root in a society that had known relatively little privation and cultural diversity in the past. The real test came with industrialization and the arrival of the immigrant poor. From the early 1840s onward, Boston became a prime destination for non-Anglo-Saxon peoples seeking admission to the United States. In 1836, before the great transatlantic migration, nine out of ten Bostonians were still of English descent. At midcentury, the number of foreign-born residents had climbed to almost 40 percent of the population. The vast majority were dispossessed and hungry Irish peasants, complemented by smaller groups of emigrants from Scotland, France, Italy, and the German-speaking regions of Europe. Finally, Boston also provided shelter to a small but stable African American community.[6]

For Boston's conservative establishment, this ethnic sprawl in its midst was nothing short of alarming. Districts formerly dominated by white middle-class families mutated into overcrowded slums, bearing witness to the proletarian status of their new inhabitants. Fort Hill and South Cove, near the wharfs and offering cheap rent, became the preferred areas of an overwhelmingly Irish immigrant population. Outlying suburbs too felt the residential shift. In 1847, South Boston still trumpeted that it counted among its residents "no single colored family" and only immigrants "of that better class who [would] not live in cellars"; ten years later, the evolution toward a more socially mixed neighborhood was undeniable. The North Side of Beacon Hill experienced a similar transition. By the late 1850s, more than a half of the city's black population had found lodging there. Due to the squalid houses and shabby quarters that its residents had to cope with, the borough soon earned the odious nickname "Nigger Hill."[7]

City authorities were badly equipped to deal with the mass influx of strangers from overseas. Appalled by the unsanitary living conditions among the poorer newcomers, many native-born Bostonians feared that these people would transform their home into a giant mud hole. "Foreign paupers are rapidly accumulating on our hands," warned Mayor John Prescott Bigelow in 1850, seeing a mounting hazard in their "filth and wretchedness." To the *Boston Daily Advertiser*, the Irish seemed a particularly "vicious, criminal, profligate, and abandoned" people, prone to begging, stealing, and other "degrading practices."[8]

In this vortex of antiforeign resentment, Boston's German immigrants tried to avoid conflict as best they could. Here their low numbers certainly proved advantageous. Throughout the antebellum and Civil War periods, they never comprised more than 3 percent of the city's total population. Another attribute that blurred their ethnic profile was their occupational dispersion. Adding strength to the region's burgeoning industrial labor force, German immigrants also found employment as tailors, coopers, shoemakers, teachers, and physicians. Nonetheless, comparable to other German American communities, Boston's Germans did develop a group consciousness, traces of which survive in the records of various associations. Those enamored of Mozart, Beethoven, and Hayden listened to the performances of the Germania Orchestra. German charitable societies, established as early as November 1846, aided countrymen stricken by unemployment or disease. Pastime was tendered by the annual turkey shoot of the Germania Shooting Society, and radical workers looking for physical exercise and political debate enlisted in the local chapter of the national Turner confederation.[9]

The few political refugees of 1848 who found asylum in New England contributed actively to the formation of this small but vibrant German American public sphere, according to Heinzen "the most decent in the United States, and the most genuinely interested in radical causes." Among the first to make their presence felt were Eduard Schläger and Bernhard Domschke, both journalists involved in the founding of the left-leaning abolitionist *Neu England Zeitung*. After Schläger and Domschke moved west, the editorship of the paper was passed on to Philipp Wagner, who managed the *Zeitung* until its demise in the mid-1850s. In the meantime, members of Boston's German intelligentsia involved themselves in the city's academic and literary life. Foremost in embracing this opportunity was the novelist and scholar Reinhold Solger. His ability to address people in fluent English secured Solger an audience outside the immigrant community. Most prominently, it won him an invitation to deliver a series of lectures at the renowned Lowell Institute between 1857 and 1859.[10]

As the sectional strife over the westward expansion of slavery grew more turbulent, Boston's German American radicals took up the standard of the free-soil and abolitionist causes. Their proposal often went further than those coming out of other immigrant communities. A German anti-Nebraska platform timbered at William's Hall not only disapproved of Senator Douglas's bill but vowed opposition to tyranny all over the world. In July 1854, a group of exiles echoed Garrison's critique of Lajos Kossuth by publicly denouncing the Hungarian's "frosty and only theoretical denial of American slavery, as a mean and cowardly act." Two years later, a festival sponsored by the Boston Turnverein on the eve of the presidential elections of 1856 drew a crowd of at least two thousand spectators. The speakers, Adolf Douai, Gustav Struve, Karl Friedrich Kob, and Senator Henry Wilson, railed against the incursion of proslavery settlers into Kansas and urged a predominantly German audience to "seek redress for the outrages thus inflicted upon their countrymen by casting their votes for John C. Frémont." Douai and Kob furthermore assumed the task of cooperating with the New England Emigrant Aid Company to promote the transfer of European free-soil immigrants to the embattled plains of Kansas.[11]

The ambitions of Boston's political refugees, however, were not limited to their adopted homeland. That much became obvious in their response to the execution of Felice Orsini in the spring of 1858. Orsini and a group of comrades, persuaded that Napoleon III was a chief obstacle to Italian independence, hurled three bombs at his carriage as the emperor was on his way to the opera. Orsini's death on the scaffold of French monarchy caused a stir among European revolutionists across the United States, rousing painful recollections of their own persecution ten years earlier. In this sentiment, Boston's foreign-born democrats assembled in the evening hours of April 29, 1858, at Turner Hall, where they venerated Orsini's failed bid for Italian freedom. The polyglot gathering was called to order by an Italian American named Urbino, the first on a long list of eulogists featuring the Italian nationalist Francis Piccaroli, the French republicans Leon Chautard and Pierre Fouquet, and the German democrat Adolf Douai. Their speeches were greeted with spirited applause as was an open letter from William Lloyd Garrison, who had been unable to attend but nevertheless seized the occasion to bond with the cosmopolitan revolutionists. "It is true, I do not believe in killing any man — not even so great a monster as Louis Napoleon," Garrison wrote, reaffirming his philosophy of nonviolent resistance. But in his hatred of tyranny little seemed to distinguish the senior abolitionist from the foreign radicals. "I am not only an abolitionist for the chattelized slave, but an emancipationist for the whole human race," the editor of the *Liberator* pledged. "I am no advocate for one-sided liberty, or mere national independence; but wherever tyranny exists, I loathe and execrate it, and proclaim liberty to be the inalienable right of every human being — liberty of person, of locomotion, of thought, of speech, of the press — liberty in all things, under all circumstances, in all lands, for all peoples, through all time, and to all eternity." Surely this was a declaration of human rights to which even the most eccentric agitator would have acquiesced, even somebody as eccentric as Karl Heinzen.[12]

Equal Rights for the Immigrant

For their aggressive politics, Boston's German American democrats had to expect a serious backlash. Although the Irish were most frequently pilloried in nativist accounts, Massachusetts's Yankee elites were equally wary of foreign newcomers who challenged their way of life from a secular or anti-Christian position. The radical Forty-Eighters, as one nativist mouthpiece claimed, were a particularly defiant class of immigrants. It likened the agitators from abroad to a "festering boil" and asserted, "Their atheism produce[s] a pest, wherever they go." In a similar mood, the *Boston Courier* lashed out at the protagonists of the Orsini meeting, vilifying them as rabble-rousers who could conceive of no other mode of settling human problems than outright murder. A people confusing equal rights with uncurbed license, and freedom with political terror, the *Courier* insisted, violated "every enlightened doctrine upon which rest the ennobling institutions of the American republic." Such troublemakers, the article concluded, should not be tendered the rights of American citizens.[13]

Although Know-Nothings in the Bay State pushed hard to keep the immigrants out of the body politic, they acted surprisingly liberal on other issues. When controlling the state legislature in 1855, the American Party collaborated with Conscience Whigs, Free-Soilers, and old Liberty Party men, passing a series of remarkable laws: they abolished imprisonment for debt, enacted legislation prohibiting child labor, and almost eliminated the death penalty. Responding to the arrest of fugitive slave Anthony Burns, which had set Bostonians afire the previous year, the legislature passed one of the most generous personal liberty laws ever devised. It was this coalition with Massachusetts's antislavery and abolitionist politicians that allowed the Know-Nothings to pursue their anti-immigrant agenda long after their prime. In 1855 steps were taken toward adopting a twenty-five-year residency requirement for foreign-born voters. Four years later, nativist delegates who had allied themselves with moderate Republicans pushed for an amendment to the state constitution that would withhold from naturalized citizens the right to vote or hold office until two years after they had acquired citizenship.[14]

The "two-year amendment," as it came to be known, hit the foreign-born like a bombshell. Those who had been lauding the young Republican Party for its outspoken free-labor and free-soil policies were consternated. Protests against the referendum poured in from immigrant organizations throughout the North.

Carl Schurz, the rising star of German American republicanism in the West, bellowed that the measure "upset the whole theory on which the Republican Party rest[ed]." The Democratic *Wisconsin Banner und Volksfreund*, trying to make the most of this affair, cited it as proof that native-born Republicans had no qualms about "degrad[ing] the German to a scale below that of a nigger." Meanwhile, Boston's German American radicals held their own indignation meeting on March 3, 1859. Under the auspices of Karl Heinzen, those present implored the state legislature to rescind the discriminatory act and vowed to support only the party that did "not measure civil rights by place of birth, or human rights by color of skin." It was all in vain. Later that spring, Massachusetts voters endorsed the amendment.[15]

Not quite three months after coming to Boston, the editor of the *Pionier* flung himself into the heat of another political battle. The opponent was a familiar one. Heinzen, though never oblivious to the shortcomings of his fatherland, proudly weighed his German heritage against that of the native-born white American. True, men of Anglo-Saxon stock had penned the Declaration of Independence, yet the idea that a people cut off from modern tastes and knowledge by the bigotries of Protestantism should feel superior seemed ludicrous to Heinzen. Like many of his fellow refugees, he ascribed to German culture a redemptive quality and believed that "German festivity and art, radicalism and science, enlightenment and humanity" were proper instruments to belittle the Know-Nothings. The model he favored was accommodation, not assimilation. "We want to live and strive next to and with the Americans, but never beneath them," Heinzen clarified. "We want to give them what we have, and not let them take away what is ours. We want to receive what they have to offer, but not as charity. We do not want more than they have, but we do not want less either." A better vindication of America's democratic ideals fanned by a heightened ethnic awareness was hard to find.[16]

Now that Boston's conservative establishment seemed to have become infested with Know-Nothingism, voices in the German American radical milieu calling for separate political action were getting louder. Heinzen, however, kept looking for reliable partners on the other side of the ethnic fence. Then he remembered Garrison. Heinzen's relationship with America's radical abolitionists was never easy. Both stood on common ground in that they spoke out aggressively against chattel slavery and other forms of human oppression. Yet blatant differences remained and appeared impossible to bridge at first. So it seemed during a brief but momentous encounter with Arthur Tappan, cofounder of the American and Foreign Anti-Slavery Society, which Heinzen described with this revealing statement: "When I was editing my first abolitionist paper in

New York, I received a visit from the wealthy abolitionist Tappan, who died just recently. He had come to offer me some assistance, supposing that I was a Christian. But when I told him that I was a decided atheist, the pious man replied that I could not be a true abolitionist. He then left me with a sad face."[17]

The scene bears symbolic value for the difficulties attending the transactions between Old World radicalism and New World reform. For Heinzen, people like Tappan were tragicomic fellows — decent, upright citizens fighting for an honorable end with dangerously flawed means. Again religion was a major bone of contention: what evangelical abolitionists identified as a vital source of moral inspiration seemed to Heinzen a relic of medieval thought. Why invoke a God in whose name the most terrible crimes had been perpetrated when there were far more compelling arguments available to combat a social evil such as chattel slavery? The Christian reformers' obsession with scriptural truth, Heinzen diagnosed, had turned them into "Bible slaves" and made them blind to the accomplishments of modern science and philosophy. He agreed with Gustav Struve that the philosophy of "Christian patience" had estranged American abolitionists from other revolutionary movements in the Atlantic world inspired by "a hatred of tyranny" inherited from ancient Greece. Evangelical abolitionists portrayed themselves as liberators, but what they really needed, according to Heinzen, was liberation from a worldview that chained them hopelessly to a superstitious past.[18]

It was in this state of mind that Heinzen addressed a letter to the office of the *Liberator* on March 22, 1859. Garrison, whose paper was printed just a few blocks away from Heinzen's, received with delay, for he did not circulate it until April 8. In an unusually polite and diplomatic tone, the editor of the *Pionier* began by congratulating the abolitionist leader on his "vigorous and consistent defence of the rights of colored men." Yet Heinzen was no sweet-talker. "Allow me to utter my astonishment," he went on, "at your passing over in silence a violation of the rights of *white* men, that goes on before your eyes." While crusading for the social advancement of blacks deserved praise, Heinzen conceded, a glaring discrepancy among Garrisonians nonetheless remained: their lack of outrage that the descendants of "Mazzini, Ledru Rollin, even Humboldt, Liebig, &c." would not be given the franchise "except after seven years of residence." Was Garrison a hypocrite? The German radicals in the United States were waiting for a clear answer.[19]

The reply came swiftly. Amazed that somebody dared to lecture him on human rights, Garrison stressed, even though "we do not go to the polls ourselves (having long since withdrawn from them as a matter of conscience), we, nevertheless, strongly condemn an act of political injustice like that referred to by the editor of the 'Pionier.'" To underpin his statement, he attached to it an editorial censuring the politicians responsible for the amendment as well an appeal by Toledo's German American Republicans denouncing the Massachusetts legislature for discriminating between native- and foreign-born citizens.[20]

Reassuring enough for the immigrant radical, Garrison had proven himself not dedicated to black liberation alone. However, Garrison disagreed with his German interrogator that nativism was simply an upshot of American intolerance. In his opinion, it was inextricably bound up with chattel slavery and the inertia of large parts of the immigrant population regarding its existence. Even if there was no justification for barring foreigners from the polls, abolitionists like Garrison had little sympathy for the naturalized citizen who, by voting Democratic, prolonged the misery of the black man. The Irish, the *Liberator* bewailed, had on the whole degenerated into "allies of the slave-breeders and slave-hunters," and only recently had parts of the German American electorate begun to support the Free Soil and Republican parties. Garrison credited this realignment primarily to the efforts of refugee intellectuals like Heinzen and Schurz, whose lecture "True Americanism" at Faneuil Hall received much applause for echoing the abolitionist vision of a multiethnic and cosmopolitan American republic. In perspective, though, these were only small steps on the road to adopting the motto "No Union with Slaveholders," without which, Garrison asserted, "love of liberty [was] nothing but personal selfishness."[21]

Garrison's deliberations were favorably reviewed by Heinzen. He responded to them on April 30, ten days prior to the referendum. The editor of the *Liberator*, that much had become clear, was not indifferent to the lot of the immigrants, nor did he seem to have much in common with the nativist hardliners, whom Heinzen had assailed in earlier accounts. Instead, Garrison's anti-Irish views converged smoothly with Heinzen's depiction of Irish Catholics as "raw" and "uncouth" minions of the slave power. Both also locked horns with conservative German immigrants, who allegedly cared nothing about bringing freedom to those who needed it most. In light of such unexpected analogies, disagreements that persisted appeared less strident than earlier. Heinzen continued to object that the Garrisonians associated slavery with sin rather than crime, but the language in which he did so became more conciliatory. "We can assure the 'Liberator' that the German Radicals . . . have always heartily acknowledged the honorable attitude of the American Abolitionists," he affirmed, regretting that both parties had been unable to meet on more cordial terms because of their religious disputes.[22]

The fledgling entente between the *Liberator* and the *Pionier* did not stop voters from approving the controversial two-year amendment. Yet it spawned a dialogue between culturally diverse radicalisms that had hitherto evolved all but separately from each other. Once instigated, this dialogue absorbed a growing number of participants and continued to do so as national developments inflamed the political climate in the Bay State.[23]

Boston's Civil War

After the storm over the Know-Nothing referendum had petered out, Heinzen entered into a brief period of relative ease and stability. Financial difficulties still plagued him, but friends managed to bail him out of most of his quandaries. With the help of one of his admirers, the lithographer Louis Prang, Heinzen was able to find more-generous lodging for his family at 419 Washington Street. The Heinzens became good friends with the wealthy Prangs, who contributed to virtually all the causes that the editor of the *Pionier* championed with his pen. Another valuable companion who helped Heinzen adjust was the Polish American physician and women's rights activist Marie E. Zakrzewska, who declared Heinzen "equal to William Lloyd Garrison" in his commitment to universal freedom. Making her home a social center for the city's leading radicals from Europe and North America, the polyglot doctor became Heinzen's loyal confidant on issues ranging from women's rights to the abolition of slavery and actively introduced him to a wider circle of Boston intellectuals.[24]

Although Heinzen welcomed his new acquaintances, especially his relationship with Garrison, with whom he frequently played whist at Zakrzewska's house, the journalist liked best the quiet of his workplace, where he was always striving to perfect his "organ of radicalism." A city as energetic and colorful as antebellum Boston provided ample material to ponder. Its streets were teeming with self-anointed prophets, mystics, humanitarians, philanthropists, and moral practitioners from all walks of life whose presence could not but leave a deep imprint on Heinzen. Here in "The Hub," the German revolutionist was one among many competing architects of progress. Rivalries were quite common, and those with no significant affiliations had even greater difficulties recruiting followers in this hodgepodge of professional do-gooders and world improvers. Heinzen became aware of this as he scanned the city's reform-oriented segments for potential allies.

His first impressions, though, were not very encouraging. When, in October 1859, telegraph stations cabled that John Brown and his band had spilled blood for the liberation of Virginia's slaves, Heinzen quivered with excitement. Finally an abolitionist who backed up his revolutionary words with revolutionary deeds! Tired of northern conciliators, Heinzen hailed Brown as "the pride and disgrace of this Republic, its most courageous martyr and hero in the cause of liberty." Just as Orsini had given his life for a free and unified Italy, Brown's feat evinced that there was no middle ground between freedom and slavery. "There he hangs," Heinzen wrote after learning of Brown's execution, "and will hang and dangle in the wind, until revenged. . . . A gallows now separates North from South. That gallows will be the signpost for the politics of this land. It will either move down to South Carolina, or up to Massachusetts."[25]

Other Bostonians were more cautious in their appraisals. The Garrisonians in particular saw themselves confronted with a fundamental dilemma: How could one sympathize with Brown and advocate nonviolence at the same time? Lydia Maria Child held that Brown had been "sadly mistaken in his mode of operation," yet his willingness to die for the rights of others turned him into a Christlike figure. Clearly, pacifists in the movement were dancing on a tightrope, and after Brown had completed his martyrdom, peace principles in the movement proved even more difficult to vindicate. On December 2, 1859, the day of Brown's execution, nearly four thousand abolitionist mourners, black and white, met for prayer at Tremont Temple. At last, Garrison himself mounted the speakers' platform and found words that acknowledged Brown's valor yet allowed him to utter his belief in nonviolent protest: "As a peace man . . . I am prepared to say, 'Success to every slave insurrection at the South, and in every slave country.' And I do not see how I compromise or stain my peace profession in making that declaration."[26]

Heinzen could only shake his head as he watched Garrison and those identifying with his peace doctrines wriggle their way through the present crisis. To him, advocating revolution without violence was like trying to make an omelet without breaking eggs. In the heydays of the European uprisings, Heinzen had stunned readers with the statement that terror and tyrannicide were valid means in the struggle for greater democracy. Conditions in the United States, he proclaimed, warranted no less militant an approach. If the stalemate between freedom and slavery could not be unlocked with words, then arms should do the talking; those departing from this logic merely strengthened the evil they had sworn to combat. Heinzen applied this line of reasoning explicitly to the nonresistant abolitionists, whom he found paralyzed by a delusive Christian faith. "How much intellectual, reformatory, yes revolutionary talent do we see assembled in men such as Parker, Emerson, and W. Phillips," he noted. But how sad to see them "bow down feebly in a chapel of superstition" every other Sunday.[27]

Then again, as Brown and his men abundantly showed, not all native-born abolitionists loathed physical resistance. Even in the cradle of Garrisonianism, one could easily run into activists who favored harsher measures. Five of the famous Secret Six, wealthy philanthropists who funded the Harpers Ferry operation, resided in or near Boston. Outside the city's liberal white intelligentsia, a yet louder chorus of approval rose from the African American quarters. Black pastor J. Sella Martin, who attended the December 2 meeting at Tremont Temple, spoke for many of his parishioners when he rejoiced that Brown's actions had finally aroused "the slumbering might of the volcano." Espousing armed resistance, in the case of Boston's blacks, was less a result of pompous theories than a response to concrete dangers. The rising anger over the Fugitive Slave Law led black activists to join their white allies in storming the federal courthouse where Anthony Burns was held captive. Shortly afterward, in August 1854, a group of black Bostonians, anxious to defend themselves against further white aggression, formed the Massasoit Guard, the first in a series of black volunteer units that remained in service until after the Civil War.[28]

Contrary to most of his fellow exiles, Heinzen acknowledged a separate African American agency in the movement to abolish slavery. As early as 1855, he gave credit to black agitators whose contention that rising up against oppression was a universal right deviated sharply from the moral-suasion rhetoric of their white partners. Endowed with an "unvarnished sense of right," the free blacks, Heinzen suggested, had a clearer understanding of what was at stake than the white "peace tootlers," who had never suffered under a tyrant's rod. Like the radical democrats from overseas, they did not wait for a moral revolution but courageously opted for a political one, sensing that this was the only way to lift themselves and their fellow blacks out of misery. This, according to Heinzen, was the essence of true radicalism, and it was high time that Garrison and his consorts began to tilt in that direction.[29]

Slowly and reluctantly they did. After the standoff at Harpers Ferry, sectional animosities rose to new extremes. Eighteen sixty was election year, and southern congressmen warned their northern colleagues that secession loomed unless voters turned their back on Abraham Lincoln, the candidate of the antislavery Republicans. But most northerners would not listen. Eventually, the Republican platform received 39.8 percent of the popular vote — enough for Lincoln to claim the White House and for southern extremists to take action. As Boston's abolitionists were preparing for the first anniversary of Brown's death on the gallows, fire-eaters in South Carolina made final arrangements to lead their state out of the Union.

Wendell Phillips's response to the impending clash with the slaveholding South seesawed somewhere between discomfort and anticipation. A loyal Garrisonian, the forty-nine-year-old Brahmin Calvinist had come to support all of that faction's principal tenets: moral suasion, nonviolent resistance, disunionism, renunciation of party politics, and women's involvement. Phillips was destined to serve the law as his father had done but gave up his career in 1837 after identifying himself as an abolitionist. The speech that catapulted him into the upper echelons of the movement and gained him the reputation as the "Golden Trumpet of Abolition" occurred at a Faneuil Hall meeting in honor of the slain Illinois editor Elijah Lovejoy. His sparkling and fervid oratory turned Phillips into Garrison's most important coworker, and his lectures marked the high point of nearly every annual convention of the American Anti-Slavery Society. "We have no orator in England who can compare with him," a reporter for the *London Times* admitted after seeing Phillips in his element. "He is the most eloquent speaker living." Phillips's family, however, thought that he had lost his mind and tried to confine him to a lunatic asylum.[30]

Abolitionists like Phillips saw nothing glorious in the politics that carried Lincoln all the way to the presidency. It bore too much the stigma of opportunism and lacked the righteousness that elevated the abolitionist cause above the Republican one. Yet the immediate result of Lincoln's victory tallied nicely with a policy that the Garrisonians had been preaching for decades. These people did not care that the Union was falling apart. Regarding any attempt to negotiate with slaveholders as a bargain with evil, they had little compassion for unionists striving to protect the Constitution at all costs. The prevailing attitude among Boston's native-born abolitionists was if the southern states wished to secede, let them go, and nobody shed a tear at their departure. It was better to build a new, smaller nation untainted by the curse of slavery than to continue to live under the old leviathan that had proven deaf to pleas for moral improvement.[31]

Northerners favoring compromise were infuriated to hear men and women in their vicinity pronounce disunionist sentiments. Most had legitimate reasons for trying to appease their departing countrymen. Already southerners were canceling orders for northern goods and strangulating the cotton trade, on which Massachusetts's textile mills relied. Prices soared, and wages were cut; the shoemakers and textile workers of Lynn, Marblehead, and Haverhill went on strike. White capitalists and workers were commonly affected by the mounting national calamity, and the unionist coalition they constituted vowed to bash out of town anyone who added fuel to the fire. Phillips and his friends remained undeterred by such threats. Branded an enemy of the state, Phillips went on to call for separation and was planning to do so at the upcoming anniversary memorial of John Brown's death, where he was to be featured as one of the main speakers.[32]

December 3, 1860, commenced like every other Boston day that fall — cold, windy, yet overall serene. But the shouts and hisses from angry bystanders greet-

Abolitionists ejected from Tremont Temple, *Harper's Weekly*, December 15, 1860. Comparing conservative Bostonians to Europe's antiliberal establishment, immigrant Turners formed a body-guard to protect local abolitionists from physical harm.

ing the abolitionists headed for Tremont Temple were anything but tranquil. Black and white activists had defied caveats not to assemble; now they were in deep trouble. Hardly had Frederick Douglass, J. Sella Martin, Franklin Sanborn, and other illustrious Brown sympathizers ascended the platform than the doors flew open, giving way to a howling pack of unionists determined to break up the meeting. After three hours of mayhem, with both parties trying to out-yell and out-muscle the other, the mayor ordered the police to clear the hall. A group of conservative businessmen then regained control of the meeting and passed resolutions that stamped the abolitionist gathering "a public nuisance" and condemned its organizers as "irresponsible persons and demagogues" who "disturb[ed] the public peace and misrepresent[ed them] abroad."[33]

When Heinzen got word that the abolitionists were being heckled out of Tremont Temple by a mob of Irish and native-born unionists, he instantly swung into action. This was not the occasion for petty bickering. Whatever their flaws, the Garrisonians, with their moral rectitude and avowed fidelity to universal democracy, still seemed light-years ahead of their enemies. Accompanied by a cohort of Turners, Heinzen rushed to the scene of the brawl, only to find the Temple deserted. Had he come too late? Not quite. The ejected, he was told, had regrouped in the heart of black Boston at J. Sella Martin's Joy Street Church. Heinzen followed them to the new location. It was the first time he had set foot in a house of worship in America; there was no greater tribute that the militant atheist could pay to the cause. He did not regret it, for the spectacle unfolding before his eyes was unlike anything he had ever seen. The bulk of the congregation consisted of African Americans, and Heinzen noted with delight the many dark-hued women showing little restraint in voicing their approval during the service. After a few opening remarks, Wendell Phillips stepped out to a roar of recognition. Heinzen had listened to the abolitionist thunderer previously, but today's performance swept the German editor off his feet. "Every word a sword," he exulted, "that pierced to the bone the Boston millionaires . . . and kindred traitors." This was not the same man whom Heinzen had criticized in the past for his lack of courage in the face of slaveholder aggression. No, before him spoke a gallant agitator who was upholding basic civil liberties at a time of grave personal danger, a true and fearless radical who did not stop expounding his views even as another pro-Union mob was on the verge of storming the church.[34]

The dramatic events on that day changed almost everything for Boston's abolitionists. In the pandemonium of Tremont Temple and Joy Street Church, old doctrines buckled and yielded to more-flexible ones. To hear of antiblack riots and of Phillips being ushered home past a raging crowd made even the most zealous pacifist reconsider. "Why, what is the matter with us? Are we going to palliate and excuse a palpable and flagrant outrage on the right of speech — by implying that only a particular description of persons should exercise of that right?" an exasperated Frederick Douglass challenged his nonresistant brethren. Phillips, who had become the object of special vengeance, drew his own conclusions. From now on, he never left his house without a gun, vowing to use it against anyone who dared lay hand on him or his family.[35]

Boston's immigrant radicals suffered far fewer pangs of conscience when it came to the use of force. To them, recent efforts to deny abolitionists a public platform seemed a glaring memento of their own scuffles with state authorities in Europe and a wrong they could not ignore. A few days following the clash at Tremont Temple, members of the local Turnverein put together an armed task force and entrusted it with protecting the city's abolitionist leadership from further harassment. Concurrently, Heinzen's *Pionier* heaped invective after invective upon city officials, who, as he saw it, defamed Boston's revolutionary legacy by placing the moneybag and the slave whip above the precious right of free assembly.[36]

Armed with rifles and clothed in their customary white attire, the Turners swarmed out. Phillips was one of the first to realize what this meant. Looking out his bedroom window one evening, the beleaguered agitator was pleased to find "a squad" of German Turners watching his house and deflecting potential troublemakers. "That's worth being mobbed for," Phillips rejoiced weeks later in a letter to the Philadelphia abolitionist Mary Grew. "There's some good in the world, spite original sin." The first major test for Phillips's new bodyguard occurred on December 16 at Boston's Music Hall. More than three thousand people showed up to listen to a lecture by Phillips that bore the provocative title "The Mob and Education." Obviously, this speech was not going to pacify Phillips's opponents. Not long after he began pouring out blistering diatribes against the city's political and commercial elites, the anti-abolitionist segments of the crowd started jeering and stamping in their galleries. Phillips carried on despite the hullabaloo, building to a peroration that made the blood of every honest unionist boil. "Governments exist to protect the rights of minorities," he declared. If the Union fails this litmus test, "the sooner it vanishes out of the way, the better."[37]

Then the storm broke loose. At the conclusion of Phillips's address, friends jumped onto the platform and shepherded him out through a back door. On the street, the party was stopped by an angry horde of rioters. Cries such as "There he is!" "Damn him!" "Bite his head off!" filled the air as the mob tried to seize the abolitionist. Phillips, almost miraculously, got through without a scratch. In addition to the nearly two hundred policemen who were needed to calm the situation, the Turners formed a cordon around Phillips, making sure that he would not be hurt. After some minor tussling, the formation managed to break out of the gridlock and safely bore their hero to his house at 26 Essex Street. Three cheers were given by friends and relatives as Phillips arrived home. His guards, meanwhile, took up sentinel position, bayonets flashing, until the last cursing and yowling protester vanished into the night.[38]

Four days after Phillips's performance at Music Hall, South Carolina seceded. Mississippi followed on January 9, Florida on the tenth, Alabama on the eleventh, and Georgia on the nineteenth. When Phillips gave his next speech at Music Hall on January 20, the Deep South claimed it was no longer part of the country. Unmoved by these developments, the abolitionist chose a topic for his address as incendiary as ever: "Disunion." Anticipating another row, Phillips took increased measures to protect himself. His riot control force now included old-line abolitionists, black militiamen, German Turners, and idealists like the young Oliver Wendell Holmes Jr. Simultaneously, Heinzen summoned members of the Turnverein to his printing office, where he made them swear to defend "free speech and free speakers" at whatever cost. Secession, which he deemed a despicable, cowardly act, was not the issue now. This was about upholding an ideal on which intellectuals across party lines depended: that of a free and unrestricted public sphere.[39]

The scene at Music Hall on January 20, 1861, was almost identical to the one four and a half weeks earlier. Samuel Gridley Howe, one of Phillips's associates, submitted the following vivid sketch to Charles Sumner:

> About fifty hard-fisted and resolute Germans went ahead and pushed the mob to the right-left. Then followed some fourty [*sic*] or fifty determined antislavery Yankees, who arm in arm and close ranks preceded and followed Phillips. . . . It was a hard struggle down Winter St. & through Washington St. as far as the corner of Bedford St. The mob pushed against us, howling & swearing & clamouring, — a few resolute fellows pushing us against the wall, & evidently longing for a stop or melee in which they could get a lick at Phillips, who however bore himself very resolutely & bravely. Our course was to bear on steadily, saying nothing. . . . At last we got to Phillips' door & way was made for him to get in. Then there was groaning & hooting & other disgraceful acts, before the crowd dispersed.[40]

Mayor John Wightman, no friend of the abolitionists, had seen enough. Learning that this year's convention of the Massachusetts Anti-Slavery Society on January 23 was doomed to be ravaged by a unionist demonstration, he decided to intervene. Tremont Temple was studded with police as Phillips commenced speaking. The orator held his ground thanks to his stellar rhetorical skills; his successor, however, was less fortunate. Ralph Waldo Emerson was able to say only a few sentences before being booed off the stage. Unnerved by this behavior, the organizers appealed to Governor Andrew for help. The newly inaugurated Andrew, fearing additional outbursts, refused to send the state militia, and when Phillips and his cohorts returned to the Temple, they found the doors shut. The mayor had ordered the closing of the hall. Public safety, he maintained, demanded it. Wightman, who owed his election to the city's conservative magnates, agreed with the *Boston Courier*, which dubbed Phillips's speeches "a mass of poisonous and malignant trash — a thorough jail delivery of bad temper, vituperation, and hatred" — emotions, of course, that seemed detrimental to law and order.[41]

Boston's abolitionists were infuriated but not silenced. Once more they retreated to Joy Street Church and resumed their meeting there, stalwartly guarded by black militia and a company of German Turners. Karl Heinzen was spitting fire as always, calling for Wightman's removal and insisting that the state legislature pass a bill explicitly designed to protect freedom of speech and of the press. "Life and property are saved from harm in all those places where law and peace have replaced barbarism and war," Heinzen fumed. "But how can there be life without freedom of expression, and does that right have less value than a nickel or a cotton handkerchief?"[42]

By mid-February, civic unrest in the streets of Boston had largely subsided. A more ominous foe was gathering down South that absorbed all public attention. The abolitionist agitators, it seemed, had emerged victorious; yet their defiant behavior had not left them in a triumphant mood. They too had suffered enormous casualties, among them the belief that a peaceful resolution of the slavery conflict was possible. The old Garrisonian line of thinking had been that secession would allow the North to recuperate from its moral involvement in the evil of slavery. Now even Garrison was ready to admit that the entire nation, for its unparalleled iniquities, deserved "to be visited with civil and servile war." The turbulent winter of 1860/61 had turned Boston's abolitionist leaders upside down. But it had also won them stout allies. "It was men who had learned of him," Phillips praised Heinzen in an undated scrapbook entry, "that . . . passed that never to be forgotten vote, 'that they would protect Free Speech and Free Speakers.' Members of your Halle carried out that resolve, and four men by four, relieved every hour, guarded the houses of prominent abolitionists, week after week, all night long."[43]

Enforcing Freedom

In the days following the cannonade on Fort Sumter, Boston erupted into a frenzy of patriotism. Republicans and Democrats, natives and immigrants, all dashed rapaciously to the colors, burning to avenge the fall of Sumter. Each ward held its own war meetings, and political differences were momentarily cast aside. Garrison's *Liberator* also succumbed to the reality of armed conflict. "Let us break every yoke," its chief editor exclaimed. "If this war shall put an end to that execrable system, it will be more glorious in history than that of the Revolution." Speaking in Music Hall on Sunday, April 21, Wendell Phillips completed his transformation from a nonresistant Garrisonian to a prowar abolitionist. Uplifted by the cheers of four thousand listeners (many of whom had wished him dead not too long ago), Phillips burst forth: "I rejoice . . . that now, for the first time in my antislavery life, I speak under the stars and stripes, and welcome the tread of Massachusetts men marshaled for war."[44]

Heinzen noted with relief that the war had reconciled abolitionists with some of his key positions. To him, southerners were little more than barbarians, and their validations of slavery as a positive good were an upshot of the aristocratic ideas they had been taught to revere. "Brotherly reconciliation," Heinzen argued, was no viable course in such a situation. Rejecting every form of compromise, he favored coercion and an instant, all-out attack on the secessionists. Their invocation of states' rights rang hollow in Heinzen's ears, for he saw in these arguments nothing but a subterfuge for preserving a system postulating that if one man chose to enslave another, no third man should be allowed to object. The current struggle, the editor of the *Pionier* affirmed, was one of Manichean proportions, and those engaged in it needed to fight for higher goals than personal fame, riches, or restoring the status quo ante.[45]

Although his training in the Prussian army would have secured him an officer post in an ethnic unit, the radical editor refused to enlist. Heinzen's leadership in the Turner intervention in support of Boston's abolitionists had earned him the gratitude of the Garrisonians and the near unanimous backing of the city's German American community. His friend Louis Prang sold portraits of Heinzen showing him in the company of other Boston freedom fighters such as Garrison, Phillips, and Theodore Parker. Why jeopardize this rare moment of popularity? Heinzen's vocation was that of a journalist, and in that role, he was certain, he could be most useful to the war effort. To a Turner friend he replied that the blows he could deliver with his pen were at least as sharp as the blade of an army saber. Already in February, Heinzen had decided to release his southern subscribers, boasting that he would rather lose money than endanger the few remaining radicals in what was now enemy territory. Impressed by Heinzen's resolve, Garrison praised the floundering *Pionier* for its "manly and fearless utterance on all subjects" and called on readers of his own paper to help swell Heinzen's subscription list. Wendell Phillips did not ask for details. "I should ask you to put my name on your list if I read the German with any ease," he wrote to Heinzen. "But my ignorance in that direction does not blind me to the value of your labors or lessen my interest on the success of your journal." Enclosed with Phillips's letter was a twenty-dollar bill.[46]

Heinzen's *Pionier* survived the first shocks of war, yet so did the southern Confederacy. After the rout of the Union army at Bull Run, lofty hopes of a swift victory died almost overnight. Northerners had gravely misjudged the fighting spirit of the South and realized that they were in for a long, hard war. Far more frustrating to abolitionists, however, were decisions made beyond the battlefield. Garrison called Lincoln's revocation of Frémont's emancipation order "timid, depressing, suicidal" and a "serious dereliction of duty." The news of Frémont's dismissal set passions afire in the radical German American bloc as well. Together with other immigrant democrats, Heinzen spoke at a pro-Frémont rally in Boston's Turner Hall on November 12, 1861. Six hundred people cheered as Heinzen extolled the valor of his countrymen who, as he claimed, were fighting alongside Frémont to crush the rebellion and free the slaves. The resolutions adopted demanded the immediate reinstatement of the abolitionist general and branded his removal the product of a policy that "destroy[ed] justice, prompt[ed] friction, and stifle[d] true patriotism." Copies were made available in German and English to ensure publication in the city's major newspapers.[47]

Like hundreds of abolitionists and immigrant radicals, Heinzen chafed at what seemed to him squandered opportunities in the quest for emancipation. Whiteness mattered little in the radical democratic cosmology of the *Pionier*. Heinzen declared without restraint that he would rather send every proslavery German to the gallows "than consider him [his] countryman." Although he could rhapsodize over the idealism of his fellow Turners fighting for the Union, he reserved his hardest clouts for German-born soldiers who donned the uniform for purposes other than revolutionary ones. With a rancor that troubled even close associates, Heinzen called into question the military aptitude of officers he deemed politically unfit, often denouncing them as bootlickers or mere award hunters. Most notorious was his controversy with Ludwig Blenker — the rumor was that Blenker had embezzled army funds — but it was a rare jab at Franz Sigel that triggered a wave of indignation among German Americans. Sigel was a beacon of ethnic pride for Heinzen's compatriots, and they could not fathom how one could accuse the popular general of being too soft on the enemy. Not long after Heinzen's attack on Sigel, Boston's Germans censured the editor of the *Pionier* in a public meeting at Turner Hall on May 18, 1862, stating that criticizing Sigel only gave ammunition to nativists in the War Department.[48]

Heinzen's egalitarian beliefs were in no way shared by all immigrant refugees. Reinhold Solger told Phillips that "the united voice of history, science, and daily experience" confirmed that Africans could never become the equals of white men. Heinzen, on the contrary, forged ahead boldly to rebut the popular prejudice that blacks were a lazy and servile people, capable of little more than menial labor. Bristling with anger over Lincoln's colonization plans, he noted: "With respect to the European, [Lincoln] thinks it justifiable to bring to the fore principal dictates of justice. . . . People of African descent, however, are asked to forfeit their rights and are callously subjected to prejudice." Deporting African Americans, according to Heinzen, not only violated all rules of decency; worse, it wrested them away from the land they had learned to call home. To him, blacks were entitled to citizenship just like any other ethnic group stranded on America's shores, and he saw no reason why a white person should avoid their company. Garrison and Phillips benefited immensely from their relationships with black activists. Why, then, should Heinzen not follow in their footsteps and give his philosophy of radicalism a similar boost by reaching out to African Americans as well?[49]

Boston's black community seemed ideally situated for such an undertaking. Heinzen contacted black intellectuals through the Massachusetts Anti-Slavery Society, whose annual gatherings he frequented from 1861 onward. There he witnessed the impassioned oratory of the European-traveled William Wells Brown, Charles Lenox Remond, and Baptist clergyman J. Sella Martin — Martin's decision to give refuge to abolitionists during the unruly winter months of 1860/61 was a service that the editor of the *Pionier* never forgot. A still more commanding presence in Heinzen's eyes was John Swett Rock, one of Boston's most outspoken civil rights activists. A European-traveled polyglot with a medical degree and the first African American to gain admittance to the Massachusetts Bar, Rock lectured assiduously against the contention that blacks were unsuited for higher education. Heinzen first saw Rock in action in March 1860 and was immediately enamored of the eloquent black agitator. His ability to interweave the African American freedom struggle with other revolutionary quests such as the civic empowerment of women made a deep impression on the German editor. But Heinzen would not have been the journalist he was had he not seized this opportunity to hurl upon his opponents some of his choicest sarcasm. "A thinking, sophisticated, German- and French-speaking negro," he gloated. "Where is this going to end? 'Democratic' editors, have you no remedy? Where are your fists? Your heads you cannot use, for the wooly one of Dr. Rock contains more knowledge, education, and intelligence than all your pumpkins together."[50]

Despite his admiration for black luminaries like Martin and Rock, Heinzen had strong misgivings whether African Americans would ever be able to elevate themselves without the assistance of benign whites. Although he did not question their fighting spirit, he found them too vulnerable to take matters into their own hands. He supported arming blacks but also reported at length about atrocities committed by Confederates against defenseless former slaves and black prisoners of war. Just as the Garrisonians viewed themselves as fatherly tutors of a downtrodden race, Heinzen claimed a similar custodianship for the generation of Old World radicals he represented, one that was equally if not more universal in scope. Of all the weak and underprivileged, blacks, Heinzen contended, were the weakest and hence in special need of an intellectual avant-garde proficient enough to shepherd them up the evolutionary ladder — a proper task, it seemed, for an Enlightenment humanist. Declaring blacks "the touchstone of humanity" in America, Heinzen lectured: "Glorify Kosziusko, admire Garibaldi, toast the Hungarians, root for the French Revolution . . . and boast with Humboldt and Goethe if you feel like testifying your love of freedom, your education and humanity — you are liars, shameless liars and hypocrites, if you despise the negro, the poor, naked, degraded, helpless negro, and think you can do without his liberation in the great concert of human aspirations."[51]

Modern-day readers might feel tempted to fault such a statement for its latent racism. Heinzen, had he understood such a charge, surely would have dismissed it. He would have pointed to the fact that, unlike most of his contemporaries, he believed that blacks had the racial genius for self-government, and that the reasons for their current agonies were environmental, not genetic. The only thing these "fellow citizens of the fugitive world" required were people recognizing and activating their potential for growth. Thus Heinzen managed to square his egalitarian outlook with the conviction that history had bestowed on radicals like him the mission to lead all the oppressed, irrespective of rank, sex, or color, to a better future.[52]

A Union without Lincoln

When Massachusetts's Garrisonian abolitionists gathered for their annual convention on January 24, 1862, they could not be satisfied with developments on the battlefield and in the White House. Last year's military operations had failed to bring a feisty Confederacy to its knees, and the abolitionists had not managed to convince the government that harsher, more far-reaching measures were necessary. Public opinion in the North was also slow to rally behind the cause of freedom for the slaves. True, abolitionists no longer needed to preach to overwhelmingly hostile crowds. In the wake of the distressing experiences of the first war months, many northerners had come to regard the emancipators in a new light, seeing them less as the crackpot fanatics of previous years than as prophets whose vision of an Armageddon between Liberty and Slavery had come true. "The people are ready to hear," Wendell Phillips rejoiced in an address to his New England followers. "Lyceums which could not formerly endure an Abolitionist on any topic, now invite them, stipulating that they shall talk on slavery."[53]

Others were more hesitant in their appraisals. Too numerous were signals indicating that the growing support for black emancipation was not grounded in humanitarian motives but derived instead from a pragmatic desire to hamper the Confederate war machine. Even as the doctrine of liberating the slaves out of military necessity took root in northern society, the nation's leaders were yet reluctant to go that far. Speeches at the 1862 annual meetings of the anti-slavery societies of Massachusetts and New England vibrated with outrage over Lincoln's policy of leaving slavery intact where it existed, and the resolutions introduced there spoke a similar language. One protested that the president "unnecessar[ily] prolonged the war" by refusing to use his powers to destroy southern bondage; a second held the commander in chief responsible "for all the blood and money which [were] sacrificed rather for the preservation of slavery . . . than for the establishment of freedom and the benefit of the people."[54]

The author of these two resolutions was no Brahmin extremist but the immigrant radical Karl Heinzen, who began leaving his imprint on Boston's old-line abolitionist organizations as well. Although Garrison's and Phillips's constant references to the deity still irked him, he shared their impatience with the federal government's moderate policies and wasted no opportunity to express his irritation. Heinzen paid little attention to Republicans who reminded him that to defeat the South, keeping the loyalty of the slaveholding border states outweighed any rash attempt at emancipation. What America needed was a second Robespierre or John Brown, a role that, as the editor of the *Pionier* scoffed, was definitely above the powers of a lawyer from Illinois.[55]

Heinzen started hammering away at Lincoln almost immediately after the inauguration ceremonies in March 1861. His verbal assaults on the chief executive were sharper and more vitriolic than those of most other critics. Lincoln's first inaugural address was derided in the *Pionier* as "a formless, wooden, inept document," and the new head of state was portrayed as a dithering, unimaginative leader without true statesmanlike qualities. "Republican Buchanan," "heartless imbecile," and "man with a leather soul, wooden brain and stony heart" were only three examples from a long list of insults that Heinzen flung at Lincoln. The president's decision to staff his cabinet with a mix of conservative and progressive politicians maddened Heinzen as much as Lincoln's alleged preference for generals favoring a strategy of limited warfare. The attacks in the *Pionier* increased in violence, cresting in July 1861 with an editorial demanding that the troops mutiny and drive Lincoln and General Winfield Scott from office. Nothing came of it, of course, except a retort from Boston's mayor, who told Heinzen that he would have him arraigned for sedition unless he toned down his language.[56]

No stranger to repression, Heinzen was not easy to intimidate, and he continued to express his disgust with the administration. When emancipation was finally proclaimed on January 1, 1863, he did not gush phrases of adulation like hundreds of fellow northern abolitionists. Unlike Boston's Garrisonians, who spent the night before emancipation in prayer, Heinzen sat in his office, firing another heavy broadside at the president and his cabinet. "The slaves declared free by Mr. Lincoln are no less in chains on January 1 than they were on December 31," he snarled. Asserting that the proclamation had no value unless implemented by force, Heinzen penned: "To declare them free without being in the condition to free them is not a blessing but a cruelty."[57]

For a moment, the German-born radical seemed isolated even from the abolitionists closest to him. Throngs turned out to celebrate Lincoln's edict of freedom at various New Year's Day gatherings. All across the Union and in the occupied parts of the South, cries of jubilation and thanksgiving rose up as the proclamation was read to slaves, free blacks, and their white allies. Sensing that victory was at hand, Garrison hallowed the document as a great historic event, "sublime in its magnitude, momentous and beneficent in its far-reaching consequences, and eminently just and right alike to the oppressor and oppressed." In a similar vein, the young black teacher Charlotte Forten declared January 1, 1863, "the most glorious day this nation ha[d] yet seen," and Lydia Maria Child, half crazy with enthusiasm, pronounced, "Whatever battles may be lost in detail, I feel confident that the *great* Battle of *Freedom* will surely be won. It is worth living for, worth dying for."[58]

The abolitionist infatuation with Lincoln, however, did not last long. After the first surges of elation had passed, abolitionist intellectuals began examining the proclamation more closely, and many did not like what they found. Its most flagrant flaw, as they saw it, was that it outlawed slavery on Confederate territory but left it untouched in states loyal to the Union. Moreover, the proclamation, and the federal government in general, remained disturbingly silent on the situation of free blacks in the North. Although the enlistment of black troops was already under way, abolitionists were unhappy that racial segregation persisted. In most places, blacks were barred from white schools and churches, confined to low-paid jobs, forced to dwell in foul quarters, and still exposed to the menace of slave catchers. Did a president who tolerated all this deserve the title "Great Emancipator"? In fact, Lincoln hated slavery personally, but he was also a realist. First, the president did not control state law and was thus unable to move against segregation. Second, he understood that for emancipation to succeed, the proclamation had to be politically sound, militarily viable, and constitutionally watertight. Abolitionists, however, cared little about these limitations. Doubts in the movement multiplied.[59]

Meanwhile, Heinzen placed himself at the apex of a faction of German American radicals committed to preventing the reelection of Lincoln. Opposition had long been brewing among left-leaning immigrants who saw their hopes betrayed that the president would set out to remodel the country in accordance with their democratic ideals. Many were also resentful because English-language newspapers reported negatively about German American military performance. In early 1863, proposals for a new political party became louder. From New York to Milwaukee, from Washington to St. Louis, radical democratic clubs were formed, and plans for separate political action were articulated. Heinzen, assisted by Louis Prang and Marie Zakrzewska, took the lead in organizing one such club. On July 9, 1863, he supervised a meeting in Turner Hall that resulted in the founding of the German Organization Society, an association of Boston freethinkers devoted to promoting radical ideas. Besides demanding the "total abolition of slavery," it came out in favor of "complete social and political equality for all citizens of the Republic regardless of national origin, skin color, and sex."[60]

Three months later, at a national convention of German American radicals in Cleveland, these planks were incorporated almost verbatim into the delegates' final manifesto. The seventy and more participants at this gathering were by no means a homogeneous unit, and old rivalries between various Forty-Eighter veterans sporadically flared up during the proceedings. Still, the delegates managed to put aside most of their differences and forge a program for political change that was more daring and uncompromising than those of the country's Republican leaders. Its goals ranged from the "unconditional suppression of the Rebellion" to the "donation of portions of the land to the defenders of the country, of whatever color," and a lasting partnership between American democrats and the European revolutionists.[61]

Declarations of such scope and magnitude could only ignite public controversy. Conservative German Americans, unsurprisingly, tore them apart; so did Attorney General Edward Bates, who denounced the authors as living in "practical ignorance of [U.S.] political institutions and of the very meaning of the phrase 'Liberty by Law.'" Liberal immigrant organs proved equally unwilling to back Heinzen and his cohorts. Pro-Lincoln papers like the influential *Illinois Staats-Zeitung* and the Philadelphia *Freie Presse* rejected the Cleveland proposals, asserting that they only played into the hands of the Peace Democrats and the Copperheads. And when Franz Sigel, the war hero of scores of German immigrants, publicly distanced himself from the platform, the German anti-Lincoln radicals saw their chances for success go down the drain. Without support from left-leaning native-born agitators, Heinzen reckoned, their campaign would be over before it really got off the ground.[62]

In February 1864, Wendell Phillips stumbled upon a curious piece in his mail. It was a translated version of the Cleveland Platform, and attached to it was a note from one of its draftsmen, Jacob Müller, urging the prominent abolitionist to endorse the manifesto and diffuse its principles among their "radical fellow-citizens of American birth, of whom [he was] an honored representative." Müller's hopes of finding an attentive ear were warranted since Phillips had been keeping company lately with radical Republicans and abolitionists bent on driving Lincoln from office. Phillips had never been on cordial terms with the president, whom he had famously maligned as "the slave-hound from Illinois." To him, Lincoln was shrewdness personified, a conservative politician who was too soft on the Confederates and had ordered emancipation merely in the interest of restoring the Union. Phillips, expecting the war to crystallize into a crusade for black freedom, could not see that the government cared about hastening that process. By late 1863, his patience was exhausted: frustrated over Lincoln's reluctance to advance forcefully on the trail to racial equality, he too began calling for a new head of state.[63]

Phillips's step was contentious and brought disruption even into the ranks of his own organization. The row came to a head at the January 1864 meeting of the Massachusetts Anti-Slavery Society, where Garrison rose up in protest against a resolution submitted by Phillips proclaiming that the government was "ready to sacrifice the interest and honor of the North to secure a sham peace." Indeed, Garrison gauged Lincoln in a manner far more flattering to the latter, citing the Emancipation Proclamation and the recruitment of black soldiers as proof of the president's capacity for moral growth. Phillips disagreed sharply with his old mentor. A man who condoned discrimination against African Americans in the Union army and appeared to have "no desire, no purpose, no thought, to lift the freed negro to a higher status," he replied, was not fit to prepare the country for the difficult job of reconstruction. Only a candidate with a pure heart and revolutionary aspirations, Phillips insinuated, could master a task of such epic proportions.[64]

Phillips's remarks gratified Heinzen deeply. In 1860, the Brahmin abolitionist had still dodged involvement in party politics; four years later, he seized every opportunity to rebuke the current administration, espousing policies that seemed all but identical to those of the German American anti-Lincoln faction. "Let me tell you the national policy I advocate," Phillips wrote back to Cincinnati's Johann Stallo, who wanted Phillips's opinion on the qualities of a potential nominee. "Subdue the South as rapidly as possible. . . . Confiscate and divide the lands of rebels, extend the right of suffrage as broadly as possible to whites and blacks, let the Federal Constitution prohibit slavery throughout the Union, and forbid the States to make any distinction among their citizens on account of color or race." Finally, Phillips advised "an unpledged and independent convention . . . to consider public affairs, and nominate for the presidency a statesman and a patriot."[65]

By February, two national celebrities had signaled that they were ready to supplant Lincoln on a separate Republican ticket: Salmon P. Chase, the ambitious and outspokenly progressive secretary of the treasury; and John C. Frémont, who had tried to capture the White House for the Republicans in 1856. Frémont, like Chase, very much wanted to become president, even more so since his Missouri emancipation decree in 1861 had won him the hearts of the country's abolitionists. Another advantage was that Frémont had been the special hero of a large number of German American radicals, who played a vanguard role in galvanizing support for his nomination. Caspar Butz's *Deutsch-Amerikanische Monatshefte* in Chicago, the *Westliche Post* in St. Louis, the *German-American* in New York, and Heinzen's *Pionier* in Boston rooted enthusiastically for the young Frémont movement. Endorsing the "Pathfinder," they urged German American voters to band together in Frémont clubs.[66]

Heinzen, head of the Boston club, set out immediately to woo the city's abolitionists into the Frémont fold. Phillips was among the first luminaries he contacted. On February 4, 1864, Heinzen called at Phillips's house at 26 Essex Street. Finding no one at home, he left a note on the doorstep. Presenting Frémont as the only candidate who "in every respect [would] be true to the principles of liberty," Heinzen asserted that Germans all over the Union were beginning to side with Frémont, and that "with a little encouragement from the American side they [would] come out en masse." These words made a strong impact on Phillips. In the following weeks, he emerged as Heinzen's principal ally. Together they took on the task of persuading disgruntled Republicans and abolitionists in Boston and elsewhere that Frémont fulfilled the requirements of a strong national leader.[67]

The Frémont campaign was gaining momentum in other places as well. Resolutions of the heavily Germanized Frémont clubs in St. Louis and Chicago in favor of the Pathfinder's nomination were echoed by the Washington, New York, and Boston branches of the movement. On March 18, the Cooper Institute in New York hosted the largest pro-Frémont rally to date, featuring prominent immigrant and native-born abolitionist intellectuals, among them Sinclair Tousey, Spencer Kirby, Friedrich Kapp, and Horace Greeley. Six weeks later, the campaigners made their boldest move. From May 4 to 6, they issued three separate calls for a national convention in Cleveland on May 31, all with the purpose of nominating Frémont as candidate for the presidency. Signers and supporters of these calls included George Cheever, Elisabeth Cady Stanton, Frederick Douglass, Stephen S. Foster, Karl Heinzen, and Wendell Phillips,

The alliance of Karl Heinzen (right, Free Congregation [Freie Gemeinde] of Sauk County, Sauk, Wisconsin) with Wendell Phillips (left, Library of Congress) peaked in 1864, when both supported John C. Frémont's bid for the presidency. Although divided on issues of religion, the German exile and the Brahmin abolitionist shared a radical commitment to women's rights, racial equality, and cosmopolitan democracy.

who had been designated the official Frémont representative of the state of Massachusetts.[68]

Not more than four hundred Frémonters followed the invitation to assemble in Cleveland, fewer than the organizers had hoped. Yet Heinzen and the other delegates — German American radicals, old-line abolitionists, and dissatisfied War Democrats — went to work with great enthusiasm. After melding into a political body that they named "Radical Democracy," the conveners ratified thirteen resolutions. Their platform called for pursuing the war until the Confederacy surrendered unconditionally, a constitutional amendment for the abolition of slavery, aid to disabled Union veterans, encouragement of immigration, and construction of a transcontinental railroad. Due to the presence of conservative War Democrats, concessions had to be made such as striking out a specific approval of black suffrage and the distribution of confiscated lands among freedmen. A provision insisting that the federal government actively support "the freedom struggles of the European peoples" also failed to garner enough votes. The German American revolutionists and their native-born allies rallied again as the chairman read aloud a letter from Wendell Phillips.

Unable to attend the convention, Phillips implored the delegates to commit themselves to a "quick and thorough reorganization of the States, on a democratic basis, every man and race equal before the law." The gathering erupted in wild cheers as he homed in on their candidate: "If I turn to General Fremont, I see a man whose first act was to use the freedom of the negro as his weapon. I see one whose thorough loyalty to democratic institutions, without regard to race — whose earnest and decisive character, whose clear-sighted statesmanship and rare military ability, justify my confidence that in his hands all will be done to save the State that foresight, skill, decision and statesmanship can do."[69]

Following Phillips's recommendation, the delegates nominated John C. Frémont as the candidate of the Radical Democratic Party. The War Democrat John Cochrane was chosen as Frémont's running mate. Accounts of the Cleveland convention were telegraphed to newspapers across the North, most of which so far had been disinclined to take the anti-Lincoln coalition of native-born abolitionists and immigrant revolutionaries seriously. Now they opened fire. The *Boston Evening Transcript* perceived in the convention little more than an "informal gathering of Germans, radicals, and War Democrats"; the *Cleveland Herald* disparaged its organizers as "sly politicians from New York, impetuous hair-brained Germans from St. Louis, abolitionists, and personal friends and parasites of Fremont." *Harper's Weekly* portrayed the gathering as the work of reckless extremists whose actions "gratified every Copperhead and rebel in the country" as they threatened to split the ruling party in two.[70]

Another big handicap for the Frémont campaign was the refusal of many influential abolitionists to jump on its bandwagon. With the exception of the African American press, few abolitionists hailed the nomination of the Pathfinder as a victory for freedom. Most feared that if Frémont stayed in the race, he might cost Lincoln enough votes to put the Peace Democrat McClellan in the White House. Others could not understand how the Phillips wing of the movement and radical émigrés like Heinzen could take their dislike of Lincoln so far as to align themselves with the negrophobic War Democrats. Garrison held this view and demonstratively attended the Baltimore convention, which renominated the president on June 7, 1864. A similar divide ran through the ranks of the German American Left. A meeting of New York's German Republicans utterly rejected "the mongrel platform got up at Cleveland by the unholy alliance of Democratic traitors and sore-headed deserters" from Republicanism. By that time, Carl Schurz had returned from the battlefield to stump for Lincoln at the polls. Although he conceded that the government had made mistakes, Schurz expressed the views of many of his liberal countrymen when he said, "The most vital thing is that the policy of the party moves in the right direction." Whether it moved "slowly or rapidly" was a "matter of little consequence," considering the alternatives.[71]

In the wake of the Cleveland and Baltimore conventions, the disagreements between the two Republican factions became increasingly hostile. The Lincolnites urged the dissenting minority to give up their extreme opposition and join them in facing a common enemy. The Frémonters, however, tenaciously defended their stance. Heinzen, accustomed to operating from the margins, was as livid as ever about those who chose the expedient over the ideal. He called Lincoln's renomination "an insolent farce" and vilified his backers as "parasites and carnivores who [fed] on the lifeblood of the Republic." Garrison's endorsement of the Baltimore platform, which pledged the Republican Party to the extinction of slavery but said little on the social elevation of blacks, left him bitterly disappointed; so too did the many German American newspapermen who berated the Frémont campaign in their editorials. Heinzen struck back with biting sarcasm. On July 18, 1864, he published a list of German Lincoln supporters, attaching insults to their names such as "traitor in both worlds," "pathetic crony," and "beer barrel."[72]

Such polemics notwithstanding, the Cleveland Platform barely went further on the questions of slavery and black citizenship than its Baltimore counterpart. Lincoln partisans repeatedly threw this inconsistency in the face of the Radical Democracy faction, whose adherents had a hard time proving that they were not hypocrites. Wendell Phillips regretted the political compromises that were made in Cleveland, yet he advised moving forward on this path, even if it entailed a temporary alliance with the War Democrats. Whatever the outcome, Phillips was sure that the Frémont movement served its purpose. It would either force the Democrats to unite with their candidate on the basis of the Cleveland Platform or push the Republican Party toward adopting a more radical policy. "Remember I am not a politician, but mainly an agitator — my special work being to make *party progress possible*," Phillips stressed. To make "every man of every race equal . . . before the law" was an idea held high by most abolitionists; its political manifestation, however, began with "the Cleveland movement," for Phillips "the high-water mark of American politics."[73]

Further developments testified to the naïveté of Phillips's expectations. Neither the native-born nor the German American front for Lincoln crumbled, and as the Democrats were preparing their own convention, the Frémont movement came under heavy fire from two sides. Yet Phillips and Heinzen were unwilling to admit defeat. Eager to dispel rumors that Frémont was a gadget in the hands of the Copperheads, both decided to interview their hero and publicize the results. It was mid-July when the Brahmin abolitionist and the German radical headed for Frémont's country house near Nahant, Massachusetts. After a long talk in which the Pathfinder rededicated himself to the abolitionist planks in the Cleveland Platform, Heinzen and Phillips left thoroughly satisfied and reported in glowing terms of the moral decency and political fitness of their candidate. "The negroes ought to have all the rights of whites," Frémont reassured his interrogators, adding that he would never sacrifice this principle in negotiations with the Democrats.[74]

The Democratic Party, however, had no use for so radical a contender. In the last days of August, an estimated six hundred delegates assembled in Chicago and nominated McClellan as their candidate on a propeace ticket. Chances to prevail on that platform seemed quite high because northern support for the war had dropped to an all-time low. Frustration ran rampant as Sherman met stiff resistance on his march to Atlanta and newspapers printed the mounting casualty lists of Grant's Wilderness campaign. The Democratic strategy to cash in on these antiwar feelings pulled the differing Republican factions together. McClellan and Pendleton seemed infinitely worse than Lincoln and Johnson, even to a Frémont backer. One by one, Frémont's supporters flocked to the Lincoln banner, leaving behind the obstinate few determined to stick to Radical Democracy, no matter the consequences.[75]

But it was too late. Advised by close friends to pull out of the presidential race for the good of the country, the Pathfinder withdrew on September 9. In an open letter on September 17, he laid out his motives and called on his followers to cast their ballots for Lincoln. Most heeded Frémont's advice. The German clubs in Hoboken and St. Louis, which had been conspicuous in their support for the Pathfinder, were the first to change course. Not so Karl Heinzen. Like Phillips, he wanted Frémont to stay in the race. Heinzen did not care that people criticized him for his lack of political realism or considered him a modern-day Don Quixote. Because "persons are nothing and principles everything," Frémont should not have resigned because of some vague fears of a Democratic victory. More important to Heinzen was that he should have stayed in the race as a beacon of radical ideas, as a symbol of what was desirable rather than of what was feasible in politics. Heinzen regretted that Frémont's move had turned "the party founded at Cleveland [into] an army without a flag." But he told his readers not to despair: "The fate of the world is not yet sealed, and wherever there are fighters, there will always be an opportunity to fight." Lincoln might be the lesser evil for now, but as soon as his election was secured, all true radicals should double their efforts and unite in a "party of the future," ready to supplant the president's "corrupt regime."[76]

Lincoln eventually beat McClellan in a landslide. By October 1864, the tide on the battlefield had turned, and northern faith in the military capacity of their commander in chief had been largely restored. Most abolitionists rejoiced at Lincoln's victory. Phillips, admitting defeat, implored his coworkers to forget the disagreements of the past and refocus on the common goal of black freedom. The caustic disputes surrounding Lincoln's reelection, however, had left deep fissures in the movement that proved more difficult to mend than Phillips was willing to admit. Prior to emancipation, abolitionists had already been split along occupational, religious, and ethnic lines. Now conflicts about the political ramifications of abolitionism had reshuffled this set of differences, further complicating the debate about how to advance on the path to universal human equality. Old bonds withered; new ones took their place. One such bond had evolved between Karl Heinzen and Wendell Phillips, who venerated his German-born partner who had pulled him into the Frémont campaign. Heinzen, Phillips wrote in hindsight, "was foremost among a few leading men who proposed the nomination of Fremont for the presidency. . . . I shall never forget some of these conversations with Mr. Heinzen. He was so far-seeing and sagacious; he was so ingenious in contriving; his judgment so penetrating."[77]

Vocations That Never End

As Abraham Lincoln was leading a weary nation into the fifth year of war, most Bostonians hoped that victory was imminent. On all fronts, the Confederacy, stripped of more than two-thirds of its territory and deprived of nearly all its armed forces, was in full retreat. Sherman was chasing Johnston's hopelessly outnumbered troops up the Atlantic seaboard, while Grant was getting in position for his final move against the tattered remnants of Lee's Army of Northern Virginia. Simultaneously, areas in the South under Union control were witnessing the first signs of reconstruction. Northern teachers and missionaries streamed into parts of the Confederacy occupied by the Union army to assist emancipated slaves in their transition to freedom. For the same purpose, the Freedmen's Bureau, which became the leading federal agency for coordinating and administering the treatment of southern freedmen, leaped into existence. In Louisiana, one of the first Confederate states that had fallen into Union hands, the radical Free State General Committee pushed for the enfranchisement of black men.[78]

Curiously enough, instead of applauding these developments unanimously, abolitionists were deeply divided over how to assess them. Once again it was the annual convention of the Massachusetts Anti-Slavery Society that brought the disagreements into the open, and once again it was Garrison and Phillips who represented the two quarreling factions. Heinzen, as earlier, identified with those who welcomed the turn of events but did not believe that the federal government was truly committed to expanding the realm of democracy. Lincoln's second inaugural address seemed to him a case in point. Heinzen dubbed it "a prayer or an appeal to a ghost above the clouds," protesting its conciliatory language and its lack of policy statements on the burning questions of black suffrage and the treatment of southern "war criminals." When news of Lincoln's assassination shocked the country a few weeks later, Heinzen refused to shed a single tear. In life as well as in death, Lincoln was to Heinzen "a man of average ability" and by no means a politician who deserved to be apotheosized as a great leader. Those succeeding him would surely go forward on the road to human equality with greater élan than the murdered president had ever done.[79]

Only too soon did Heinzen discover how terribly mistaken he had been with this forecast. By August 1865, the *Pionier* called for the impeachment of President Johnson, who gave precedence to national reconciliation over any proposals for radical reconstruction. Heinzen's own attitude resembled that of black activists and the Phillips wing of the abolitionist movement. In addition to favoring a long-term occupation of the South in order to fundamentally transform its social infrastructure and reeducate the populace, he repeated his demands for enfranchising African Americans and redistributing southern property to Union soldiers and freedmen. Heinzen continued to voice these and other provisions in concert with native-born radicals of similar temperament. On July 4, 1865, he took part in the traditional Fourth of July picnic of abolitionists at Framingham, Massachusetts, where he listened to speakers condemn Johnson's timid policies and lament that former slaves were still exposed to white terror.[80]

In the last fifteen years of his life, Heinzen watched with trepidation the resurgence of white supremacist factions in southern legislatures and national politics at large and deplored the failure of the federal government to keep them at bay. Partly out of frustration, partly out of conviction, the editor of the *Pionier* threw his weight behind other reform causes. In May 1865, he undersigned the inaugural statutes of the Society for the Dissemination of Radical Principles, a national association of German American radicals pledged to advancing some of Heinzen's most cherished objectives such as emancipation from religion and the establishment of a national social security system. Heinzen's passion for social improvement also animated him to sharp attacks on the chief executive, whom he had come to regard as "a king in dresscoat." Rather than endorse a candidate in the presidential elections of 1868 and 1872, he unabashedly demanded the abolition of the presidency, arguing that democracies should refrain from putting so much power in the hands of a single person. With similar vigor, Heinzen joined Phillips in his campaigns for penal reform and a nationwide eight-hour-per-day work limit for laborers. Furthermore, he did not tire in emphasizing that women should benefit equally from these causes. As in previous years, he collaborated closely with Marie Zakrzewska, Ernestine Rose, Mathilde Anneke, Elizabeth Cady Stanton, and other prominent European and American-born feminists in order to stamp out the social and political disparities between men and women.[81]

Few of Heinzen's contemporaries took any real interest in the ideas he championed except to find them utterly out of touch with the world to which they had grown accustomed. Until the very end, the editor of the *Pionier* led the life of an intellectual outsider, a naysayer to the conventional wisdoms of his age, and the extreme, often rancorous style in which he propagated his views earned him much disdain. Perhaps it was this position, more than anything else, that drew him close to Wendell Phillips, whose language he never learned to master in perfection and whose Christian morality he never fully understood. And yet cooperating with the Brahmin abolitionist helped Heinzen readjust his radical European heritage to a continually evolving American reality. The experience of joint public agitation, their mutual penchant for controversy, and, most notably, the common dream of an American republic without discrimination on the grounds of race and nationality softened their differences and led both men to outline a cosmopolitan democratic ideology whose promises remain relevant to this day. In this, Heinzen and his fellow Boston radicals truly were pioneers.

CHAPTER SIX

A Revolution Half Accomplished

Building Nations, Forgetting Emancipation

Slavery is dead, the negro is not, there is the misfortune.
— *Cincinnati Daily Enquirer*, May 12, 1865

Verily, the work does not end with the abolition of slavery, but
only begins.
— FREDERICK DOUGLASS in *Douglass' Monthly*, November 1862

IMAGINE A THANKSGIVING DAY DINNER where all are invited and nobody is left
out. In a solemnly lit room, ethnic Americans from all over the world are seated
at a round table, waiting for Uncle Sam to carve the turkey and put it on the
plates of his hungry guests. German, Native American, French, Arab, British,
African, Chinese, Italian, Spanish, and Irish revelers — men, women, and children — are united in happy anticipation, having buried the animosities of the
past. On the wall behind Uncle Sam hangs a large picture of Castle Garden, the
first official U.S. immigrant center, with a cordial label that reads, "Welcome."
Joining this image are portraits of the presidents Grant, Washington, and
Lincoln, the latter with the murdered statesman's plea "with malice toward
none, with charity for all." The centerpiece of the Thanksgiving Day table is a
monument to self-government and universal suffrage, a clear reference to the
Fourteenth and Fifteenth Amendments. The placement of Columbia, the per-
sonification of American freedom, between a black man and a Chinese underscores the nation's hard-won commitment to racial equality, signaling the dawn
of a new era of inclusion.

This powerful allegory, published in the November 20, 1869, issue of *Harper's
Weekly*, was the work of the popular German immigrant cartoonist and radical
Republican Thomas Nast. Born in the Palatinate town of Landau and infused
with the democratic ideas of 1848, Nast shared much of the Reconstruction idealism of America's abolitionists. His caricatures celebrated the country's ethnic
diversity but also took an uncompromising stance against the violence and dis-

"Uncle Sam's Thanksgiving Dinner," *Harper's Weekly*, November 20, 1869. Printed to endorse ratification of the Fifteenth Amendment, Thomas Nast's cartoon promoted the vision of a politically expansive and racially inclusive United States.

crimination inflicted upon nonwhite people, especially upon the newly enfranchised African Americans. For Nast and the radicals with whom he identified, the rallying cry was "Come one, Come all," and America was less a geographical destination than the grand cosmopolitan vision of political equality for all citizens, irrespective of their roots.[1]

In the Civil War's immediate aftermath, Nast's Forty-Eighter peers beamed with pride over the downfall of slavery. When learning that Lee and Johnston had laid down their arms before Union generals in April 1865, German American liberals and radicals were in an exultant mood. Over the last four years, whether in the field or behind the lines, they had labored tirelessly for the twin causes of Liberty and Union. Now that the enemy had surrendered, it was time to evaluate the results. Ottilie Assing, spellbound by the hiss of fireworks and the jubilant thunder of cannons, predicted that nothing could stand in the way of a great future for this nation "as long as it [would] use its victory in the true republican spirit to confer equal rights upon *all* citizens, without regard to race or color." Determined to see in the war's outcome a vindication of free-labor republicanism, Forty-Eighter veteran Friedrich Hecker gushed in a letter to the *Belleviller Zeitung*: "Out of this ghastly struggle we have emerged as a mighty warrior nation, both on land and at sea. Our industry has grown with breathtaking speed . . . while youngsters and elders augment the fruits of production at home . . . so that we can now proudly exclaim, like the Romans had once done with their 'civis romanus sum': 'I am an American!'"[2]

Hecker's revelation turned out to be true in many ways. Northern industry had indeed "grown with breathtaking speed" and continued to do so in the decades after the war. Without competition from a slaveholding aristocracy, free-labor economy became the dominant form of production in the country, eventually allowing the United States to overtake Great Britain as the world's leading industrial nation. Although the gulf between the capitalist and the working classes widened in this era of big business, the period also promised boundless opportunity for venturesome white men. Those who had served and bled for the Union felt especially entitled to reap the fruits of victory. Immigrant soldiers like Hecker were not alone in demanding that Anglo-northerners acknowledge their sacrifice and recognize them as equal American citizens. Many of Hecker's old German-born comrades shared his longing for a speedy integration into the country's socioeconomic mainstream, a desire that often developed parallel to the belief that revolutionary protest and agitation belonged to the past. What they came to evince instead was a greater appreciation for the prospering middle classes or, as the radical Eduard Schläger lamented in 1871, a growing respect for "Anglo-American business methods," particularly the disagreeable ones, such as "the greed for the dollar." For their role in the politics of Reconstruction, this had profound consequences.[3]

From Protest to Conformity

After the smoke of war had cleared, abolitionists, Radical Republicans, and Forty-Eighter democrats continued working shoulder to shoulder to implement a shared ideology of universal male suffrage, which climaxed in the disputes over the civil rights legislation that constituted the Fourteenth and Fifteenth Amendments. Prospects seemed rather bright, even as dark premonitions haunted many Forty-Eighter democrats who accused President Johnson of squandering the spoils of victory and making common cause with former slaveholders. Germans in Chicago and Philadelphia turned down appointments to public office from the White House. The pro-Republican Cleveland *Wächter am Erie* charged Johnson with "restoring" the southern "Junker class" to power. Individuals of the Douai and Heinzen variety joined the outcry, claiming, as Ottilie Assing did, that the Johnson administration was "generally treating the rebels with such tender regard and concern as contrast[ed] sharply with the indifference and ruthlessness it display[ed] towards the courageous, patriotic colored people."[4]

The platforms of radical German American organizations also contained ringing indictments of the administration's prosouthern leanings. In 1866, the national Turner confederation adopted a resolution supporting federal civil rights reform and endorsing radical reconstruction measures. One year later, the Turner leadership again pressured the federal government, issuing a statement that called "for the impartial administration of justice without discrimination as to race, color, or nationality." Sharper still were the provisions formulated at the Indianapolis convention of the German Society for the Dissemination of Radical Principles, a brainchild of Karl Heinzen and his associate Ludwig Greiner. The delegates considered the Civil War not over until "the last segment of the Southern aristocracy [had] been removed" and government ceased to withhold from blacks the rights that they had earned serving the Union.[5]

In the run-up to the congressional elections of 1866, the anti-Johnson segments of the Republican Party and other dissenters campaigned vigorously to strengthen factions in both houses that strove to pass national citizenship laws that neither the president nor the states could turn down. Heinzen in Boston, Schurz in St. Louis, Douai and Kapp in New York, Stallo in Cincinnati, and Caspar Butz in Chicago took to the stump and gave scores of speeches in support of Radical Reconstruction candidates. Abolitionists rushed to the lecterns with similar zeal. Some disagreed over the effectiveness of federally mandated civic reform, yet most fell in line with the demand that Johnson needed to be removed from office. "The very first task I would set before the reassembled Congress," Wendell Phillips proposed, "is to impeach the Rebel at the White House." Theodore Tilton of the *New York Independent* confidently added, "The Radical men are neither to be conquered by the Democratic, nor trifled with, by the Republican party." Abolitionists felt that their influence had climbed to unprecedented heights. Politicians sought their advice and quoted their speeches. Their lecture tours, which spanned from New England to the western frontier, attracted new and growing audiences. Congress, they deemed, could no longer afford to ignore their popularity among the masses of northerners who were tired of bickering with a defeated but defiant South.[6]

When the ballots were cast, the desire to punish a treacherous people certainly trumped aspirations to extend the boundaries of democracy. Such distinctions, though, mattered little in the election's outcome. The Republicans routed their opponents, and having gained the two-thirds majority necessary to override a presidential veto, the door to establishing a new political order was wide open. Swiftly and resolutely, the Thirty-ninth Congress passed legislation that wrote into the statute books some of the abolitionists' most cherished principles. As early as February 1866, a civil rights bill had promised to define all persons born in the United States (except American Indians) as citizens. In January 1867, a bill enfranchising blacks in the District of Columbia became law. The Reconstruction Act of March 1867 split the former Confederacy into five districts and spelled out the terms under which the southern states could be readmitted into the Union: by drafting state constitutions that guaranteed manhood suffrage without regard to race and ratifying the Fourteenth Amendment. To enforce these measures, military rule was declared and a federal bureaucracy established. After Grant replaced the hapless Johnson in 1868, Congress's dazzling and unparalleled experiment in radical republicanism persisted for at least another two years. The Freedmen's Bureau, thanks to additional government funding, expanded its schooling projects, black participation in southern politics flourished, and in February 1869, lawmakers approved the Fifteenth Amendment, which decreed that no United States citizen could be deprived of the vote on racial grounds. Abolitionists celebrated. Their journey, it seemed, had come to a successful conclusion.[7]

At that juncture, however, America's cross-cultural coalition for establishing a slave-free republic had already begun to fall apart. One of the first factions to break with their former allies was the feminists. Politically and ideologically, women's rights activists had always been on the forefront of the fight against black bondage, not least of all because they conceived of the abolitionist movement as a corridor leading to their own empowerment. The politics of Reconstruction all but shattered these dreams. Seeing that many of their male comrades hailed the enactment of color-blind voting regulations but did not object to clauses limiting suffrage to men left women with a deep sense of betrayal. The liberal nationalism undergirding Reconstruction, historian Alison Clark Efford has observed, was unmistakably gendered. By 1868, the controversy had become so bitter that Susan B. Anthony threw in Frederick Douglass's face the statement that she would "sooner cut off [her] right hand than ask the ballot for the black man and not for women." Elizabeth Cady Stanton seconded her friend and, peppering her retort with a racial slur, called it "a serious question" whether women "had better stand aside and see 'Sambo' walk into the kingdom first." Other remarks, like those made by Mathilde Anneke, sounded less strident. Yet, for the most part, white female activists started severing their ties to the black liberation struggle, embarking on a course that would crest in an independent women's movement. To advance their cause, Stanton, Anthony, and many others had no qualms about allying themselves with the most racist elements of the defeated Confederacy.[8]

Generational change and the competitive, enterprising atmosphere of the postbellum United States further disintegrated the interethnic alliance against slavery. In the decades after the Civil War, immigration from Europe soared again, soon reaching and exceeding prewar levels. Like their forebears, most of these new arrivals were attracted by the image of the United States as the land of opportunity, which gained even greater popularity in this period of rapid industrialization. Even though the era's "gospel of wealth" was anything but all-inclusive, journals and guidebooks spilled over with names of daring individuals — not a few of them foreign-born — who had made a fortune in the country's booming economy. Apart from providing encouragement to newcomers, such accounts sent an important ideological message: America's rising glory did not spring from the radicalism of the few but was dependent on the honest work of the many and, above all, the defense of property rights and free competition.

This conservative drift made its presence felt among the country's ethnic institutions as well. Newspapers formerly in the hands of revolutionary agitators turned into mouthpieces of free-market capitalism, and their editors no longer preached socialist doctrines but criticized their fallacies. Even the Turners, German America's most eminent left-leaning organization, succumbed to this trend. "The revolutionary spirit of the 'Forty-Eighters,' which inspired the fathers," Turner chronicler Heinrich Metzner noted, "was strange and incomprehensible to their children, who had grown up in other surroundings, and had been imbued with different thoughts and feelings." The way in which members of the younger generation distanced themselves from the radical roots of their Old World predecessors manifested itself not only in the renaming of the national federation as the North American Turnerbund. Simultaneously, the social composition of the various local chapters also changed dramatically as the old proletarian leadership was increasingly replaced by small businessmen, shop owners, professionals, officeholders, and other middle-class personnel. Hence, while remaining a mainstay of German American social and cultural life, the reform conventions of the Turner confederation, as one veteran member bemoaned, were "of particular interest only to those who [were] intimately identified with the organization."[9]

The few who continued to identify with the tenets of social equality did not withdraw silently to the political sidelines. To combat the severest forms of worker exploitation, national unions emerged, and German Americans featured notably in this upsurge of organized labor. When the National Labor Union began pressing for the eight-hour workday, it had Eduard Schläger as vice president. In New York, Friedrich Sorge and Adolf Douai railed against unfair wages and placed themselves at the head of the city's postwar labor movement. Douai, investing the same revolutionary passion in the emancipation of the worker that he had put into the liberation of the slave, became an avowed Marxist. German-born workingmen also played a prominent role in the great railroad strike that began in July 1877 and disrupted the entire country. And in 1886, following the bloody riot at Chicago's Haymarket, six of the eight defendants charged with murder and inciting civic unrest were German American labor activists. Overall, however, these socialists constituted a minority within a waning minority of immigrant radicals, most of whom ultimately discarded their revolutionary philosophies in order to share in the benefits of middle-class America.[10]

Carl Schurz, for many the paragon of German American democracy, typifies this departure from European left-wing ideals best. After the war, Schurz settled in St. Louis, where he assumed the editorship of the liberal *Westliche Post*. His articles and speeches in favor of a powerful central government and universal male suffrage won national acclaim and strengthened his ties to the Radical Reconstruction movement. Schurz, troubled by painful memories of a revolution gone wrong, exhorted his followers to keep pushing for change. "Nothing renders society more restless than a . . . revolution but half accomplished," he wrote on a trip through the defeated South. On the Republican ticket, Schurz was elected United States senator in 1868; not since the founding era had an immigrant ever attained a higher office. Schurz gained more prestige still after meeting with Bismarck on a trip to Germany and trying to convince the Prussian aristocrat of the vitality of American democracy. Yet with his newly gained eminence, Schurz's political outlook altered significantly. Once a fiery spokesman for radical republicanism, Schurz, impressed by government inefficiency in the North and racial violence in the South, began supporting measures that were elitist, probusiness, and states rights' oriented.[11]

By 1872, Schurz was campaigning against Grant's reelection and demanded an end to Reconstruction with the widely quoted aphorism: "There are many social disorders which it is very difficult to cure by laws." Over the past years, Schurz had been an advocate of federal civil rights reform, assuming that once legal barriers of discrimination had been eradicated, the field of opportunity would be leveled and open to all. Persisting animosities between black and white, the revival of the Democratic Party in the South, and the rise of the Ku Klux Klan, however, made him question the sanity of enforcing civil rights from above. Rather, he now urged blacks to reach "a good understanding with their white neighbors," not by asking for more protection but by refuting racial prejudice with examples of superior conduct. More astonishing still, Schurz's newfound faith in laissez-faire politics and local self-rule led him to resist federal legislation against Ku Klux Klan terror. Such a bill, he maintained, "transgress[ed] the limits with which the Constitution hedges in the competency of the National Government, and [encroached] upon the sphere of State authority." Speaking in the Senate, Schurz suggested that northerners reach out to southern whites and imitate European elites who had granted amnesty to former insurrectionists. In their attempt to forge an American meritocracy, liberal politicians like Schurz all but abandoned their concerns for social equality. Now was the time to secure the national marketplace against assaults from the unfit and let the freedmen find their own way in a society that increasingly defined itself as exceptionalist, capitalist, and white.[12]

Unification, Reunion, and the White Nation

Schurz's evolution from a revolutionary activist to a conservative reformer was part of a growing disenchantment with Radical Reconstruction among the country's liberal white intelligentsia. Their remonstrations came to a head in the election of 1872. By the end of Grant's first term, the "hero of Appomattox" no longer enjoyed the unanimous backing of his party. The postwar expansion of central authority that made possible government-promoted social and civil reform also gave birth to special-interest politics and corporate lobbying. Entrepreneurs, civil rights advocates, and labor representatives seeking advantages from the state were swarming the halls of Congress and the White House, and burgeoning connections of legislators to big business peaked in cases of individual malfeasance and bribery. As some of these frauds became public, a growing band of reformers lost faith in big government. Some even thought that the president personally was fully corrupt. Reconstruction, they contended, had passed its prime and needed to be saved from its own excesses.[13]

The men who answered the call for an independent party convention in Cincinnati on May 1, 1872, were a heterogeneous lot: professional politicians, newspaper editors, free traders, carpetbaggers and scalawags who had broken with Grant, veteran free-soilers and abolitionists, and a large faction of old Forty-Eighters. The list of delegates brimmed over with names of prominent emancipators and antislavery fighters. Theodore Tilton, Franklin Sanborn, Oliver Johnson, Frederick Law Olmsted, and Elizur Wright carried abolitionist credentials; Carl Schurz, Friedrich Hecker, Caspar Butz, Friedrich Hassaurek, August Willich, and Johann Stallo represented the German American spectrum. What united these dissenters, who referred to themselves as Liberal Republicans, was more than the simplistic slogan "anything to beat Grant." Their rejection of state interventionism was largely anchored in an emerging middle-class consciousness that celebrated individual excellence and dreaded class conflict. Grant's favoritism, they complained, had opened the gates of civic service to hordes of mediocre spoilsmen, who solidified their power by playing upon the emotions of the "uneducated masses," particularly those of Irish workers and southern freedmen. Few took their irritation so far as to challenge the accomplishments of emancipation and black suffrage. Simultaneously, the machinations of the Tweed Ring in New York and rumors about corrupt Republican regimes in the South made most Liberal Republicans deeply skeptical about popular democracy and bolstered claims that government should be reserved for "the best men." Eventually, this also meant devising a new policy for the South.[14]

The resolve and assertiveness with which Tilton, Stallo, and the others hoisted the Liberal Republican banner confounded many, not least some of their abolitionist comrades who refused to follow their lead. Abolitionists from New England and New York overwhelmingly endorsed Grant. Despite his shortcomings, they countered, the president was at least pledged to protecting the black man's right to vote as well as to suppressing the Ku Klux Klan and kindred organizations. That Liberal Republicans strayed from this basic insight made the blood of every pro-Grant abolitionist boil. Partly in despair and partly in anger, Garrison's son Francis Lloyd labeled the detractors "some of the worst rats on the Republican ship [that] ha[d] been the first to swim to the Cincinnati raft." In a less cantankerous tone, Gerrit Smith urged the Liberal Republicans to return to the fold of the Grand Old Party, insisting, "The Anti-Slavery battle is not yet fought — and, until it is, we shall need Grant's continued leadership." Black abolitionists of the Douglass and Langston sort issued similar caveats. Accusing Liberal Republican spokesmen of playing into the hands of white supremacists, they advised black voters to cast their ballot for Grant. For them, Douglass's famous adage "the Republican Party is the ship and all else is the sea" became a catchword for future elections.[15]

Rebuke also came from German American radicals who very much feared that the proslavery phoenix, if not subdued by force, would once more rise from Confederate ashes. Civil War general Franz Sigel supported Grant's tough stance against insolent southerners and tried to mobilize the German American vote for his reelection. At a glittering pro-Grant rally at New York's Cooper Institute in October 1872, a number of Forty-Eighter exiles, among them Sigismund Kaufmann, Friedrich Lexow, and Sixtus L. Kapff, marched on stage and gave their approval to the government's reconstruction policies. Tensions were exacerbated when Sigel and his associates took aim at the German-born instigators of the Liberal Republican uprising. Ottilie Assing was particularly angered by Carl Schurz's actions. Formerly a great admirer of the German

American luminary, she now regarded him the fallen angel of German republicanism. "Germans seem to follow Schurz blindly," Assing lamented in a letter to her sister, Ludmilla, "and they either do not see or do not want to see all the contradictions and falseness of which he has been guilty during the past year, no matter how obvious."[16]

Were these accusations tenable? In fact, there is little indication that people like Willich, Stallo, and Schurz deserved the antiblack tag that Assing wanted to pin on them. Even after joining the Liberal Republican party, most Forty-Eighters did not retreat from the conviction that blacks were entitled to the same constitutional rights as whites, and that egalitarian democracy meant removing all artificial distinctions of rank and skin color. Yet they were also unwilling to back an administration that, as they believed, waved the bloody shirt for the sole purpose of preventing tariff reduction, effective anticorruption laws, civil service reform, and other policy issues dear to these ethnic leaders. August Willich fretted about the influence that monopolists had gained under the current administration, a development he found detrimental to the welfare of the working masses. Grant Republicans were also suspected of entertaining anti-immigrant sentiments, which purportedly manifested themselves in a revival of Protestant temperance agitation across the North. Charges of nativism received further nourishment from the allegation that the president and his associates denied German American war heroes proper recognition by keeping them underrepresented in public office.[17]

All these grievances, however, paled before an event that shook international politics and reconfigured the ties of German Americans to both their native and their adopted homeland. Under Bismarck's stewardship, Prussia had placed itself at the apex of the all-German cause that culminated in the Franco-Prussian War of 1870–71. In a short but decisive campaign, German divisions eliminated the bulk of the French army, thus setting the stage for the proclamation of the Second German Empire. Reports about Prussian victory and the newly founded Reich sent America's German immigrant population into paroxysms of joy. At last, age-old dreams of national unity and the establishment of a strong fatherland capable of projecting power and civilization seemed to have come true. German American newspapers, liberal and conservative ones alike, posted stories of German military bravery and vilified Napoleon III as a "perfidious traitor" and "wanton aggressor." Anti-French slogans too were ubiquitous at gaudy victory parades organized by German immigrant associations, some of which took place as early as February 1871. In New York, 40,000 Americans of German stock gathered to salute a procession consisting of 12,000 horses, 1,200 carriages, and 130 brass bands.[18]

The old Forty-Eighter intelligentsia did not remain aloof from this nationalistic frenzy. There were, as always, a few exceptions. Members of the radical Left were mindful that the bayonets that had vanquished the French were of the same steel as those that had forced them into exile. Refusing invitations to attend banquets where the Hohenzollern were toasted, Karl Heinzen mocked the idea that a nation dedicated to unity *and* freedom could ever be established by aristocrats. No less skeptical were the appraisals emerging from the correspondence between Fritz and Mathilde Anneke. "People do not realize here," Fritz contemptuously noted during his 1872 trip to Germany, "that they do not as yet have free speech, a free press, that they are still watched by the police from cradle to grave, led around by leashes like a child." Such observations erected high barriers to appreciating the Bismarck style of unification from above, at least to those genuinely and primarily interested in democratic ideas.[19]

By and large, however, the refugee generation of 1848 did share in the general rejoicing. Some even outdid their countrymen in hailing the advent of German nationhood, an idea that had always occupied center stage in their political agendas. Sins of autocracy were soon forgiven now that the rays of unification shone all the way across the Atlantic. "My creed is unity," Friedrich Hecker shouted at a German American victory parade in St. Louis. Only in a nation born of common sacrifice, Hecker emphasized, and not in the "sentimental utopia of universal brotherhood," could the ideals of equality and fraternity take root. If the new state did not yet provide all desired civil liberties, these Forty-Eighters felt, one could reasonably hope that free institutions would sprout up as time went by. Had not the goal of national unity demanded similar patience?[20]

Friedrich Kapp and August Willich thought so. Plans to return to the fatherland had ripened in Kapp's mind since the end of the Civil War. In 1870, he carried them out. Kapp had never felt at home on American soil, even though his activities had brought him into contact with some of the United States' wealthiest and most influential men. When the prominent exile left New York harbor on April 29, a crowd of about three hundred friends and sympathizers gathered at the pier to bid him farewell. His reception back home was just as exuberant; Kapp's reputation as a spokesman for German culture abroad had preceded him. Enthusiastic about the coming of the Reich, Kapp was introduced into Berlin's finest salons and high-ranking political circles. An unflinching critic of Yankee culture and the "cosmopolitan fuzziness" of some of his fellow refugees, Kapp found comfort in repatriation. A united Germany proffered him the kind of security and sense of belonging that he had always longed for, a yearning that had grown so strong in exile that it ultimately triumphed over his teenage dreams of human brotherhood. At age forty-seven, Kapp was elected to the German

A German war meeting, held at Steinway Hall, New York (*Frank Leslie's Illustrated Newspaper,* August 6, 1870). Many Forty-Eighters supporting German unification eventually turned away from Radical Reconstruction and put their revolutionary legacies in the service of a boastful ethnic nationalism.

Reichstag in the fall of 1871 on the ticket of the National Liberal Party. The revolutionary of the 1850s, it seemed, had become completely reconciled with Bismarck's Germany.[21]

August Willich, the socialist, was probably less susceptible to this kind of rightward shift, but even he could not resist the chauvinistic tide. The news that war with France was imminent reached the Civil War veteran on a trip through the German states. Without further ado, Willich went to Berlin and presented his saber to William I. The Prussian king turned down his offer — the official reason was that he was too old — leaving Willich bitterly disappointed. After spending another year at Humboldt University, where he studied philosophy, Willich returned to Ohio. In his final years, disheartened by political developments in his adopted country, he led the quiet life of a bachelor in the small town of St. Marys. He died there on January 22, 1878.[22]

Molded in the violent convulsions of revolution and nation making, the ethnic patriotism of people like Kapp and Willich helps to explain why rigid forms of nationalism and empire, rather than transethnic cosmopolitan ideals, were the primary products of mid-nineteenth-century mobility and migration. Just as Charles Loring Brace and Mary Booth became more conscious of their nationality abroad, the Forty-Eighters acquired a better understanding of what it meant to be German in their American exile. While learning to interact cordially with the ethnic other, many also became more convinced than ever of ethnic otherness. This conviction did not immediately or necessarily result in an antagonistic nationalism. Yet friendships between activists of diverse origins, even as they suggested the possibility of a democratic cosmopolitanism, demonstrated the inherent difficulties attending the peaceful assimilation of cultures and furthered a language of national identity that could easily swell to extremes.

The boisterous rise of a new, competitive nationalism triggered the development of more-aggressive racial ideologies, including anti-Semitism. Although Forty-Eighters had maintained on the eve of revolution that German Jews deserved full civic equality, associations of Jewishness with capitalist exploitation were common in popular left-wing rhetoric. Quite a few Forty-Eighters, moreover, resorted to negative stereotypes such as that of the "wandering Jew" to express fears of homelessness and isolation in exile. One who went yet further was Wilhelm Marr, the patriarch of modern German anti-Semitism. A radical democrat who fought for a unified German republic in 1848, Marr turned into a vicious antiblack racist and anti-Semite after spending ten years in the United States and Central America. Adapting racial ideas to traditionally religious anti-Jewish discourses upon his return to Germany, Marr set the tone for future exclusionist theories and exemplified the ways in which racial belief systems from both sides of the Atlantic could overlap and influence each other. Marr was by all accounts the most rabid Jew-hating Forty-Eighter, but many others remained ambivalent about the notion of innate differences that set Jews apart from other Germans.[23]

Those of Marr's countrymen who stayed in the United States became embroiled in the country's postwar party machines, but most did not want to relinquish their Germanness. Scanning the field for sympathizers with the all-German cause, they found few supporters in the Grant administration. German American approval of the president hit rock bottom when it became known that the War Department had violated American declarations of neutrality by selling surplus arms and ammunition to the French. Parts of the German immigrant press had long charged Grant with clandestinely backing the French and trying to sabotage the German unification movement; the recent transactions of his secretary of war were all the evidence they needed. Consequently, German American spokesmen of the Liberal Republican movement stepped up their rhetoric against the party in power. "Mr. Schurz's object of course," the *New York Times* astutely noted, was to "exasperate the German sentiment by showing that the Government sympathized with and aided the French." With similar intentions, Gustav Körner declared that "as a German" he could not support a head of state who permitted the sale of rifles and bullets to Napoleon III and had "perhaps 100,000 brave Germans on his conscience."[24]

The rift caused by the Franco-Prussian War also widened the gulf between the pro-Grant abolitionists and flag-waving German American patriots. When Wendell Phillips came out in favor of the French republicans after Napoleon III had been deposed, calling unto heaven to "destroy the German armies by pestilence, leaving neither peasant nor prince living to tell the tale at Berlin," the German immigrant community fumed with anger. Again Körner led the charge, censuring the "insane twaddle of Mr. Phillips" and reasserting the right of his people to prepare for battle whenever the freedom and independence of their fatherland was at stake.[25]

Native-born Liberal Republicans, by contrast, seemed largely untainted by anti-German feelings. They also appeared less averse to sharing the speakers' platform with ethnic leaders who were delighted over the progress of German unification. In fact, the idea of a united German nation dovetailed neatly with a theme that was being recited with growing enthusiasm at Liberal Republican meetings: that of American reconciliation and reunion. As personal memories of the Civil War faded, many northerners began asking themselves how fraternal feelings between the sections could be restored. Lincoln's legacy, they recalled, had included not just freedom for the slaves but also finding a way "to bind up the nation's wounds." No orator hammered home this message with greater passion than Horace Greeley, the presidential nominee of the Liberal Republicans. Like most of his party friends, Greeley dreamed of a morally and economically superior American republic that would draw the envy of the civilized world. Such prominence, he emphasized, was near unattainable as long as radicals continued to divide the nation into victors and vanquished. The war was over, slavery abolished, the freedmen's rights secured, but unless veterans "clasped hands over the bloody chasm" and white southerners were readmitted into the body politic, a lasting peace remained out of reach.[26]

Greeley's message was immensely popular with old Confederates, who were desperately trying to reinstate home rule, which also meant chipping away at black civil rights. North of the Mason-Dixon Line, however, where Grant Republicans kept insisting that Ku Klux Klan outrages required prolonged federal presence in the South, Greeley failed to carry a single state. Within months after Grant's victory, the Liberal Republicans vanished from sight. Their ideas, on the other hand, survived and were a prelude of things to come. Once ingrained in the public mind, the belief that America's national greatness depended on persistent efforts to reunite the sections proved impossible to eradicate, spelling doom for the abolitionist project of building an interracial democracy. The story of Reconstruction's demise is a complex and complicated one and has been masterfully retold from different angles by John Hope Franklin, Eric Foner, David Blight, and other scholars. Let it suffice to say that, in the long run, the transformation of the war's meaning into a romantic national drama drowned out voices maintaining that its historic importance lay in the liberation of four million black slaves. By the end of the century, the notion that the Civil War was a heroic but ultimately avoidable conflict fought by gallant white soldiers, each patriotic in his own way, had begun to be memorialized in both marble and letters, reminding Americans that the nation they were living in was, and had always been, destined to be "one and indivisible."[27]

For blacks and other groups not perceived as genuinely American, this notion had dire consequences. In an era that witnessed an increasing convergence of the terms "American" and "white," failure to produce the image of whiteness immediately marked somebody as alien and thus as incapable of partaking in the national romance of reconciliation and reunion. Such narratives gave white northerners comfort in a time of rapid economic transformation and mounting social and ethnic diversity and allowed white southerners to return to the national mainstream by fashioning themselves as protectors of a racially untarnished white nation. African Americans, however, though technically enfranchised, did not belong in this framework. Nor did immigrants unless they managed to "become white," that is, become part of a history stressing allegiance to the Union and the need to conform to Anglo-Saxon culture.[28]

Few abolitionists assisted the former bondsmen in their battle for equality beyond the 1870s. Most were either dead, retired into private life, or fell under the sway of an ideology of racial Anglo-Saxonism that they had opposed earlier in their lives. Solidarity with the black liberation movement declined at an even faster rate in America's German immigrant communities. Contrary to many of their older kinsmen, the next generation of arrivals from German lands had no personal recollections of emancipation and were easily susceptible to postwar mythologies reinterpreting the Civil War as a tragic ordeal in the history of a white nation. Pressure to succumb to the white American majority was further magnified by the influx of new immigrant groups — Italians, Eastern Europeans, Russian Jews — who were quickly dismissed as unassimilable outsiders. To avoid identification with these "white others," German Americans, albeit on their own ethnic terms, overwhelmingly came to present themselves as loyal patriots and good Americans, thereby hoping to be confirmed in their claims to citizenship. This not only meant disassociating themselves from the foreign newcomers. For many, it also meant learning to despise the country's black population — men and women who had gained their freedom but were yet to gain equal social and political standing.[29]

White humanitarians of the nineteenth century did not think that the "African way of life" was as good as their own. To be progressive was to believe that by careful training blacks and other nonwhite people could be uplifted and taught how to share in the blessings of Euro-American civilization. Letting them be the architects of their own fate, many reformers warned, only meant consigning them to misery. Even as white abolitionists were appalled by slavery and invidious practices of antiblack discrimination, racial paternalism made it difficult for them to think about their relationships to blacks in any way other than that of a benevolent teacher to a willing student. Most Forty-Eighter democrats, moreover, saw in the South's "peculiar institution" little more than an offspring of Old World feudalism. To them, overthrowing slavery was less about fighting racial injustice than furthering a campaign for self-determination born in the upheavals of post-Napoleonic Europe. Because national belonging in the Atlantic world began to hinge more than ever on race, whiteness, and ethnicity, true and absolute interracial equality was rarely achieved and never emerged as a chief concern. Once slavery was outlawed, large portions of America's liberal intelligentsia believed that blacks could earn their full equality by emulating white middle-class values. But their optimism was badly misplaced. Antiblack terror and intimidation prevailed, and paternalist postures did little to ease the situation.

Frederick Douglass could recount an anecdote. In 1872, the year that Douglass's Rochester home mysteriously went up in flames, the city became the scene of violent confrontations between German Americans and African Americans. Rochester's German immigrant community was like that of most northern Little Germanies at the time: highly diversified by class, regional origins, religious beliefs, and political outlooks. A large portion of its male residents had fought in the Civil War to preserve the Union. Only few had enlisted for the sake of black emancipation. This widespread disregard for African American suffering degenerated into racial hatred when papers carried the story of a ten-year-old German American girl who had allegedly been raped by a local black man named William Howard. Promptly arrested, Howard faced greater perils still, for a mob of more than one thousand men — many of German descent — stood jeering outside the jail, demanding that he be lynched. Before long, the militia was called in to disperse the rioters, who then randomly assaulted blacks on the streets. Douglass, though not directly targeted by the Rochester mob, felt the wrath of the German American community as well.

With articles such as "Fred Douglass and His Whitewashing Brigade at New Orleans," the local press launched an unprecedented defamation campaign against the black abolitionist and well-known supporter of the Grant administration. Even radical German American papers, stout allies once, had no reservations about subjecting Douglass to the vilest slander. Relationships between the two were never the same again.[30]

These were no isolated incidents, and the fact that some of the Forty-Eighter intelligentsia played an active role in the whitening of their ethnic group indicates how far they had moved away from their radical origins. Most Forty-Eighters had become abolitionists as Germans *and* democrats, but most ended up as white German Americans. There were, to be sure, other foreign-born revolutionists who continued portraying the black freedom struggle as the extended arm of the struggle to abolish slavery. Such accounts naturally clashed head-on with prevailing explanations of the sectional conflict. The story that began to dominate national memory held that the Civil War had only temporarily interrupted the ascent of an exceptional, yet racially bounded, American democracy. The other story, that the war marked the zenith of a multiethnic movement committed to bestowing equal rights upon all men, irrespective of race, slowly sunk into oblivion.

NOTES

Introduction

1. Honorary Doctorate Certificate James W. C. Pennington, December 19, 1849, University of Heidelberg Archives. On Pennington's colorful life and achievements, see Thomas, *James W. C. Pennington*.

2. On the mid-nineteenth-century peace movement, see Linden, *International Peace Movement*. Women's rights are the subject of Bonnie S. Anderson, *Joyous Greetings*. Transatlantic socialist networks are examined in Messer-Kruse, *Yankee International*. Gemme, *Domesticating Foreign Struggles*, and Roberts, *Distant Revolutions*, discuss the impact of the 1848 revolutions in Europe on American politics and culture.

3. The place of American slavery in the Atlantic economy is masterfully discussed in the works of David Brion Davis, most notably in *The Problem of Slavery in the Age of Revolution*, *The Problem of Slavery in Western Culture*, and *Inhuman Bondage*. Hammond, *Selections from the Letters and Speeches*, 311–22.

4. Douglass, "The Anti-Slavery Movement: An Address Delivered in Rochester, March 19, 1855," in Blassingame, *Frederick Douglass Papers*, 3:48–49. Classic accounts of the Anglo-American antislavery network are Fladeland, *Men and Brothers*; Clare Taylor, *British and American Abolitionists*; and Blackett, *Building an Antislavery Wall*.

5. Good overviews of the German American Forty-Eighters are Brancaforte, *German Forty-Eighters in the United States*, and Levine, *Spirit of 1848*. Also valuable, albeit of older age, are Zucker, *Forty-Eighters*, and Wittke, *Refugees of Revolution*. Approximately ten thousand expatriates can be directly linked to persecutions following the popular upsurges in 1848–49; more-conservative estimates speak of four thousand to six thousand political refugees. See Theodore Hamerow, "The Two Worlds of the Forty-Eighters," in Brancaforte, *German Forty-Eighters in the United States*, 20–22. Palmer, *Age of the Democratic Revolution*, 1:4.

6. Differences between the two camps are stressed in Wittke, *Refugees of Revolution*; Levine, *Spirit of 1848*; and Keller, *Chancellorsville and the Germans*.

7. Wiebe, "Framing U.S. History," 242.

8. The present study draws inspiration from several excellent histories on antebellum abolitionism, among them James Brewer Stewart, *Holy Warriors*; Drescher, *Capitalism and Antislavery*; Stauffer, *Black Hearts of Men*; Davis, *Inhuman Bondage*; and McCarthy and Stauffer, *Prophets of Protest*.

9. Mazzini quoted in Hunt, *Inventing Human Rights*, 177. On the cultural foundations of modern nationalism, see the seminal study of Benedict Anderson, *Imagined Communities*.

10. Webster, "Second Reply to Hayne," in *Speeches and Writings of Daniel Webster*, 6:75; Lincoln, "A House Divided," in Basler, *Collected Works of Abraham Lincoln*, 2:461; Heinzen quoted in Levine, *Spirit of 1848*, 149; Sumner, "The Crime against Kansas," in *Works of Charles Sumner*, 4:243. The expression *slave baron* figured prominently in the German American radical press of the time. Nineteenth-century liberals, as defined by Leslie Butler, shared a faith in popular government, an identification with progress, and a commitment to orderly change; see Butler, *Critical Americans*, 10.

11. On the origins of the concept of herrenvolk democracy, see Van den Berghe, *Race and Racism*, 18. On the converging histories of race, democracy, and nation building in the nineteenth century, see also Roediger, *Wages of Whiteness*, and Bruce Baum, *Rise and Fall of the Caucasian Race*.

12. My distinction between ethnic and civic nationalism is inspired by Ignatieff, *Blood and Belonging*.

13. McPherson, "The Second American Revolution," in *Abraham Lincoln*, 3–7; Levine, *Spirit of 1848*, 256.

14. Fredrickson, *Arrogance of Race*, 73. On the distinctions and imbrications of abolition and antislavery, see James Brewer Stewart, *Holy Warriors*, 78.

1. Entanglement Is Certain

1. Hugo, *1848*, 263; Schurz, *Reminiscences of Carl Schurz*, 1:139. On pro-American sentiments among the German revolutionaries of 1848, see Franz, *Das Amerikabild der deutschen Revolution*, 104–9, and Wellenreuther, "Die USA," 23–41.

2. *Liberator*, April 21, 1848; Moltmann, *Atlantische Blockpolitik im 19. Jahrhundert*, 62, 69–87, 365; Moore, *Works of James Buchanan*, 8:32–37.

3. Pease, *Speeches, Lectures, and Letters of Wendell Phillips*, 1:29; Charles Sumner to George Sumner, November 26, 1850, in Pierce, *Memoir and Letters of Charles Sumner*, 3:230.

4. *Liberator*, May 19, 1848; *Annual Report of the American and Foreign Anti-Slavery Society, 1848*, 7. See also Morrison, "American Reaction to European Revolutions," and Roberts, *Distant Revolutions*, 83–86.

5. Edward Everett to George Bancroft, April 4, 1849, and George Ticknor to George S. Hilliard, July 17, 1848, both quoted in Morrison, "American Reaction to European Revolutions," 121. George Sanders's comments are taken from the *United States Magazine and Democratic Review* 26 (1850): 385, 392.

6. Horsman, *Race and Manifest Destiny*, 225. On antebellum nativism, see Anbinder, *Nativism and Slavery*, and Levine, "Conservatism, Nativism, and Slavery," 455–88.

7. Morse, *Foreign Conspiracy*, 57–58; American Unitarian Association, *Works of William E. Channing*, 471.

8. Roediger, *Wages of Whiteness*, 133, 134–63. See also Knobel, *Paddy and the Republic*,

82–99; Ignatiev, *How the Irish Became White*; and Jacobson, *Whiteness of a Different Color*, 39–90.

9. Conzen, "Germans," 405–25; Löher, *Geschichte und Zustände*, 319; Lincoln, "Address before the Wisconsin State Agricultural Society, September 30, 1859," in Basler, *Collected Works of Abraham Lincoln*, 3:479.

10. Nourse, *Remarks on the Past*, 39; Marsh, *Goths in New England*.

11. *Der Westbote*, June 22, 1855, quoted in Jacobson, *Whiteness of a Different Color*, 47; *New York Daily Tribune*, January 19, 1859; *Douglass' Monthly*, August 1859.

12. *New York Independent*, October 12, 1854; *Cleveland Express*, May 30, 1855, quoted in Wittke, *Refugees of Revolution*, 185.

13. Anonymous writer quoted in Sanderson, *Republican Landmarks*, 227; Whitney, *Defence of the American Polity*, 169–70, 177.

14. *Atlantis*, February 1855, 86–90. See also Wittke, *Refugees of Revolution*, 122–46.

15. Beecher, "The Reign of the Common People," in Hillis, *Lectures and Orations by Henry Ward Beecher*, 102–3; "German Emigration to America," *North American Review* 170 (1856): 267; House of Representatives Committee on Foreign Affairs, "Foreign Criminals and Paupers, August 16, 1856," in Cochran et al., *New American State Papers*, 2:29.

16. "Satzungen des sozialistischen Turnerbundes von Nord-Amerika," Sozialistischer Turnerbund Papers, New York Public Library; Metzner, *Brief History*, 7–16. See also Levine, *Spirit of 1848*, 91–94.

17. *New York Daily Times*, September 20, 1853; *Turn-Zeitung*, July 15 and October 15, 1853.

18. Assing quoted in Diedrich, *Love across Color Lines*, 104; Struve quoted in Reiß, *Radikalismus und Exil*, 270–71.

19. Fröbel, *Die deutsche Auswanderung*, 35, 46, 78–101; Christian Esselen quoted in Wittke, *Refugees of Revolution*, 179; Kapp, *Aus und über Amerika*, 1:330.

20. Öfele, *German-Speaking Officers*, 4; Körner, *Memoirs of Gustav Körner*, 549; *Wisconsin Banner und Volksfreund*, June 7, 1854.

21. Carl Schurz to Malwida von Meysenburg, in Bancroft, *Speeches, Correspondence and Political Papers of Carl Schurz*, 1:6.

22. Emerson, "Address to the Citizens of Concord on the Fugitive Slave Law, May 3, 1851," in Gougeon and Myerson, *Emerson's Antislavery Writings*, 53.

23. See also Davis, *Inhuman Bondage*, 250–96; James Brewer Stewart, *Holy Warriors*, 147–77; Stauffer, *Black Hearts of Men*, 8–44; and Grant, *North over South*, 74–80.

24. American Anti-Slavery Society, *Proceedings of the Seventh Annual Meeting*; Philip S. Foner, *Life and Writings of Frederick Douglass*, 120; O'Connell, *Daniel O'Connell upon American Slavery*, 38–40.

25. Davis, *Inhuman Bondage*, 48–76; Roediger, *Wages of Whiteness*, 133–50; Knobel, *Paddy and the Republic*, 93, 179; Hochgeschwender, *Wahrheit, Einheit, Ordnung*, 135–67.

26. Ignatiev, *How the Irish Became White*, 134–36; William Lloyd Garrison to Richard Davis Webb, March 1, 1845, quoted in Osofsky, "Abolitionists," 906; Parker quoted in Bean, "Puritan versus Celt," 71.

27. *Frederick Douglass' Paper*, September 1855; Douglass, "The Present and Future of the Colored Race in America, Brooklyn, on 15 May 1863," in Blasingame, *Frederick Douglass Papers*, 3:578–79; "Colonizationist Measures, New York, on 24 April 1849," in Blasingame, *Frederick Douglass Papers*, 2:164–65.

28. Parker, *Rights of Man in America*, 22; Knobel, *Paddy and the Republic*, 31. The connections of German and New England thought are investigated in Vogel, *German Literary Influences*.

29. *National Anti-Slavery Standard*, August 22, 1856; American Anti-Slavery Society, *Anti-Slavery Tracts*, 17–18. The interview with the *New York Evening Post* quoted in Keil, "German Immigrants," 146. See also Philip S. Foner, *Alexander von Humboldt*, 30–58.

30. For abolitionist critiques of Father Mathew, see Osofsky, "Abolitionists," 906. On Kossuth in America, see Roberts, *Distant Revolutions*, 146–67.

31. *National Anti-Slavery Standard*, December 11, 1851, and January 22, 1852; "Resolutions by a Committee of Philadelphia Blacks," in Ripley et al., *Black Abolitionist Papers*, 4:69; Garrison, "Letter to Kossuth," in Merrill, *Letters of William Lloyd Garrison*, 4:98, 100.

32. Roberts, *Distant Revolutions*, 150; Douglass, "Letter to Kossuth," in Philip S. Foner, *Life and Writings of Frederick Douglass*, 2:171.

33. Ebeling, *Erdbeschreibung und Geschichte von Amerika*, 7:294; Rotteck, *Lehrbuch des natürlichen Privatrechts*, 147–51; Heinrich Heine quoted in Musgrave, "Heinrich Heine's Anti-Slavery Thought," 91.

34. Spevack, *Charles Follen's Search*, 206–49; Heinzen, "Republik und Sklaverei," in *Teutscher Radikalismus in Amerika*, 4:139; Schurz, "The Doom of Slavery," in Bancroft, *Speeches, Correspondence and Political Papers of Carl Schurz*, 1:157; "Verhandlungen der Turner-Tagsatzung zu Buffalo, vom 24. bis 27. September 1855," Sozialistischer Turnerbund Papers.

35. Tolzmann, *German-American Forty-Eighters*, 98–105.

36. The Clayton amendment was named after nativist Senator John Clayton from Delaware. See also Levine, *Spirit of 1848*, 155–56.

37. The account relies heavily on Levine, *Spirit of 1848*, 149–209; Johannson, *Stephen A. Douglas*, 419; *National Era*, January 24, 1854.

38. *Pittsburger Courier*, February 13, 1854; *New York Daily Times*, March 4, 1854; *Chicago Daily Tribune*, March 18 and 20, 1854; *Daily Cincinnati Gazette*, February 24, 1854; *New York Daily Tribune*, February 28, 1854.

39. Überhorst, *Turner unterm Sternenbanner*, 50; Betz, "Die Deutschen und die Sklaverei," 575; *New York Daily Tribune*, February 23 and 24, 1854.

40. See Wittke, *German-Language Press*, 139.

41. Pelz and Rödel quoted in Levine, *Spirit of 1848*, 221; Assing, "The Presidential Election and Slavery," in Lohmann, *Radical Passion*, 73.

42. See also Eric Foner, *Free Soil, Free Labor, Free Men*, 1–45; Keil, "German Immigrants," 142–43; Roediger, *Wages of Whiteness*, 80–84; Gienapp, *Origins of the Republican Party*, 355–59; Wilentz, *Rise of American Democracy*, 671–77.

43. *Baltimore Wecker,* January 19, 1856; *Belleviller Volksblatt,* August 30, 1856; *Mississippi Blätter,* October 9, 1859, in Rowan, *Germans for a Free Missouri,* 85–86.

44. *Philadelphia Demokrat* quoted in Betz, "Die Deutschen und die Sklaverei," 584.

45. Mueller, *Memoirs of a Forty-Eighter,* 29–30.

46. *Trenton (Ohio) State Gazette,* December 6, 1851, quoted in Levine, *Spirit of 1848,* 150; *Ohio State Journal,* December 5, 1851.

47. "Proceedings of the Convention of the Colored Freemen of Ohio, Cincinnati, January 14, 15, 16, 17, and 19, 1852," in Philip S. Foner and Walker, *Proceedings of the Black State Conventions,* 277; *Douglass' Monthly,* August 1859; Smith, "The German Invasion," *Anglo-African Magazine,* March 1859, 83–86; *Weekly Anglo-African,* July 27, 1861.

48. On Assing and Douglass, see Diedrich, *Love across Color Lines;* Keil quoted in Paul, *Kulturkontakt und Racial Presences,* 61–62; Jacobs and Keil, "African Americans and Germans," 174–75.

49. Fröbel, *Aus Amerika,* 124–88; *Atlantis,* May 1856, 278–87.

50. *Sociale Republik,* May 1 and September 4, 1858; Struve quoted in Reiß, *Radikalismus und Exil,* 330, 375, 396.

51. *Atlantis,* January 1855, 16–17; Assing, "Colored People in New York," in Lohmann, *Radical Passion,* 58. See also Diedrich, *Love across Color Lines,* 120–28.

52. See Rice and Crawford, *Liberating Sojourn,* and Sollors, *Neither Black nor White yet Both,* 339.

2. A Firm Phalanx of Iron Souls

1. Olmsted spent a total of fourteen months in the South, writing seventy-five letters for the *New York Daily Times* and the *New York Daily Tribune* and completing four books: *A Journey in the Seaboard Slave States* (1856), *A Journey through Texas; Or, A Saddle-Trip on the South-Western Frontier* (1857), *A Journey in the Back Country* (1858), and *Cotton Kingdom* (1861). The fullest account of Olmsted's life is Roper, *FLO.*

2. *New York Daily Times,* January 26, 1854.

3. Frederick Law Olmsted to Anne Charlotte Lynch, March 12, 1854, Frederick Law Olmsted Papers, Manuscript Division, Library of Congress, Washington, D.C.; unless otherwise indicated, all letters to and from Frederick Law and John H. Olmsted are taken from this collection. Achenbach, *Tagebuch meiner Reise,* 133–35. Comprehensive histories of German immigration to Texas are Biesele, *History of the German Settlements,* and Jordan, *German Seed in Texas Soil.*

4. In 1850, the German-speaking element in Texas rose above thirty thousand people, equaling about 20 percent of the state's white population. See Biesele, *History of the German Settlements;* Jordan, *German Seed in Texas Soil,* 50; and Kamphoefner, "German Texans," 119–38.

5. *New York Daily Times,* April 24, 1854.

6. On antebellum European travel, see Stowe, *Going Abroad.*

7. Frederick Law Olmsted to Charles Loring Brace, December 1, 1853, in Beveridge et al., *Papers of Frederick Law Olmsted*, 2:232–38; *New York Daily Times*, April 28 and June 30, 1853, January 26 and February 25, 1854.

8. Olmsted, *Journey through Texas*, 181; Jordan, "Germans and Blacks in Texas," 89–97; Campbell, *Empire for Slavery*, 214–16.

9. Quoted in Biesele, "Texas State Convention," 252; Adolf Douai to John H. Olmsted, September 4, 1854.

10. The only comprehensive biography of Douai is Randers-Pehrson, *Adolf Douai*. Biesele, "Texas State Convention," 247–55.

11. Siemering quotation from *Neu Braunfelser Zeitung*, April 21, 1854. Kapp and Siemering quotation from *San Antonio Zeitung*, April 1, 1854.

12. Olmsted to Brace, December 1, 1853; Olmsted, "Letter to a Southern Friend, December 29, 1856," in *Journey through Texas*, vii–xxix; Olmsted, *Journey through Texas*, 133, 187–88; *New York Daily Times*, April 24, 1854.

13. Biesele, "Texas State Convention," 255–61; *Austin State Gazette*, June 24, 1854 ("very few active fanatics").

14. Douai quotation from Adolf Douai to John H. Olmsted, September 4, 1854; see also Douai, "Autobiography," 117, Adolf Douai Papers, Center for American History, University of Texas, Austin; Charles Riotte to Frederick Law Olmsted, October 14, 1854; Eduard Degener to John H. Olmsted, November 2, 1854. According to the joint resolution of Congress of March 1, 1845, Texas could, by consent of its citizens, be divided into as many as five separate states. Olmsted referred to this possibility in the *New York Daily Times*, June 3, 1854.

15. Olmsted, "An Appeal for Funds for the *San Antonio Zeitung*" (October 1854), Frederick Law Olmsted Papers; Adolf Douai to Frederick Law Olmsted, December 16, 1854; Adolf Douai to John H. Olmsted, September 15, 1854; John H. Olmsted to John Olmsted, October 31, 1854; Adolf Douai to John and Frederick Law Olmsted, March 28, 1855; *New York Daily Tribune*, November 9, 1854; *New York Daily Times*, January 6 and 19, 1855.

16. *Anti-Slavery Bugle*, July 28 and August 19, 1855; *National Anti-Slavery Standard*, November 17, 1855; *Proceedings of the Convention of Radical Political Abolitionists*, 55.

17. *National Anti-Slavery Standard*, April 4, 1854; Charles Loring Brace, *Home-Life in Germany*, iv–vi. Not everybody in the Anglo-American reform community agreed with Brace's favorable depiction of the Germans. Asserting that German sociability licensed drunkenness, the protemperance *New York Independent* speculated that Brace came to his conclusions "lying under the table with his German friends"; see Emma Brace, *Life of Charles Loring Brace*, 129.

18. Kapp, *Die Sklavenfrage in den Vereinigten Staaten*, 173–85; *New York Daily Times*, January 15, 1855; Frederick Law and John H. Olmsted to John Olmsted, January 22, 1855. Kapp quotation from *New York Daily Tribune*, January 20, 1855. The only major biographical treatment of Kapp is Hinners, *Exil und Rückkehr*.

19. Eric Foner, *Free Soil, Free Labor, Free Men*, 30–45; Gienapp, *Origins of the Republican Party*, 356–57.

20. Olmsted, *Journey through Texas*, 432; *New York Daily Times*, January 26, 1854.

21. *New York Daily Tribune*, November 7, 1854.

22. *National Anti-Slavery Standard*, April 4, 1854; Kapp, "Die Deutschen Ansiedlungen im westlichen Texas und der Mainzer Verein deutscher Fürsten, Grafen und Herren," in *Aus und uber Amerika*, 1:290; *San Antonio Zeitung*, January 5, 1855; Douai to Frederick Law Olmsted, December 16, 1854.

23. Kapp, *Die Sklavenfrage in den Vereinigten Staaten*, 20; Friedrich Kapp to Friedrich Kapp sen., March 24, 1851; Friedrich Kapp to Eduard Cohen, December 9, 1856, both in Friedrich Kapp Papers, Manuscript Division, Library of Congress, Washington, D.C.

24. Charles Loring Brace to Asa Gray, February 6, 1851, in Emma Brace, *Life of Charles Loring Brace*, 116, 151.

25. Olmsted to Brace, December 1, 1853. On the concept of wage slavery in proslavery discourse, see Faust, *Ideology of Slavery*. On the economic visions of antebellum reform, see Walters, *American Reformers*, 175–96.

26. *San Antonio Zeitung*, July 5, 1853; Adolf Douai to Frederick Law Olmsted, August 26, 1854.

27. Eduard Degener to John H. Olmsted, November 2, 1854 ("infuriated southerners"); Douai quotation from Adolf Douai to Frederick Law Olmsted, August 26, 1854.

28. Olmsted, *Journey through Texas*, xx; Kapp, *Die Geschichte der Sklaverei*, 514.

29. Beveridge et al., *Papers of Frederick Law Olmsted*, 2:20; Degener to John H. Olmsted, November 2, 1854.

30. Douai to Frederick Law Olmsted, December 16, 1854; Eduard Degener to Frederick Law Olmsted, January 11, 1856; *New York Daily Times*, March 31 and June 3, 1854.

31. Adolf Douai to Frederick Law Olmsted, December 7, 1854.

32. Adolf Douai to Frederick Law Olmsted, October 28, December 7, and December 16, 1854.

33. Adolf Douai to Frederick Law Olmsted, November 7, and December 16, 1854; *San Antonio Zeitung*, November 25, 1854, and May 5, 1855. Olmsted quotation from *San Antonio Zeitung*, December 23, 1854.

34. Friedrich Kapp, "Die Geschichte der deutschen Ansiedlungen des westlichen Texas und deren Bedeutung für die Vereinigten Staaten," *Atlantische Studien* 8 (1857): 177–86; Olmsted, *Journey through Texas*, 172–77; August Siemering, "Erinnerungen aus Texas," *Atlantische Studien* 6 (1855): 17–23; Degener to John H. Olmsted, November 2, 1854.

35. Shields, *Civil Tongues & Polite Letters*, xiii–xxxii; Douai to Frederick Law Olmsted, October 28 and December 7, 1854; Siemering, "Erinnerungen aus Texas," 19; Degener to John H. Olmsted, November 2, 1854; Douai, "Autobiography," 106, 111.

36. Friedrich Kapp, "Home Life in Germany," *Atlantische Studien* 3 (1853): 106–18; Friedrich Kapp to Frederick Law Olmsted, October 19, 1860. In a letter to his father, Kapp writes that joining the antislavery cause has helped him "win many friends, even among Americans"; see Kapp to Friedrich Kapp sen., January 24, 1855, Friedrich Kapp Papers. Frederick Law Olmsted and John H. Olmsted to John Olmsted, January 22, 1855; Frederick Law Olmsted to John Olmsted, February 9, 1855; Friedrich Kapp to Frederick Law Olmsted, February 22 and July 12, 1861; Kapp, *Die Geschichte der Sklaverei*, 3.

37. Friedrich Kapp to Ludwig Feuerbach, May 30, 1851, and December 12, 1856, Friedrich Kapp Papers; Kapp, *Die Sklavenfrage in den Vereinigten Staaten*, 184–85; Kapp, *Die Geschichte der Sklaverei*, 217–18.

38. Douai to Frederick Law Olmsted, December 16, 1854; *Der Pionier*, October 5, 1856.

39. Douai to Frederick Law Olmsted, December 16, 1854.

40. Douai to Frederick Law Olmsted, December 16, 1854, and March 28, 1855. On the intersections between evangelicalism, antislavery, and antebellum reform, see Noll, *God and Mammon*, and McKivigan and Snay, *Religion and the Antebellum Debate over Slavery*.

41. Charles Loring Brace, *Home-Life in Germany*, 272; see also Frederick Law Olmsted to Charles Loring Brace, March 25, 1848, in Beveridge et al., *Papers of Frederick Law Olmsted*, 1:316–17; *New York Daily Times*, July 10, 1856.

42. Kapp, *Die Sklavenfrage in den Vereinigten Staaten*, 3, 184; Kapp, *Die Geschichte der Sklaverei*, 3.

43. Friedrich Kapp to Becker, January 2, 1857, Friedrich Kapp Papers.

44. *Austin State Gazette*, June 12, 1855; *Texas State Times*, March 31, 1854; Fitzhugh, *Cannibals All!* 287.

45. Kapp, *Die Geschichte der Sklaverei*, ix. See also Nadel, *Little Germany*, 126–27; Friedrich Kapp to Ludwig Feuerbach (undated, perhaps 1856), Friedrich Kapp Papers: "As a foreigner I am going to confront the narrow-minded American and show him, by presenting facts rather than arguments, what he owes to the 'damned foreigners' and 'Dutchmen.'"

46. *Der Pionier*, October 5, 1856; *San Antonio Zeitung*, January 6 and May 5, 1855; Kapp, *Die Geschichte der Sklaverei*, 26–27.

47. Friedrich Kapp, "Die erste politische Hinrichtung in den USA: John Brown," *Demokratische Studien* 1 (1860): 289–312, contains a tribute to Frederick Douglass. See also *Die Geschichte der Sklaverei*, 512–13.

48. Adolf Douai to Frederick Law Olmsted, November 17 and December 16, 1854. Douai, "Autobiography," 112.

49. Douai quotation from *Der Pionier*, October 5, 1856. See also Douai, *Land und Leute*, 308–12. Inspired by Stowe, Douai also produced some antislavery fiction of his own. In 1859, he published *Der Abolitionist*, a novella about a German American philanthropist who travels south to help slaves escape to freedom. Even though the story has a white male as main character, it also recounts cases of black heroism. The novella was serialized in the January 6 to April 13, 1859, issues of *Der Pionier*.

50. Charles Loring Brace, *Races of the Old World*, 441; Emma Brace, *Life of Charles Loring Brace*, 211, 239; Frederick Law Olmsted to Charles Loring Brace, October 4, 1862, in Beveridge et al., *Papers of Frederick Law Olmsted*, 4:451.

51. *New York Daily Times*, April 5, 1853; Olmsted quotation from *New York Daily Times*, February 13, 1854; Frederick Law Olmsted to Abraham Lincoln, March 8, 1862; Frederick Law Olmsted to Edwin M. Stanton, April 13, 1862, both in Beveridge et al., *Papers of Frederick Law Olmsted*, 4:286–87, 292–302.

52. On the Douai-Agassiz controversy, see *Der Pionier*, July 2–23, 1859; Kapp, *Die Geschichte der Sklaverei*, iii, 517.

53. Riotte quoted in Frederick Law Olmsted to Edward Everett Hale, February 19, 1857, in Beveridge et al., *Papers of Frederick Law Olmsted*, 2:401. Douai to Frederick Law Olmsted, November 17, 1854; Douai, *Land und Leute*, 324. See also Douai's prize-winning novella *Fata Morgana*, which synthesizes his views on Germanness, Enlightenment humanism, and racial uplift.

54. Douai to Frederick Law Olmsted, December 16, 1854.

55. Douai to John H. Olmsted, September 4, 1854. In his January 6, 1855, letter to John H. and Frederick Law Olmsted, Douai reported, "The Spanish paper is to be started soon."

56. Riotte to Frederick Law Olmsted, October 14, 1854; Degener to John H. Olmsted, November 2, 1854. Douai quotation from Adolf Douai to Frederick Law Olmsted, September 4, 1854. See also Adolf Douai to Frederick Law Olmsted, November 17 and December 16, 1854.

57. Heinzen quotation from *Der Pionier*, May 13, 1854; Olmsted quotation from Frederick Law Olmsted to John Olmsted, January 22, 1855; Adolf Douai to John H. Olmsted and Frederick Law Olmsted, February 9, 1855. See also Douai, "Autobiography," 115; *San Antonio Zeitung*, February 9, 1855.

58. *Texas State Times*, May 19, 1855. *Austin State Gazette* and Louisiana paper quoted in *Anti-Slavery Bugle*, July 28, and December 29, 1855.

59. Douai, "Autobiography," 120. See also *San Antonio Zeitung*, December 12, 1855.

60. Douai, "Autobiography," 118–19. The proslavery attacks on Douai and his newspaper are also mentioned in Olmsted, *Journey through Texas*, 436–39.

61. Biesele, "Texas State Convention," 260; Philip S. Foner, *American Socialism and Black Americans*, 21; Campbell, *Empire for Slavery*, 216; *San Antonio Ledger*, September 8 and October 6, 1855; Douai, "Autobiography," 119; Douai to Frederick Law Olmsted, August 4, 1855.

62. Douai quotation from Adolf Douai to Frederick Law Olmsted, August 4, 1855. See also Adolf Douai to Frederick Law Olmsted, August 26, 1855; Charles Riotte to Frederick Law Olmsted, August 19, 1855.

63. Frederick Law Olmsted to James B. Abbot, October 7, 1855. On the Emigrant Aid Company's support of German settlers, see Baron and Seeger, "Moritz Hartmann," 1–22; Bondi, "Excerpts from the Autobiography," 87–159; Frederick Law Olmsted to Edward Everett Hale, August 23, 1855; Edward Everett Hale to Frederick Law Olmsted (perhaps November 1855).

64. Douai to Frederick Law Olmsted, February 9, 1855. Douai's appraisal of the situation squares with demographic estimates used in Jordan, *German Seed in Texas Soil*, 50.

65. Charles Riotte to Frederick Law Olmsted, January 25, 1856; *New York Daily Times*, January 31, 1856; Frederick Law Olmsted to Edward Everett Hale, January 17, 1856; Charles Riotte to Frederick Law Olmsted, February 25, 1856. These diverging viewpoints are also the subject of an editorial in the December 8, 1855, edition of the *San Antonio Zeitung*.

66. Riotte to Frederick Law Olmsted, February 25, 1856.

67. Degener to Frederick Law Olmsted, January 11, 1856.

68. Douai, "Autobiography," 119; *San Antonio Zeitung*, February 16, 1856; Douai to John H. Olmsted, January 27, 1856.

69. Philip S. Foner, *American Socialism and Black Americans*, 22; Douai, "Autobiography," 127; "A Letter from Mr. Oswald," *San Antonio Herald*, May 24, 1856, Adolf Douai Papers; John H. Olmsted to Frederick Law Olmsted, May 4, 1856.

70. Douai, "Autobiography," 133. See also Randers-Pehrson, *Adolf Douai*, 232–50, 315–33.

71. Kapp quotations from *New York Daily Tribune*, August 22 and October 8, 1856, and *New York Herald*, August 22, 1856. See also Randers-Pehrson, *Adolf Douai*, 232–34; Friedrich Kapp to Ludwig Feuerbach, December 12, 1856, Friedrich Kapp Papers; Levine, *Spirit of 1848*, 215–22; Kapp to Frederick Law Olmsted, October 19, 1860; *New York Daily Tribune*, October 19, 1860; *New York Daily Times*, October 19, 1860.

72. Frederick Law Olmsted to Edward Everett Hale, January 10, 30, 1857, in Beveridge et al., *Papers of Frederick Law Olmsted*, 2:397–400. A German translation of *A Journey through Texas* appeared later that year. Frederick Law Olmsted to Samuel Cabot Jr., June 29 and 30, July 4 and 26, August 18, September 14, and October 27, 1857; Frederick Law Olmsted to the Secretaries of the Cotton Supply Associations of Manchester and Liverpool, July 6, 1857, all in Beveridge et al., *Papers of Frederick Law Olmsted*, 2:431–56.

73. *New York Daily Tribune*, July 11, 1857; Douai, "Autobiography," 150–51; see also Randers-Pehrson, *Adolf Douai*, 236–37.

74. Unidentified New York paper quoted in Wittke, *Refugees of Revolution*, 188–89. Douai, "Autobiography," 126.

75. *Neu Braunfelser Zeitung* quoted in Jordan, "Germans and Blacks in Texas," 92.

76. Friedrich Kapp to Frederick Law Olmsted, September 20, 1861; Frederick Law Olmsted to Oliver Wolcott Gibbs, November 5, 1862; Charles Riotte to Frederick Law Olmsted, March 14 and 23, April 16, and June 10, 1861; Frederick Law Olmsted to Charles Sumner, April 5, 1861. Kapp also asked Olmsted to assist him in getting a post in the new administration, but his application for U.S. consul to Frankfurt was denied. It was not until 1870 that Kapp returned to Germany; Friedrich Kapp to Frederick Law Olmsted, May 8 and 17, 1861.

77. Marten, *Drawing the Line*, 222–36, has a more comprehensive analysis of German Texan unionism during the Civil War. Friedrich Kapp to Frederick Law Olmsted, November 20, 1862.

78. Charles Riotte to Frederick Law Olmsted, January 22, 1867. Douai, "Autobiography," 130.

3. The Only Freedom-Loving People of This City

1. Gilman, Journals and Miscellaneous Notebooks of Ralph Waldo Emerson, 14:333.

2. On John Brown's death and legacy, see Oates, *To Purge This Land with Blood*, 354–55; Reynolds, *John Brown*, 402–37; and Finkelman, *His Soul Goes Marching On*.

3. *Cincinnati Daily Enquirer*, December 6, 1859.

4. *Cincinnati Republikaner*, December 2, 3, and 5, 1859.

5. *Cincinnati Republikaner*, December 5, 1859; Conway, *Autobiography, Memories and Experiences*, 1:269.

6. *Cincinnati Daily Enquirer*, December 6, 1859; *Cincinnati Volksfreund*, December 6, 1859.

7. Bertaux, "Structural Economic Change," 130; Bremer quoted in Benson, *America of the Fifties*, 246–47.

8. Bird, *Englishwoman in America*, 119–20; Cist, *Sketches and Statistics . . . 1851*, 24; Cist, *Sketches and Statistics . . . 1859*, 165; Wittke, "Germans of Cincinnati," 3; Levine, *Spirit of 1848*, 183–88; Körner, *Das Deutsche Element*, 177–237.

9. Easton, *Hegel's First American Followers*; Reemelin, *Life of Charles Reemelin*; Körner, *Das Deutsche Element*, 182–92.

10. Franz von Löher, "Landscape and People of Cincinnati," 42.

11. Bird, *Englishwoman in America*, 120.

12. Baughn, "Bullets and Ballots," 267–72; Hochgeschwender, *Wahrheit, Einheit, Ordnung*, 190–91. For reports on clashes between Cincinnati Turners and local nativists, see "Die Vorgänge in Covington und Newport," in Metzner, *Jahrbücher der Deutsch-Amerikanischen Turnerei*, vol. 2, bk. 3, 112–19.

13. See also Nikki M. Taylor, *Frontiers of Freedom*, 20, 28–37; and Henry Louis Taylor Jr. and Dula, "Black Residential Experience," 99.

14. Hearn, *Children of the Levee*, 32; Henry Louis Taylor Jr., "On Slavery's Fringe," 26–30; Cist, *Sketches and Statistics . . . 1851*, 44.

15. Nikki M. Taylor, *Frontiers of Freedom*, 118–26.

16. *Cincinnati Daily Commercial*, May 12, 1860.

17. Levine, "Community Divided," 70–71; Hochgeschwender, *Wahrheit, Einheit, Ordnung*, 224–76, 361; Körner, *Das Deutsche Element*, 186, 208–12; Reemelin, *Life of Charles Reemelin*, 87–88.

18. Quotation from Daily Cincinnati Gazette, February 27, 1854. See also Levine, "Community Divided," 72–82; Levine, *Spirit of 1848*, 191–99; *Daily Cincinnati Gazette*, February 25 and 28, 1854; *Cincinnati Daily Enquirer*, March 3, 1854.

19. *Daily Cincinnati Gazette*, February 25, 27, and 28, and March 24 and 25, 1854; *Cincinnati Daily Enquirer*, March 25, 26, and 28, 1854.

20. *Der Wahrheitsfreund*, June 16, 1853; *Cincinnati Volksfreund*, February 9, 1856, and December 23, 1859.

21. "Proceedings of the Convention of the Colored Freemen of Ohio, Cincinnati, January 14, 15, 16, 17, and 19, 1852," in Philip S. Foner and Walker, *Proceedings of the Black State Conventions*, 277; Wittke, *Refugees of Revolution*, 89; *New Yorker Staats-Zeitung*, February, 21, 1852.

22. See the May 1858 editions of the *Daily Cincinnati Gazette*, the *Cincinnati Daily Times*, the *Cincinnati Daily Enquirer*, and the *Cincinnati Daily Commercial*. German-language newspapers at the trial were the *Cincinnati Volksfreund* and the *Cincinnati Tägliches Volksblatt*.

The *National Anti-Slavery Standard* informed a larger abolitionist reading public about the Connelly case. Conway, *Autobiography, Memories and Experiences*, 253.

23. *Ohio State Journal*, June 12, 1858; *Cincinnati Daily Commercial*, June 12, 1858; *Anti-Slavery Bugle*, June 19, 1858; *National Anti-Slavery Standard*, June 26, 1858; *Kansas Herald of Freedom*, July 17, 1858.

24. Conway, *Autobiography, Memories and Experiences*, 253; Mary Elisabeth Burtis, *Moncure Conway*; d'Entremont, *Southern Emancipator*; Easton, *Hegel's First American Followers*, 123–58.

25. Conway, *Autobiography, Memories and Experiences*, 255–62.

26. Easton, "Hegelianism in Nineteenth-Century Ohio," 362–63; Herz, "Influence Transcending Mere Numbers," 15–16.

27. Rattermann, *Johann Bernhard Stallo*, 2–10; Stallo, "Drei Sängerfestreden: Cincinnati, Juni 1856," in *Reden, Abhandlungen und Briefe*, 154.

28. Herz, "Influence Transcending Mere Numbers," 15–16.

29. Easton, *Hegel's First American Followers*, 136–41; *Dial*, January, April, and July 1860.

30. Conway, *Autobiography, Memories and Experiences*, 268, 272, 275.

31. Stewart, "Bachelor General," 131–54; Easton, *Hegel's First American Followers*, 159–203; Reinhart, *August Willich's Gallant Dutchmen*, 3–13; Lattek, *Revolutionary Refugees*, 110–36.

32. Conway, *Autobiography, Memories and Experiences*, 269; *Cincinnati Republikaner*, December 6, 1858.

33. *Cincinnati Republikaner*, February 26, and July 30, 1859.

34. *Daily Cincinnati Gazette*, May 2 and June 13, 1859; *Cincinnati Daily Commercial*, August 22, 1860; Wittke, "Germans of Cincinnati," 4–10; Harsham, "Community Portrait," 63–72.

35. Conzen, "German-Americans," 148–59; Conzen, "Ethnicity and Festive Culture," 44–76. The Orsini demonstration is covered in the May 18, 1858, issues of the *Cincinnati Daily Enquirer*, the *Cincinnati Daily Commercial*, and the *Cincinnati Tägliches Volksblatt*. Enthusiasm for Garibaldi is mentioned in the July 7, 1860, editions of the *Daily Cincinnati Gazette* and the *Cincinnati Daily Enquirer*.

36. *Daily Cincinnati Gazette*, November 12, 1859; *Cincinnati Daily Times*, November 11, 1859; *Cincinnati Daily Commercial*, November 11, 1859; *Cincinnati Republikaner*, November 12, 1859; *Dial*, December 1860.

37. Conway quotations from *Daily Cincinnati Gazette*, November 12, 1859, and *Cincinnati Daily Commercial*, November 14, 1859. See also *Cincinnati Daily Times*, November 14, 1859.

38. Hoadly quoted in Stange, *Patterns of Antislavery*, 180–81. Conway, *East and West*, 8; *Dial*, March, June 1860.

39. D'Entremont, *Southern Emancipator*, 122.

40. *Daily Cincinnati Gazette*, April 20 and May 2, 1859; d'Entremont, *Southern Emancipator*, 122–24; Herz, "Influence Transcending Mere Numbers," 10–11.

41. *Cincinnati Republikaner*, December 31, 1858; December 8, 1859.

42. *Cincinnati Republikaner*, December 8, 1859.

43. *Cincinnati Republikaner*, March 21 and May 11, 1859.

44. Willich quotation from *Cincinnati Republikaner*, February 2, 1860. Conway, *Autobiography, Memories and Experiences*, 281–85, 295–98; Conway, *Emerson at Home and Abroad*, 1–17; d'Entremont, *Southern Emancipator*, 127–31; *Cincinnati Republikaner*, January 5, 1860.

45. Conway, *Autobiography, Memories and Experiences*, 304.

46. Quotations from *Cincinnati Daily Enquirer*, February 1, 1860. See also *Cincinnati Daily Commercial*, January 31, 1859; *Cincinnati Daily Enquirer*, January 30, 1859; *Cincinnati Daily Times*, January 31, 1859; *Cincinnati Republikaner*, January 31, 1859; *Cincinnati Daily Times*, January 30, 1860; *Cincinnati Daily Commercial*, January 30, 1860; *Cincinnati Republikaner*, January 30, 1860; Kistler, "German-American Liberalism," 81–91.

47. Conway, *Thomas Paine*; Conway, *Autobiography, Memories and Experiences*, 305.

48. Gerber, "Peter Humphries Clark," 173.

49. Local newspaper quoted in Frederickson and Herz, "Matter of Respect," 25–36. Gaines, "What Is the Duty?" 8; Grossman, "In His Veins," 79–95; Gerber, "Peter Humphries Clark," 173–90.

50. Unitarian meeting quoted in Stange, *Patterns of Antislavery*, 223–25. Frederickson and Herz, "Matter of Respect," 28–29; Gerber, "Peter Humphries Clark," 181; d'Entremont, *Southern Emancipator*, 115; Conway, *Autobiography, Memories and Experiences*, 274.

51. D'Entremont, *Southern Emancipator*, 85–87. The event was overshadowed by the recent arrest of fugitive slave Anthony Burns. Conway, *Testimonies Concerning Slavery*, 79; Conway, *Autobiography, Memories and Experiences*, 340–41.

52. Conway, *Testimonies concerning Slavery*, 56–74, esp. 64 and 71. Conway is also quoted in *Boston Commonwealth*, October 18, 1862. See also Conway's tribute to the black astronomer Benjamin Banneker in *Atlantic Monthly* 11 (1863): 79–84.

53. Conway, *Testimonies Concerning Slavery*, 76–77.

54. "Proceedings of the Convention of the Colored Freemen," 277.

55. Quotations from *Cincinnati Republikaner*, October 3, 1859; see also the May 18 and July 3, 1860 issues of the *Republikaner*.

56. Quotation from the *Cincinnati Republikaner*, December 3, 1859. See also the October 22 and December 9, 1859, issues of the *Cincinnati Republikaner*. The October 22 issue was partly translated and reprinted in the *Liberator*, December 9, 1859.

57. Conway, *Autobiography, Memories and Experiences*, 300; *Cincinnati Daily Commercial*, December 6, 1859.

58. *Dial*, January 1860.

59. Willich quotation from *Cincinnati Republikaner*, December 5, 1859. Willich also reminded abolitionists who criticized Brown "that progress [could not] be made in rocking chairs"; *Cincinnati Republikaner*, October 22, 1859. See also *Cincinnati Daily Enquirer*, December 6, 1859; *Cincinnati Volksfreund*, December 6, 1859; *Weekly Anglo-African*, December 17, 1859.

60. *Cincinnati Republikaner*, December 20 and 26, 1859.

61. *Cincinnati Republikaner*, July 9, 1860; *Cincinnati Volksfreund*, December 25, 1859. See

also *Cincinnati Republikaner*, December 24, 1859, and *Cincinnati Volksfreund*, December 29, 1859.

62. *Cincinnati Republikaner*, March 11 and December 26, 1859.

63. *Sociale Republik*, September 25, 1858; Reiß, *Radikalismus und Exil*, 334–35; *Cincinnati Republikaner*, December 27, 1859.

64. Minutes of the Turner Meeting, December 29, 1859, Cincinnati Turnverein Papers, Cincinnati Historical Society.

65. *Cincinnati Volksfreund*, April 16, 1861; *Daily Cincinnati Gazette*, April 23, 1861; Conway, *Autobiography, Memories and Experiences*, 324–25; *Cincinnati Daily Commercial*, April 16, 1861; *Daily Cincinnati Gazette*, April 16, 1861.

66. *Cincinnati Volksfreund*, April 19, 1861; Wittke, "The Ninth Ohio Volunteers," *Ohio Archeological and Historical Quarterly* 35 (1926): 402–17.

67. Reinhart, *August Willich's Gallant Dutchmen*, 22–23.

68. Ibid., 51–52, 58–60; Barnett, "Willich's Thirty-second Indiana Volunteers," 48–70.

69. August Willich to Fritz Anneke, January 31, 1862, Fritz and Mathilde Anneke Papers, Archives and Rare Book Division, State Historical Society of Wisconsin, Madison.

70. D'Entremont, *Southern Emancipator*, 155–56. In July 1862, Conway demonstrated that he was also a man of action. He escorted a group of Virginia slaves to freedom and helped them find housing and employment in Yellow Springs, Ohio; Conway, *Autobiography, Memories and Experiences*, 357–63.

71. Conway, *Rejected Stone*, 75–80, 110. See also Conway, *Autobiography, Memories and Experiences*, 341; *Liberator*, February 28, 1862; Frederickson and Herz, "Matter of Respect," 29.

72. *Cincinnati Daily Commercial*, November 25, 1861; *Cincinnati Daily Enquirer*, November 24, 1861; *Cincinnati Volksfreund*, November 24, 1861; *Liberator*, December 20, 1861; Conway, *Autobiography, Memories and Experiences*, 342–43. On German American unionism in Civil War Missouri, see McPherson, *Battle Cry of Freedom*, 291–93.

73. *New York Herald*, November 28, 1861; Clark, *Black Brigade of Cincinnati*, 4–5.

74. Klement, "Sound and Fury," 100; Harding, "Cincinnati Riots of 1862," 229–39.

75. *Liberator*, April 4, 1862; "Wendell Philipps und die Turner von Cincinnati," in Metzner, *Jahrbücher der Deutsch-Amerikanischen Turnerei*, vol. 3, bk. 3, 97–99; Minutes of the Turner Meeting of March 25, 1862, Cincinnati Turnverein Papers; Clark, *Black Brigade of Cincinnati*, 3.

76. Turner resolution quoted in *Cincinnati Daily Enquirer*, August 28, 1862. Hatch quoted in Clark, *Black Brigade of Cincinnati*, 6. See also *Cincinnati Daily Enquirer*, August 31, 1862; *Cincinnati Daily Commercial*, August 27, 1862; Clark, *Black Brigade of Cincinnati*, 9–14; *Cincinnati Volksfreund*, August 17, 1862.

77. *Cincinnati Volksfreund*, May 20, 1863; d'Entremont, *Southern Emancipator*, 180–82; Conway, *Autobiography, Memories and Experiences*, 388–90.

78. *Dayton Herald*, September 26, 1873; Willich, *Army*, 23.

79. Stallo, "Ein Votum über die Negerstimmrechtsfrage," in *Reden, Abhandlungen, und*

Briefe, 211–31; Gutman, "Peter H. Clark," 413–18; Conway quoted in d'Entremont, *Southern Emancipator*, 221.

4. Why Continue to Be the Humble Maid?

1. Mary Booth to Jane Corss, February 15, 1859; Mary Booth to Adeline P. Corss, March 4, 1859, both in Booth Family Papers, Archives Department, University of Wisconsin at Milwaukee. Unless otherwise indicated, all letters to and from Sherman and Mary Booth are taken from this collection.

2. Schurz, *Reminiscences*, 1:196. On Fritz and Mathilde Anneke, see Schmidt, *Mathilde und Fritz Anneke*; Stuecher, *Twice Removed*; Piepke, *Mathilde Franziska Anneke*; and Maria Wagner, *Mathilde Franziska Anneke*.

3. Mathilde Anneke to Franziska Hammacher, April 3, 1850; Mathilde Anneke to Fritz Anneke, May 1859 (undated), and July 15, 1859, all in Fritz and Mathilde Anneke Papers, Archives and Rare Book Division, State Historical Society of Wisconsin, Archives and Rare Book Division Madison. Unless otherwise indicated, all letters to and from Fritz and Mathilde Anneke are taken from this collection.

4. Gurda, *Making of Milwaukee*; Conzen, *Immigrant Milwaukee*; Ortlepp, *Auf denn, Ihr Schwestern!* 31–47.

5. Koss, *Milwaukee*, 112, 158. German immigrants constituted 36.4 percent of Milwaukee's total population in 1850, and 35.3 percent in 1860; see Conzen, *Immigrant Milwaukee*, 14, 31, 128; and Ortlepp, *Auf denn, Ihr Schwestern!* 34.

6. Conzen, *Immigrant Milwaukee*, 172.

7. Ibid., 172–84. A social highlight in pre–Civil War Milwaukee was the 1857 *Turnfest*, with reportedly more than seven thousand delegates from the midwestern states.

8. Schurz, *Reminiscences*, 2:45; *Wisconsin Banner und Volksfreund*, August 16, 1854.

9. Koss, *Milwaukee*, 382–83.

10. See Baker, *Rescue of Joshua Glover*, 17–25; on Sherman Booth's politics, see Diane S. Butler, "Public Life and Private Affairs," 166–97; and Blue, *No Taint of Compromise*, 117–37, Booth quoted on 128.

11. *Wisconsin Banner und Volksfreund*, March 15, 1854; Koss, *Milwaukee*, 444–46.

12. See also Blue, *No Taint of Compromise*, 117–20.

13. Sherman Booth to Adeline Corss, November 17, 1848, quoted in Diane S. Butler, "Public Life and Private Affairs," 173–74.

14. *Wisconsin Free Democrat*, January 1, 1852, quoted in Blue, *No Taint of Compromise*, 125. The *Wisconsin Free Democrat* became the *Milwaukee Free Democrat* in 1856. See also Diane S. Butler, "Public Life and Private Affairs," 175. On the role of antislavery politics and the beginnings of the Republican Party in Wisconsin, see McManus, *Political Abolitionism in Wisconsin*.

15. *Wisconsin Free Democrat*, September 6, 1855, quoted in Blue, *No Taint of Compromise*, 130. See also Trefousse, *Carl Schurz*, 66.

16. The newspapers that engaged Fritz and were to publish his correspondence were the *Milwaukee Sentinel*, the *Atlas*, and the *Milwaukee Free Democrat*. Mathilde's bitterness over Fritz's departure becomes evident in her letter to him dated January 16, 1860.

17. *Trial of Sherman M. Booth*, 11, 19; Diane S. Butler, "Public Life and Private Affairs," 187–90; Mary Booth to Adeline Corss, August 8, 1859. Mathilde quotation from Mathilde to Fritz Anneke, July 15, 1859. See also Mathilde to Fritz Anneke, August (undated) and September 26–30, 1859; Mary Booth to Adeline Corss, March 4, 1859; Mary Booth to Jane Corss, May 3, 1859; Mary Booth to Ella Booth, June 27 and October 2, 1859.

18. Carl to Margarethe Schurz, March 2, 1860, in Bancroft, *Speeches, Correspondence and Political Papers of Carl Schurz*, 1:108–9; see also McManus, *Political Abolitionism in Wisconsin*, 180–81; Sherman Booth to his mother and Ella Booth, April 26, 1859.

19. *Trial of Sherman M. Booth*, 11; Diane S. Butler, "Public Life and Private Affairs," 188–89.

20. Mary Booth to Adeline Corss, August 8, 1859; Bonnie S. Anderson, *Joyous Greetings*, 4–6; Mathilde Anneke, "Woman in Conflict with Society," in Piepke, *Mathilde Franziska Anneke*, 36.

21. On gender norms in nineteenth-century German society, see Hausen, "Die Polarisierung der 'Geschlechtscharaktere,'" 363–93. For the American scene, see Welter "Cult of True Womanhood," 151–74. See also Chused, "Married Women's Property Law," 1359–1425.

22. The phrase "civilly dead" is used in the 1848 Seneca Falls Declaration of Sentiments. For differing conceptions of female self-determination among European and American women's rights activists, see Bonnie S. Anderson, *Joyous Greetings*.

23. Welter, "Cult of True Womanhood"; Mary Booth to Adeline Corss, January 29, 1860.

24. Mary Booth to Ella Booth, October 2, 1859; Mathilde to Fritz Anneke, September 26–30, 1859; Mary Booth to Jane Corss, May 3, 1859. Mathilde quotation from Mathilde to Fritz Anneke, January 16, 1860. See also Mary Booth to Adeline Corss, March 4, 1859. I take issue with Dorothea Stuecher's view that Mathilde simply "Germanized" Mary; see Stuecher, *Twice Removed*, 142. On the connections between sentimentalism and antebellum reform, see Douglas, *Feminization of American Culture*; and Tompkins, "Sentimental Power," 122–46.

25. Mathilde to Fritz Anneke, January 28, 1860 (includes a postscript by Sherman Booth). See also Mathilde to Fritz Anneke, January 16, 1860; Mary Booth to Adeline Corss, August 8 and October 14, 1859.

26. Mathilde to Fritz Anneke, January 28, 1860 (parts of the letter bear Mary Booth's handwriting); *Milwaukee Free Democrat*, January 3, 1860; Fritz quotation from Fritz Anneke to Mary Booth, July 1, 1859, Fritz and Mathilde Anneke Papers.

27. Mathilde quotation from Mathilde to Fritz Anneke, January 16, 1860. See also Mathilde to Fritz Anneke, September 26–30, 1859; May 14, 1860; and Fritz to Mathilde Anneke, May 1, 1860. Fritz's expectations went even further. He hoped that a stay in Europe might convert Mary altogether to the tenets of the radical European Enlightenment: "Indeed, Maria, I am certain, you will say then: 'Farewell, America, with thy trist, gloomy churches and priesthood

and sundays, with thy tedious prairies and woods and lakes, with all thy social nonsense; I know now what beauty of nature, what social life and what enjoyment of life is'"; Fritz Anneke to Mary Booth, July 1, 1859.

28. See the coverage in the December 3, 4, and 6 editions of the *Milwaukee Sentinel*, the *Milwaukee Free Democrat*, and the *Wisconsin Banner und Volksfreund*. Maria Wagner, *Mathilde Franziska Anneke*, 100.

29. Booth quotation from *Atlas*, December 17, 1859. See also McManus, *Political Abolitionism in Wisconsin*, 173–82; and Blue, *No Taint of Compromise*, 132–33.

30. Mathilde to Fritz Anneke, March 31, 1860. Fritz quotation from Fritz to Mathilde Anneke, May 1, 1860. On the Annekes' feud with Carl Schurz, see Mathilde to Fritz Anneke, September 26–30 and November 12, 1859.

31. Mathilde to Fritz Anneke, August 17, 1859, and March 31, 1860.

32. Mary Booth to Fritz Anneke, May 14, 1860, Fritz and Mathilde Anneke Papers; "Franziska Maria" was Mary's pet name for Mathilde; *Liberator*, August 3, 1860; *Atlas*, July 3, 1860; *Milwaukee Daily Sentinel*, June 2, 1860. Most of Booth's letters from jail were first published in the *Milwaukee Free Democrat* and then cited by other newspapers, among them the *Liberator* and the *New York Daily Tribune*.

33. Mathilde to Fritz Anneke, July 4, 1860; Mary Booth to Adeline Corss, July 8, 1860.

34. *Milwaukee Daily Sentinel*, July 6, 1860; *Atlas*, July 6, 1860.

35. Mathilde to Fritz Anneke, July 4, 1860; *Milwaukee Daily Sentinel*, July 6, 1860.

36. Mathilde to Fritz Anneke, May 14, 1860.

37. Anneke, "Erinnerungen vom Michigan-See," in Maria Wagner, *Die gebrochenen Ketten*, 191.

38. Mary to Ella Booth, September 3, 1860.

39. Schneebeli, *Zürich*; Keller quoted in Craig, *Triumph of Liberalism*, 12–13.

40. The Herweghs, Moleschott, Rüstow, and their Italian connections are frequently mentioned in the Annekes' and Mary's letters from Switzerland.

41. Mary Booth to Jane Corss, November 16, 1860; Mathilde Anneke, diary entry, December 1860, quoted in Maria Wagner, *Mathilde Franziska Anneke*, 136; Mathilde Anneke to Elisabeth Giesler, undated (perhaps January 1861).

42. Mathilde Anneke to Annette Giesler, April 21, 1861; Mary Booth to Adeline Corss, November 8, 1861.

43. Mary Booth to Adeline Corss, June 6, 10, and November 8, 1861.

44. Mathilde Anneke to Elisabeth Giesler, perhaps January 1861 (undated).

45. *Daily Life*, September 28 and October 5, 1861; Gottfried Kinkel to Fritz Anneke, August 16, 1861; Mary Booth to Adeline Corss, August 25, 1861; Mathilde to Fritz Anneke, September 18, 1861. For Anneke's commission in Wisconsin, see also Öfele, *German-Speaking Officers*, 15.

46. Mary Booth to Adeline Corss, August 25, 1861; Mathilde to Fritz Anneke, September 24, 1861.

47. *Milwaukee Free Democrat*, November 28, 1860; "I'm Dying, Comrade," in Booth, *Wayside Blossoms*, 74–75.

48. Fritz Anneke, *Der zweite Freiheitskampf*, v–vii.

49. *Augsburger Allgemeine Zeitung*, June 26, 29, August 20, 22, and September 17, 1861. Mathilde claims authorship of these articles in her December 21, 1861, letter to the editor of the *Augsburger Allgemeine Zeitung*, Georg Cotta. Mary Booth to Adeline Corss, August 25, 1861; Mathilde quotation from Mathilde to Fritz Anneke, perhaps December 1861 (undated).

50. *Das Ausland*, nos. 46, 48, 49 (1862). Mathilde quotation from *Das Ausland*, no. 34 (1863). See also Mathilde Anneke to Elisabeth Giesler, September 26, 1862, in which Mathilde complains about the "racial hatred" and "stupid prejudices" of the masses.

51. *Das Ausland*, no. 3 (1861); Mathilde to Fritz Anneke, perhaps December 1861 (undated); January 30, 1862; July 1862 (undated).

52. *Daily Life*, January 4, 1862. Mary also reprinted the harangue of a Swiss woman who startled her with the remarks, "So, so? Interesting news we have from your Republican America? If your land was united, as we are, you wouldn't make yourselves so ridiculous in the eyes of other nations."

53. *Daily Life*, February 21, 1863 ("incendiary"). Mary Booth to Adeline Corss, February 12, 1861, and March 4, 1863; Mary Booth to Ella Booth, December 26, 1862. Mary's greatest tribute to Garibaldi is her poem "A Mountain Monument," which is dedicated to the Italian revolutionary. It is included in her published volume *Wayside Blossoms*, 27–32. In this poem, Mary fuses American abolitionism and European liberalism into a cosmopolitan radical tradition. See also *Daily Life*, October 24, 1863; April 9, 1864. Mary quotation from Mary Booth to Mathilde Anneke, August 1, 1863, Fritz and Mathilde Anneke Papers.

54. *Daily Life*, November 14, 1861.

55. Mary Booth to Adeline Corss, March 4, 1863; Mathilde to Fritz Anneke, November 6, 1863.

56. Mathilde to Fritz Anneke, December 4, 1861; August 2, 1863; Mathilde Anneke to Georg Cotta, December 21, 1861. Mathilde quotation from Mathilde to Fritz Anneke, June 5, 1863. See also Maria Wagner, *Mathilde Franziska Anneke*, 158.

57. Mary Booth to Adeline Corss, November 8, 1861; Mary Booth to Jane Corss, April 29, 1862; Mathilde to Fritz Anneke, March 1, 1862, perhaps July 1862 (undated). Gerrit Smith's political relationship with Sherman Booth is discussed in Blue, *No Taint of Compromise*, and McManus, *Political Abolitionism in Wisconsin*.

58. Mary Booth to Adeline Corss, June 6, 1861; Mary Booth to Jane Corss, April 29, 1862.

59. The stories were published serially in the following German and German American newspapers: "Die Sclaven-Auction," *Didaskalia*, June 25 to 29, 1862; "Die Gebrochenen Ketten," *Milwaukee Herold*, July 9 to 16, 1864; "Uhland in Texas," *Illinois Staats-Zeitung*, April 15 to June 3, 1866. Edited versions of these stories are available in Maria Wagner, *Die gebrochenen Ketten*. Excerpts of the "Sturmgeiger" manuscript were translated by Mary and appeared in scattered issues of the *Daily Life* throughout 1863. Mathilde to Fritz Anneke, December 20, 1863.

60. See also Douglas, *Feminization of American Culture*; Tompkins, *Sensational Designs*; and Samuels, *Culture of Sentiment*.

61. Maria Wagner, "Feminismus, Literatur und Revolution," 122.

62. *Daily Life*, January 4, 1862.

63. Mathilde to Fritz Anneke, August 2, 1863; see also Maria Wagner, *Mathilde Franziska Anneke*, 384–85; and Stuecher, *Twice Removed*, 141–42; *Daily Life*, March 29, 1862; Mary Booth to Ella Booth, January 1, 1864; Mathilde to Fritz Anneke, December 20 and 21, 1863.

64. Mathilde Anneke, "Die Sclaven-Auction," in Maria Wagner, *Die gebrochenen Ketten*, 38.

65. Mathilde Anneke, "Die gebrochenen Ketten," in Maria Wagner, *Die gebrochenen Ketten*, 18. On the importance of Gerrit Smith and his family, see Mathilde Anneke to Georg Cotta, December 21, 1861; Mathilde Anneke to Elisabeth Giesler, September 25, 1862; Mathilde to Fritz Anneke, September 25, 1862; Mary Booth to Adeline Corss, August 25, 1861. Mary's poem "A Little Blossom" is a special homage to Gerrit Smith, which is included in her *Wayside Blossoms*, 23–26.

66. Mathilde Anneke, "Woman in Conflict with Society," 31–34.

67. Mathilde Anneke, "Die Sclaven-Auction," 37. Rensellar seems to have taken the quote from a speech by Gerrit Smith against the Kansas-Nebraska Act.

68. Mathilde Anneke, "Uhland in Texas," in Maria Wagner, *Die gebrochenen Ketten*, 190.

69. Ibid., 148.

70. Gilmore's slaves are bilingual, well bred, and several of them have Greek or Roman names (Caesar, Cleopatra, Romulus, Remus). See Mathilde Anneke, "Uhland in Texas," 84–87. The role of the revolutionary slave in *Uhland in Texas* is played by Marzell, Wallenstein's loyal servant whose heritage is black-Indian. His negotiations with a local Indian tribe prove instrumental in defeating the Confederate besiegers of Uhland.

71. *Daily Life*, February 14, 1863.

72. Mary Booth to Mathilde Anneke, not dated (perhaps 1863), Fritz and Mathilde Anneke Papers. On the nineteenth-century concept of romantic female friendship, see Hansen, *Very Social Time*, 52–78; and Bonnie S. Anderson, *Joyous Greetings*, 60.

73. Fritz Anneke to Elisabeth Giesler, April 20, 1863; Fritz Anneke to Edwin A. Stanton, August 22, 1863; Fritz to Mathilde Anneke, September 15, 1863; Mathilde to Fritz Anneke, September 21, 1862; September 10 and 20, 1863.

74. Mary Booth to Adeline Corss, June 6, 1861.

75. Mary Booth to Jane Corss, April 29, 1862; Mathilde to Fritz Anneke, undated (perhaps October 1862), and February 9 and 19, 1864.

76. Mathilde to Fritz Anneke, July 2, 1864.

77. Mathilde Anneke to her sister Johanna Weißkirch, March 30, 1865.

78. See, for instance, Mathilde's address at the 1869 anniversary conference of the American Equal Rights Association in Anthony, Gage, and Stanton, *History of Woman Suffrage*, 2:392–94.

5. Let Us Break Every Yoke

1. *Boston Daily Globe*, November 16, 1880. See also Wittke, *Against the Current*, 320–21.

2. *Boston Daily Advertiser*, February 23, 1881; *Boston Evening Transcript*, February 23, 1881. Parts of Phillips's speech are also reprinted in Wittke, *Against the Current*, 323–24; and Heinzen, *Teutscher Radikalismus in Amerika*, 1:12–14.

3. Wittke, *Against the Current*, remains the standard biography of Karl Heinzen.

4. *Der Pionier*, June 1, 1856; January 6, 1859.

5. Holmes, "The Professor at the Breakfast-Table," in *Works of Oliver Wendell Holmes*, 2:83; and Holmes, "The Autocrat of the Breakfast-Table," *Works*, 1:125. The term *Brahmin* referring to Boston's native-born white upper class was coined by Oliver Wendell Holmes Sr. in "The Professor's Story," *Atlantic Monthly*, January 1860, 91–93. See also Menand, *Metaphysical Club*, 4–22.

6. Handlin, *Boston's Immigrants*, 8–11, 53, 241; Lankevich, *Boston*, 36, 43; Horton and Horton, *Black Bostonians*, 2, 77.

7. Handlin, *Boston's Immigrants*, 88–100.

8. John Bigelow quoted in Lupo, *Liberty's Chosen Home*, 22; O'Connor, *Boston Irish*, 59–63; Handlin, *Boston's Immigrants*, 132–33, 173–74; Steven Taylor, "Progressive Nativism," 179–85. *Boston Daily Advertiser* quoted in O'Connor, *Boston Irish*, 63.

9. See the data on census and occupational distribution listed in Handlin, *Boston's Immigrants*, 243–45, 250–52, for the years 1850, 1855, 1860, and 1865; *Boston Daily Courier*, November 23, 1846.

10. *Der Pionier*, June 1, 1856; Levine, *Spirit of 1848*, 203; Philipp Wagner, *Ein Achtundvierziger*, 287–95; Zucker, *Forty-Eighters*, 343–44; Kapp, *Aus und über Amerika*, 356–80.

11. Baron, "German Republicans and Radicals," 5–11. "Exiles" quoted in *Liberator*, April 7, July 21, 1854. "Speakers" quoted in *Boston Daily Atlas*, September 12, 1856.

12. *Boston Daily Courier*, April 30, 1858; *Liberator*, May 7, 1858. Garrison's letter was also partly or fully reprinted in the April 30 and May 15 editions of the *Boston Daily Courier* and the *Anti-Slavery Bugle*. See also Wittke, *Against the Current*, 267; *Liberator*, July 9, 1858.

13. Nativist newspaper quoted in Wittke, *Refugees of Revolution*, 182; *Boston Daily Courier*, April 30, 1858.

14. On the Know-Nothing movement in Massachusetts, see Steven Taylor, "Progressive Nativism," 167–85; Von Frank, *Trials of Anthony Burns*, 236–43; Anbinder, *Nativism and Slavery*, 90–95; Dale Baum, "Know-Nothingism," 959–86.

15. Carl Schurz to Edward L. Pierce, March 26, 1859, in Bancroft, *Speeches, Correspondences, and Political Papers of Carl Schurz*, 1:42; *Wisconsin Banner und Volksfreund*, October 17, 1859; Wittke, *Against the Current*, 289. See also Eric Foner, *Free Soil, Free Labor, Free Men*, 250–56; and Levine, *Spirit of 1848*, 241.

16. Heinzen, *Teutscher Radikalismus in Amerika*, 1:59. See also Wittke, *Refugees of Revolution*, 179–80; and Heinzen, *Die Teutschen und die Amerikaner.*

17. Heinzen, *Erlebtes, 2. Theil*, 456.

18. "We would welcome those Christian fighters against slavery as allies . . . if they did not hate so bitterly, no less than slavery itself, that truly free endeavor, the 'infidel' antislavery movement," Heinzen commented at the 1855 annual convention of the Ohio Anti-Slavery Society (Heinzen, *Teutscher Radikalismus in Amerika*, 1:90). Reiß, *Radikalismus und Exil*, 261.

19. *Liberator*, April 8, 1859.

20. Ibid.

21. *Liberator*, April 22, 1859. On Schurz's 1859 Faneuil Hall lecture, see Trefousse, *Carl Schurz*, 73–75.

22. See Mayer, *All on Fire*, 213–39; *Der Pionier*, April 30, 1859. A translated version of this article appeared in the May 20, 1859, edition of the *Liberator*.

23. See also Dale Baum, "Know-Nothingism," 976.

24. Wittke, *Against the Current*, 102–5. Heinzen's friendship with Marie Zakrzewska is explored in Tuchman, *Science Has No Sex*.

25. *Der Pionier*, December 10, 1859.

26. Lydia Maria Child to William Lloyd Garrison, October 28, 1859, in Meltzer and Holland, *Lydia Maria Child: Selected Letters*, 326; Oates, *To Purge This Land with Blood*, 355; *Liberator*, December 16, 1859.

27. Heinzen, *Die Teutschen und die Amerikaner*, 39. "If you have to blow up half a continent and cause a bloodbath to destroy the party of barbarism," Heinzen wrote in 1849, "you should have no scruples of conscience. Anyone who would not joyously sacrifice his life for the satisfaction of exterminating a million barbarians is not a true republican." Quote taken from a manuscript by Heinzen titled "Der Mord," in Karl Heinzen Papers, University of Michigan Libraries, Ann Arbor.

28. Sella Martin quotation from *Liberator*, December 9, 1859. See also *Weekly Anglo-African*, December 17, 1859; Horton and Horton, "Affirmation of Manhood," 146–52; and Kantrowitz, "Fighting like Men," 23–29.

29. Heinzen, *Teutscher Radikalismus in Amerika*, 1:89–90; *Der Pionier*, September 27, 1856; September 6, 1857.

30. *London Times* reporter quoted in Brockett, *Men of Our Day*, 146. There are several important biographies of Phillips, particularly Irving H. Bartlett, *Wendell Phillips*; James Brewer Stewart, *Wendell Phillips*; and Hofstadter, *American Political Tradition*, 135–61.

31. On Phillips and disunion, see "Can Abolitionists Vote or Take Office under the United States Constitution," in Ruchames, *Abolitionists*, 192–96.

32. See also Menand, *Metaphysical Club*, 29–31; and Lader, *Bold Brahmins*, 257.

33. The disruption of the John Brown anniversary memorial in Boston was covered in papers throughout the North. "Businessmen" quotation from *New York Daily Tribune*, December 4, 1860; see also *Liberator*, December 7, 1860; *National Principia*, December 8, 1860; *National Anti-Slavery Standard*, December 15, 1860; *Douglass' Monthly*, January 1861; *New Yorker Demokrat*, December 4, 1860.

34. *Der Pionier*, December 6, 1860; *Liberator*, December 10, 1860.

35. Douglass, "A Plea for Freedom of Speech in Boston, December 9, 1860," in Blassingame, *Frederick Douglass Papers*, 3:423.

36. *Der Pionier*, December 20, 1860. See also "Wendell Philipps und die Turner in Boston" in Metzner, *Jahrbücher der Deutsch-Amerikanischen Turnerei*, vol. 2, bk. 4, 81.

37. Wendell Phillips to Mary Grew (undated, perhaps early January 1861), quoted in Martyn, *Wendell Phillips*, 306; *Liberator*, December 21, 1860; Phillips, "The Mob and Education," in Pease, *Speeches, Lectures, and Letters of Wendell Phillips*, 1:346–47.

38. "Wendell Philipps und die Turner in Boston," 81–82; *Liberator*, December 21, 1861; *Boston Daily Journal*, December 17, 1860. See also Irving H. Bartlett, *Wendell Phillips*, 228–30; and Sherwin, *Prophet of Liberty*, 418–19.

39. See also Stewart, *Wendell Phillips*, 214; Sherwin, *Prophet of Liberty*, 419; Wittke, *Against the Current*, 177.

40. Samuel G. Howe to Charles Sumner, January 20, 1861, quoted in Irving H. Bartlett, *Wendell Phillips*, 231.

41. *Boston Daily Courier*, January 25, 1861; *Boston Daily Journal*, January 24, 1861. The *Boston Courier* is cited in the *Liberator*, December 28, 1860.

42. *Der Pionier*, January 31, 1861; see also *Liberator*, November 22, 1861.

43. William Lloyd Garrison to Oliver Johnson, January 19, 1861, in Merrill, *Letters of William Lloyd Garrison*, 5:6. Phillips's scrapbook entry is cited in Sherwin, *Prophet of Liberty*, 717.

44. *Liberator*, May 3, 1861; *Boston Advertiser*, April 22, 1861; *New York Times*, April 28, 1861.

45. *Der Pionier*, February 21 and April 26, 1861. See also Heinzen's lectures "Die sybillinischen Bücher" and "Salomonische Weishheit," in *Teutscher Radikalismus in Amerika*, 2:122–51, 152–91.

46. *Der Pionier*, February 21, 1861; *Liberator*, February 22, 1861. The Heinzen-Phillips correspondence is reprinted in the February 28, 1861, issue of *Der Pionier*. See also Heinzen, *Teutscher Radikalismus in Amerika*, 1:256–57; Wittke, *Against the Current*, 179.

47. *Liberator*, September 20, 1861; Douglass, "Fighting the Rebels with One Hand, January 14, 1862," in Blassingame, *Frederick Douglass Papers*, 3:484; *Der Pionier*, November 14, 1861.

48. Heinzen quotation from Heinzen, *Die Teutschen und die Amerikaner*, 30; see also Heinzen, *Teutscher Radikalismus in Amerika*, 1:140–42; *Boston Daily Journal*, May 17, 1862. On Heinzen's sallies against German American Civil War officers, see Wittke, *Against the Current*, 180–84.

49. Reinhold Solger to Wendell Phillips, March 7, 1859, Wendell Phillips Papers, Houghton Library, Harvard University, Cambridge, Mass.; Heinzen, *Teutscher Radikalismus in Amerika*, 2:47–48.

50. *Der Pionier*, March 29, 1860. On John S. Rock, see Logan and Winston, *Dictionary of American Negro Biography*, 529–31.

51. Heinzen, *Teutscher Radikalismus in Amerika*, 2:58–59; *Der Pionier*, July 16, 1862; January 28, April 15, and July 15, 1863; Karl Heinzen to Wendell Phillips, February 4, 1864, Wendell Phillips Papers; McPherson, *Struggle for Equality*, 143–47.

52. The phrase "fellow citizen of the fugitive world" appears in Heinzen's play *Die teutschen Organisten der Bildung in Amerika*, a biting satire against the *New Yorker Staats-Zeitung*, and is used to address a fugitive slave; in Heinzen, *Gesammelte Schriften, zweiter Band*, 207.

53. Phillips quotation from *Liberator*, January 31, 1862; *New York Daily Times*, January 25, 1862.

54. *Der Pionier*, May 28, 1862; *Liberator*, June 3, 1962. See also McPherson, *Struggle for Equality*, 102–17.

55. See also Heinzen's lecture "Die Menschheit als Verbrecherin," published in *Der Pionier*, February 19, 1864.

56. Wittke, *Against the Current*, 186–87; Heinzen, *Teutscher Radikalismus in Amerika*, 2:96–97. See also Heinzen's lecture "Public Opinion," which was reprinted in the April 19 and 26, 1863, issues of the *Liberator*.

57. *Der Pionier*, January 1, 1863.

58. *Liberator*, January 2, 1863; Charlotte Forten quoted in Quarles, *Negro in the Civil War*, 163; Lydia Maria Child to William Lloyd Garrison Haskins, December 28, 1862, in Meltzer and Holland, *Lydia Maria Child*, 423.

59. Finkelman, "Lincoln," 349–87, provides a well-argued defense of Lincoln's politics of emancipation. The Fugitive Slave Act was not revoked until 1864.

60. *Der Pionier*, July, 15, 1863. On German American opposition to the Lincoln administration, see also Nagler, *Fremont contra Lincoln*. On the nativist attacks against German-born soldiers that became endemic after the Union defeat at Chancellorsville in May 1863, see Keller, *Chancellorsville and the Germans*.

61. *Der Pionier*, October 28, 1863; *Liberator*, November 6, 1863. See also Nagler, *Fremont contra Lincoln*, 149–59.

62. Cf. Wittke, *Against the Current*, 189–92; Nagler, *Fremont contra Lincoln*, 155–57. Edward Bates quoted in Vorenberg, *Final Freedom*, 40.

63. Jacob Müller to Wendell Phillips, January 28, 1864, Wendell Phillips Papers.

64. *Liberator*, February 5, 1864.

65. Wendell Phillips to Johann Stallo, April 21, 1864, quoted in Austin, *Life and Times of Wendell Phillips*, 232.

66. See also Nagler, *Fremont contra Lincoln*, 161–91; McPherson, *Struggle for Equality*, 262–65; Wittke, *Against the Current*, 191–93; *Der Pionier*, March 11 and April 13, 1864.

67. Karl Heinzen to Wendell Phillips, February 4, 1864, Wendell Phillips Papers. Heinzen's key outlets for promoting Frémont's candidacy were *Der Pionier* and the Boston Organisations-Verein, over which he presided. The resolutions of the Organisations-Verein were printed in the March 18 and April 20, 1864, editions of the *Pionier*. Phillips spoke for

Frémont in Boston and New York on several occasions; see McPherson, *Struggle for Equality*, 266–69; S. Wolf to Wendell Phillips, June 14, 1864; David Plumb to Wendell Phillips, June 13, 20, 1864, Wendell Phillips Papers.

68. *Liberator*, March 25, 1863, and April 1, 1864. See also Nagler, *Fremont contra Lincoln*, 182–83, 191–98.

69. Nagler, *Fremont contra Lincoln*, 214–16. Heinzen's letter to Charles Sumner dated February 7, 1864, Karl Heinzen Papers, is a particularly urgent appeal for an interventionist foreign policy against the European monarchies. A German version of this letter is reprinted in the April 27, 1864, issue of *Der Pionier*. *Liberator*, June 3, 1864; *Boston Daily Journal*, May 31 and June 2, 1864; see also Heinzen's editorial correspondence from Cleveland in the June 1 and 8 editions of his *Pionier*.

70. *Boston Evening Transcript* and *Cleveland Herald* quoted in Ruhl J. Bartlett, *John C. Frémont*, 104; *Harper's Weekly*, June 18, 1864. The *New York Independent* also opposed the Frémont movement.

71. The *Douglass' Monthly* responded positively to the Frémont ticket; see also the New York *Anglo-African*, June 4 and August 6, 1864. For Garrison's support of Lincoln in 1864, see McPherson, *Struggle for Equality*, 266–71. *Liberator*, August 5, 1864; Abraham Lincoln to Carl Schurz, March 23, 1864, in Basler, *Collected Works of Abraham Lincoln*, 7:262–63; Carl Schurz to Theodor Petrasch, October 12, 1864, in Bancroft, *Speeches, Correspondences, and Political Papers of Carl Schurz*, 1:249.

72. *Der Pionier*, June 15, 25, and July 13, 1864.

73. *New York Independent*, June 30 and July 7, 1864. Both letters were widely circulated and commented on in the antislavery press, most significantly in the *Liberator* and the *National Anti-Slavery Standard*.

74. Wittke, *Against the Current*, 194; *Der Pionier*, July 20, 1864; Frémont quotation from McPherson, *Struggle for Equality*, 279.

75. On the Democratic national convention and its aftermath, see Williams, *Lincoln and the Radicals*, 328–29; and Paludan, *Presidency of Abraham Lincoln*, 283–85.

76. *Der Pionier*, September 14 and October 19, 1864. Fremont's letter of withdrawal is reprinted in the September 30 issue of the *Liberator*.

77. Cf. McPherson, *Struggle for Equality*, 285–86; Heinzen, *Teutscher Radikalismus in Amerika*, 1:13.

78. Eric Foner, *Reconstruction*, 35–76; Eric Foner, *Forever Free*; McPherson, *Struggle for Equality*, 178–91, 238–59.

79. Heinzen's comments on Lincoln's second inaugural quoted in Wittke, *Against the Current*, 195; *Der Pionier*, April 28, 1865.

80. *Liberator*, July 15, 1865. According to the *Liberator*, Heinzen donated two dollars to a fund for the establishment of black schools in the South. *Der Pionier*, May 31, July 12, August 22, and December 13, 1865.

81. See also Wittke, *Against the Current*, 202–21; *Der Pionier*, May 31, 1865; Heinzen, *Teutscher Radikalismus in Amerika*, 2:416–17, 250 ("king in dresscoat").

6. A Revolution Half Accomplished

1. *Harper's Weekly*, November 20, 1869.

2. Assing, "Thrills of Victory and Depth of Mourning," April 1865, in Lohmann, *Radical Passion*, 308; Hecker quoted in Freitag, *Friedrich Hecker*, 300.

3. Schläger, *Die soziale und politische Stellung*, 16–17.

4. Wittke, *Refugees of Revolution*, 248; Assing, "Victorious South — Half- and Whole-Hearted — Black Literacy Institute," November 1865, in Lohmann, *Radical Passion*, 324.

5. *Der Pionier*, May 31, 1865; Metzner, *Brief History*, 24–25; Levine, *Spirit of 1848*, 262.

6. See also Trefousse, *Carl Schurz*, 161–62; Randers-Pehrson, *Adolf Douai*, 273–74; Hinners, *Exil und Rückkehr*, 200–201; Wittke, *Against the Current*, 196–98; Wittke, *Refugees of Revolution*, 248–49; on Johann Stallo, see Rattermann, *Johann Bernhard Stallo*, 5–12; *New York Tribune*, October 27, 1866; *New York Independent*, November 15, 1866.

7. For a more detailed account of laws passed in the period of Congressional Reconstruction (1866–72), see Eric Foner, *Reconstruction*, 228–80, 346–411; Eric Foner, *Forever Free*, 107–80; and McPherson, *Struggle for Equality*, 341–432.

8. Susan B. Anthony quoted in McFeely, *Frederick Douglass*, 266; Elizabeth Cady Stanton quoted in Philip S. Foner, *Frederick Douglass on Women's Rights*, 26; Efford, "German Immigrants," 76. There is no evidence that Anneke, unlike many other white feminists, fretted about the Fifteenth Amendment in a way that led her to reject black suffrage. See also Ortlepp, *Auf denn, Ihr Schwestern!* 180–84; and Maria Wagner, *Mathilde Franziska Anneke*, 332–66.

9. Metzner, *Brief History*, 22–30; Levine, *Spirit of 1848*, 263–65. On the small faction of the Turner movement that kept alive the radical ideals of 1848, see Ralf Wagner, "Turner Societies," 221–39.

10. See also Levine, *Spirit of 1848*, 269; Keil, "German Working-Class Radicalism," 37–48; Randers-Pehrson, *Adolf Douai*, 283–303. An excellent account of the Haymarket Affair is Green, *Death in the Haymarket*.

11. Schurz, "Report on the Condition of the South," in Bancroft, *Speeches, Correspondence and Political Papers of Carl Schurz*, 1:354; Schurz, *Reminiscences*, 3:274–80.

12. Eric Foner, *Reconstruction*, 499; Schurz, "The Issues of 1874, Especially in Missouri," in Bancroft, *Speeches, Correspondence and Political Papers of Carl Schurz*, 3:89–90. See also Efford, "German Immigrants," 68; Trefousse, *Carl Schurz*, 196–209.

13. See Eric Foner, *Reconstruction*, 451–95. For a more general evaluation of postwar expansions of federal power, see Bensel, *Yankee Leviathan*.

14. McPherson, "Grant or Greeley?" 136–57; Wittke, *Refugees of Revolution*, 250–51; Nagler, "Deutschamerikaner," 415–38. On the genteel ideology of the Liberal Republican movement, see Eric Foner, *Reconstruction*, 499–511.

15. Smith and Francis L. Garrison quoted in McPherson, "Grant or Greeley?" 50–51.

16. *New York Times*, October 31, 1872; Nagler, "Deutschamerikaner," 436; Ottilie Assing to Ludmilla Assing, April 16, 1872, quoted in Diedrich, *Love across Color Lines*, 305.

17. For these and other ethnocultural aspects that influenced German American voting behavior in the 1870s, see Nagler, "Deutschamerikaner," 419–25. On Willich's postwar career, see Reinhart, *August Willich's Gallant Dutchmen*, 180–81.

18. Rippley, "German Assimilation," 129. A broader array of responses to the Franco-Prussian War is discussed in Trefousse, "German-American Immigrants," 160–75.

19. Wittke, *Against the Current*, 272, 299–300; Fritz to Mathilde Anneke, August 30, 1872, Fritz and Mathilde Anneke Papers.

20. Hecker, *Friedrich Hecker's Festrede*.

21. Kapp, *Leben*, iii. Kapp's return to Germany and his infatuation with the German Reich are more fully investigated in Hinners, *Exil und Rückkehr*, 235–55.

22. On Willich's last years, see Easton, *Hegel's First American Followers*, 197–203; and Reinhart, *August Willich's Gallant Dutchmen*, 180–81.

23. A striking example of the "wandering Jew" metaphor in Forty-Eighter literature can be found in Douai, *Fata Morgana*, 13. See also Freitag, *Friedrich Hecker*, 399–401; Herzig, "Judenhass," 1–18; and Bruns, *Towards a Transnational History of Racism*.

24. *New York Times*, February 13, 1872; Körner quoted in Wittke, *Refugees of Revolution*, 251.

25. Körner, *Memoirs of Gustav Körner*, 515–18.

26. On Greeley's ill-fated candidacy, see Downey, "Horace Greeley and the Politicians," 727–50; Eric Foner, *Reconstruction*, 501–11.

27. On race and memory in postbellum America, see Silber, *Romance of Reunion*; Blight, *Race and Reunion*; Fahs and Waugh, *Memory of the Civil War*.

28. On the relationship between immigration, whiteness, and late nineteenth-century American nationalism, see Jacobson, *Whiteness of a Different Color*, 39–90.

29. On German American postwar integration, see also Öfele, *German-Speaking Officers*, 209–28. German immigrant efforts to retain an ethnic identity while becoming "white" American citizens are analyzed in Keller, *Chancellorsville and the Germans*, 146–67.

30. Diedrich, *Love across Color Lines*, 304–6; *New York Times*, January 4, 1872.

BIBLIOGRAPHY

MANUSCRIPT COLLECTIONS

Anneke, Fritz and Mathilde, Papers. Archives and Rare Book Division, State Historical Society of Wisconsin, Madison.

Booth Family Papers. Archives Department, University of Wisconsin at Milwaukee.

Cincinnati Turnverein Papers. Cincinnati Historical Society.

Douai, Adolf, Papers. Center for American History, University of Texas, Austin.

Heinzen, Karl, Papers. University of Michigan Archives, Ann Arbor.

Honorary Doctorate Certificate James W. C. Pennington. University of Heidelberg Archives.

Kapp, Friedrich, Papers. Manuscript Division, Library of Congress, Washington, D.C.

Olmsted, Frederick Law, Papers. Manuscript Division, Library of Congress, Washington, D.C.

Phillips, Wendell, Papers. Houghton Library, Harvard University, Cambridge, Mass.

Sozialistischer Turnerbund Papers. New York Public Library.

NEWSPAPERS AND PERIODICALS

American (English-Language)

Anglo-African Magazine (New York), *Anti-Slavery Bugle* (Salem, Ohio), *Atlantic Monthly* (Boston), *Austin (Tex.) State Gazette*, *Boston Commonwealth*, *Boston Daily Advertiser*, *Boston Daily Atlas*, *Boston Daily Courier*, *Boston Daily Globe*, *Boston Daily Journal*, *Boston Evening Transcript*, *Chicago Daily Tribune*, *Cincinnati Daily Commercial*, *Cincinnati Daily Enquirer*, *Cincinnati Daily Times*, *Cleveland Express*, *Cleveland Herald*, *Daily Cincinnati Gazette*, *Daily Life* (Milwaukee), *Dayton Herald*, *The Dial* (Cincinnati), *Douglass' Monthly* (Rochester, N.Y.), *Frederick Douglass' Paper* (Rochester, N.Y.), *Harper's Weekly* (New York), *Hartford Courant*, *Kansas Herald of Freedom*, *The Liberator* (Boston), *Milwaukee Free Democrat*, *Milwaukee Sentinel*, *National Anti-Slavery Standard* (New York), *National Era* (New York; Washington, D.C.), *National Principia* (New York), *New York Daily Times*, *New York Daily Tribune*, *New York Herald*, *New York Independent*, *New York Times*, *New York Tribune*, *North American Review* (Boston), *Ohio State Journal* (Columbus, Ohio), *San Antonio Ledger*, *Texas State Times* (Austin), *Trenton (Ohio) State Gazette*, *United States Magazine and Democratic Review* (New York), *Weekly Anglo-African* (New York), *Wisconsin Free Democrat* (Milwaukee).

215

American (German-Language)

Atlantis (Detroit; Buffalo), *Atlas* (Milwaukee), *Baltimore Wecker, Belleviller Volksblatt, Cincinnati Republikaner, Cincinnati Tägliches Volksblatt, Cincinnati Volksfreund, Deutsch-Amerikanische Monatshefte* (Chicago), *Illinois Staats-Zeitung* (Chicago), *Milwaukee Herold, Mississippi Blätter* (St. Louis), *Neu Braunfelser Zeitung, New Yorker Criminal-Zeitung und Belletristisches Journal, New Yorker Demokrat, New Yorker Staats-Zeitung, Der Pionier* (Louisville, Ky.; Cincinnati; New York; Boston), *Philadelphia Demokrat, Pittsburger Courier, San Antonio Zeitung, Sociale Republik* (New York), *Turn-Zeitung* (New York; Baltimore), *Der Wahrheitsfreund* (Cincinnati), *Der Westbote* (Columbus, Ohio), *Wisconsin Banner und Volksfreund.*

German

Atlantische Studien (Göttingen), *Augsburger Allgemeine Zeitung, Das Ausland* (Munich), *Demokratische Studien* (Hamburg), *Didaskalia* (Frankfurt).

PRIMARY SOURCES AND EDITED COLLECTIONS

Achenbach, Hermann. *Tagebuch meiner Reise, in d. Nordamerikanischen Freistaaten oder das neue Kanaan.* Düsseldorf: G. H. Beyer, 1835.

American Anti-Slavery Society. *Anti-Slavery Tracts,* series 2, nos. 1–14, 1860. Westport, Conn.: Greenwood Press, 1970.

———. *Proceedings of the Seventh Annual Meeting.* New York: American Anti-Slavery Society, 1840.

American Unitarian Association. *The Works of William E. Channing, D.D.* Boston: Unitarian Association, 1875.

Anneke, Fritz. *Der zweite Freiheitskampf der Vereinigten Staaten von Nordamerika.* Frankfurt: J. D. Sauerländer, 1861.

The Annual Report of the American and Foreign Anti-Slavery Society, Presented at New York, May 9, 1848. New York: American and Foreign Anti-Slavery Society, 1848.

Anthony, Susan B., Matilda J. Gage, and Elizabeth Cady Stanton. *History of Woman Suffrage.* 6 vols. New York: S. B. Anthony, 1882.

Bancroft, Frederic, ed. *Speeches, Correspondence and Political Papers of Carl Schurz.* 6 vols. New York: G. P. Putnam's Sons, 1913.

Basler, Roy P., ed. *The Collected Works of Abraham Lincoln.* 8 vols. New Brunswick, N.J.: Rutgers University Press, 1953–55.

Benson, Adolph B., ed. *America of the Fifties: Letters of Fredrika Bremer.* New York: American Scandinavian Foundation, 1924.

Beveridge, Charles E., et al., eds. *The Papers of Frederick Law Olmsted.* 6 vols. Baltimore: Johns Hopkins University Press, 1977–92.

Bird, Isabella L. *The Englishwoman in America.* Edited by Andrew Hill Clark. Madison: University of Wisconsin Press, 1966.

Blassingame, John W., ed. *The Frederick Douglass Papers: Speeches, Debates, and Interviews.* 5 vols. New Haven, Conn.: Yale University Press, 1979–92.

Bondi, August. "Excerpts from the Autobiography of August Bondi." *Yearbook of German-American Studies* 40 (2005): 87–159.

Booth, Mary C. *Wayside Blossoms among Flowers from German Gardens.* Heidelberg: Bangel & Schmitt, 1864.

Brace, Charles Loring. *Home-Life in Germany.* New York: C. Scribner, 1853.

——— . *The Races of the Old World: A Manual of Ethnology.* New York: C. Scribner, 1863.

Brace, Emma. *The Life of Charles Loring Brace.* New York: Arno Press, 1976.

Brockett, L. P. *Men of Our Day; or Biographical Sketches of Patriots, Orators, Statesmen, Generals, Reformers, Financiers, and Merchants.* Philadelphia: Ziegler & McCurdy, 1872.

Cist, Charles E. *Sketches and Statistics of Cincinnati in 1851.* Cincinnati: W. H. Moore, 1851.

——— . *Sketches and Statistics of Cincinnati in 1859.* Cincinnati, 1859.

Clark, Peter H. *The Black Brigade of Cincinnati.* Cincinnati: J. B. Boyd, 1864.

Cochran, Thomas C., et al. *The New American State Papers: Labor and Slavery.* 7 vols. Wilmington, Del.: Scholarly Resources, 1972.

Conway, Moncure Daniel. *Autobiography, Memories and Experiences.* 2 vols. Boston: Houghton & Mifflin, 1904.

——— . *East and West: An Inaugural Discourse, Delivered in the First Congregational Church, Cincinnati, O., May 1, 1859.* Cincinnati, 1859.

——— . *Emerson at Home and Abroad.* Boston: J. R. Osgood, 1882.

——— . *The Rejected Stone.* Boston: Walker, Wise, 1862.

——— . *Testimonies concerning Slavery.* London: Chapman & Hall, 1864.

——— . *Thomas Paine: A Celebration.* Cincinnati: Office of The Dial, 1860.

Douai, Adolf. *Fata Morgana.* St. Louis: Anzeiger des Westens, 1858.

——— . *Land und Leute in der Union.* Berlin: O. Janke, 1864.

Ebeling, Christoph Daniel. *Erdbeschreibung und Geschichte von Amerika: Die vereinten Staaten von Nordamerika.* 7 vols. Hamburg: Bohn, 1794–1816.

Fitzhugh, George. *Cannibals All! Or, Slaves without Masters.* Richmond, Va.: A. Morris, 1857.

Foner, Philip S., ed. *Alexander von Humboldt on Slavery in the United States.* Berlin: Humboldt-Universität, 1981.

——— , ed. *Frederick Douglass on Women's Rights.* Westport, Conn.: Greenwood Press, 1976.

——— , ed. *The Life and Writings of Frederick Douglass.* 5 vols. New York: International Publishers, 1950.

Foner, Philip S., and George E. Walker, eds. *Proceedings of the Black State Conventions, 1840–1865.* Philadelphia: Temple University Press, 1979.

Fröbel, Julius. *Aus Amerika: Erfahrungen, Reisen und Studien.* 2 vols. Leipzig: J. J. Weber, 1857.

——— . *Die deutsche Auswanderung und ihre culturhistorische Bedeutung: Fünfzehn Briefe an den Herausgeber der Allgemeinen Auswanderungs-Zeitung.* Leipzig: F. Wagner, 1858.

Gaines, John I. "What Is the Duty of the Colored American Parent?" In *Ninth Annual Report of the Board of Trustees for the Colored Public Schools of Cincinnati*. Cincinnati, 1858.

Gilman, William H., et al., eds. *The Journals and Miscellaneous Notebooks of Ralph Waldo Emerson*. 16 vols. Cambridge, Mass.: Belknap Press of Harvard University, 1960–82.

Gougeon, Len, and Joel Myerson, eds. *Emerson's Antislavery Writings*. New Haven, Conn.: Yale University Press, 1995.

Hammond, James Henry. *Selections from the Letters and Speeches of the Hon. James H. Hammond, of South Carolina*. New York: John F. Trow, 1866.

Hearn, Lafcadio. *Children of the Levee*. Edited by O. W. Frost. Lexington: University of Kentucky Press, 1957.

Hecker, Friedrich. *Friedrich Hecker's Festrede, Gehalten bei der Deutschen Friedens-Feier zu St. Louis, March 12, 1871*. Frankfurt, 1871.

Heinzen, Karl. *Erlebtes. 2. Theil: Nach meiner Exilirung*. Boston, 1874.

———. *Gesammelte Schriften, zweiter Band*. New York, 1858.

———. *Die Teutschen und die Amerikaner*. Boston, 1860.

———. *Teutscher Radikalismus in Amerika*. 3 vols. Boston: Verein zur Verbreitung Radikaler Prinzipien, 1879.

Hillis, Newell Dwight, ed. *Lectures and Orations by Henry Ward Beecher*. New York: AMS Press, 1970.

Holmes, Oliver Wendell, Sr. *The Works of Oliver Wendell Holmes*. 13 vols. Boston: Houghton & Mifflin, 1892.

Hugo, Victor. *1848: Ein Revolutionsjournal*. Edited and translated by Jörg Rademacher. Berlin: Elfenbein Verlag, 2002.

Kapp, Friedrich. *Aus und über Amerika: Thatsachen und Erlebnisse*. 2 vols. Berlin: J. Springer, 1876.

———. *Die Geschichte der Sklaverei in den Vereinigten Staaten von Amerika*. New York: L. Hauser, 1860.

———. *Leben des Amerikanischen Generals Friedrich Wilhelm von Steuben*. Berlin: O. Janke, 1858.

———. *Die Sklavenfrage in den Vereinigten Staaten; Geschichtlich Entwickelt*. New York: L. W. Schmidt, 1854.

Körner, Gustav. *Das deutsche Element in den Vereinigten Staaten von Nordamerika, 1818–1848*. Cincinnati: A. E. Wilde, 1880.

———. *Memoirs of Gustav Körner, 1809–1896*. Edited by Thomas I. McCormack. 2 vols. Cedar Rapids, Iowa: Torch Press, 1909.

Koss, Rudolf H. *Milwaukee*. Milwaukee: Herold, 1871.

Löher, Franz von. *Geschichte und Zustände der Deutschen in Amerika*. Göttingen: Wigand, 1855.

———. "The Landscape and People of Cincinnati, 1846–47." Translated by Frederic Trautmann. In *Ethnic Diversity and Civic Identity: Patterns of Conflict and Cohesion in Cincinnati since 1820*, edited by Henry D. Shapiro and Jonathan D. Sarna, 39–47. Urbana: University of Illinois Press, 1992.

Lohmann, Christoph. *Radical Passion: Ottilie Assing's Reports from America and Letters to Frederick Douglass.* New York: Peter Lang, 1999.

Marsh, George P. *The Goths in New England: A Discourse Delivered at the Anniversary of the Philomathesian Society of Middlebury College.* Middlebury, Vt.: J. Cobb, 1843.

Meltzer, Milton, and Patricia G. Holland, eds. *Lydia Maria Child: Selected Letters, 1817–1880.* Amherst: University of Massachusetts Press, 1982.

Merrill, Walter M., ed. *The Letters of William Lloyd Garrison.* 6 vols. Cambridge, Mass.: Belknap Press of Harvard University, 1975.

Metzner, Heinrich. *Jahrbücher der Deutsch-Amerikanischen Turnerei.* 3 vols. New York: 1890–94.

Moore, John Bassett, ed. *The Works of James Buchanan, Comprising His Speeches, State Papers, and Private Correspondence.* 12 vols. Philadelphia: Lippincott, 1908–11.

Morse, Samuel F. B. *Foreign Conspiracy against the Liberties of the United States.* New York: Arno Press, 1977.

Mueller, Jacob. *Memories of a Forty-Eighter: Sketches from the German-American Period of Storm and Stress in the 1850s.* Edited and translated by Steven Rowan. Cleveland: Western Reserve Historical Society, 1996.

Nourse, James D. *Remarks on the Past and Its Legacies to American Society.* Louisville: Morton & Griswold, 1847.

O'Connell, Daniel. *Daniel O'Connell upon American Slavery.* New York: American-Antislavery Society, 1860.

Olmsted, Frederick Law. *A Journey through Texas; Or, A Saddle-Trip on the South-Western Frontier.* New York: Mason Bros., 1857.

Parker, Theodore. *The Rights of Man in America.* Boston: American Unitarian Association, 1854.

Pease, Theodore C., ed. *Speeches, Lectures, and Letters of Wendell Phillips.* 2 vols. Boston: Lee & Shepard, 1891.

Pierce, Edward L., ed. *Memoir and Letters of Charles Sumner.* 5 vols. Boston: Roberts Brothers, 1877–93.

Proceedings of the Convention of Radical Political Abolitionists, Held at Syracuse, N.Y., June 26th, 27th, and 28th, 1855. New York: Central Abolition Board, 1855.

Rattermann, Heinrich. *Johann Bernhard Stallo: Denkrede gehalten im Deutschen Literarischen Klub von Cincinnati, am 6. November 1901.* Cincinnati, 1902.

Reemelin, Charles. *Life of Charles Reemelin, in German: Carl Gustav Rümelin.* Cincinnati: Weier & Daiker, 1892.

Ripley, C. Peter, Roy E. Finkenbine, et al., eds. *The Black Abolitionist Papers.* 5 vols. Chapel Hill: University of North Carolina Press, 1991.

Rotteck, Carl von. *Lehrbuch des natürlichen Privatrechts.* Stuttgart: Brockhaus, 1840.

Rowan, Steven, ed. and trans. *Germans for a Free Missouri: Translations from the St. Louis Radical Press, 1857–1862.* Columbia: University of Missouri Press, 1983.

Ruchames, Louis, ed. *The Abolitionists: A Collection of Their Writings.* New York: Putnam, 1963.

Sanderson, John P. *Republican Landmarks: The Views and Opinions of American Statesmen on Foreign Immigration*. Philadelphia: Lippincott, 1856.

Schläger, Eduard. *Die sociale und politische Stellung der Deutschen in den Vereinigten Staaten*. Berlin: Puttkammer & Mühlbrecht, 1871.

Schurz, Carl. *The Reminiscences of Carl Schurz, 1829–1852*. 2 vols. New York: McClure, 1907–8.

Stallo, Johann Bernhard. *Reden, Abhandlungen und Briefe*. New York: Steiger, 1893.

Sumner, Charles. *The Works of Charles Sumner*. 15 vols. Boston: Lee & Shepard, 1870–83.

The Trial of Sherman M. Booth for Seduction: Evidence and Summing Up of Counsel in the Case of the State versus S. M. Booth, for Seducing Caroline N. Cook. Milwaukee, 1859.

Wagner, Maria. *Die gebrochenen Ketten: Erzählungen, Reportagen und Reden (1861–1873)*. Stuttgart: H. D. Heinz, 1983.

———. *Mathilde Franziska Anneke in Selbstzeugnissen und Dokumenten*. Frankfurt: Fischer, 1980.

Wagner, Philipp. *Ein Achtundvierziger: Erlebtes und Gedachtes*. Brooklyn: Otto Wigand, 1882.

Webster, Daniel. *The Writings and Speeches of Daniel Webster*. 18 vols. Boston: Little, Brown, 1903.

Whitney, Thomas R. *A Defence of the American Polity*. New York: De Witt & Davenport, 1856.

Willich, August. *The Army, Standing Army or National Army*. Cincinnati, 1866.

SECONDARY LITERATURE

Anbinder, Tyler. *Nativism and Slavery: The Northern Know Nothings and the Politics of the 1850s*. New York: Oxford University Press, 1992.

Anderson, Benedict. *Imagined Communities: Reflections on the Origin and Spread of Nationalism*. London: Verso, 1991.

Anderson, Bonnie S. *Joyous Greetings: The First International Women's Movement, 1830–1860*. New York: Oxford University Press, 2000.

Austin, George Lowell. *The Life and Times of Wendell Phillips*. Chicago: Afro-Am Press, 1969.

Baker, H. Robert. *The Rescue of Joshua Glover: A Fugitive Slave, the Constitution, and the Coming of the Civil War*. Athens: University of Ohio Press, 2006.

Barnett, James. "Willich's Thirty-second Indiana Volunteers." *Cincinnati Historical Society Bulletin* 37 (1979): 48–70.

Baron, Frank. "German Republicans and Radicals in the Struggle for a Slave-Free Kansas: Charles F. Kob and August Bondi." *Yearbook of German-American Studies* 40 (2005): 3–26.

Baron, Frank, and G. Scott Seeger. "Moritz Hartmann (1817–1900) in Kansas: A Forgotten German Pioneer of Lawrence and Humboldt." *Yearbook of German-American Studies* 39 (2004): 1–22.

Bartlett, Irving H. *Wendell Phillips: Brahmin Radical.* Boston: Beacon Press, 1961.

Bartlett, Ruhl J. *John C. Frémont and the Republican Party.* Columbus: Ohio State University, 1930.

Baughn, William A. "Bullets and Ballots: The Election Day Riots of 1855." *Bulletin of the Historical and Philosophical Society of Ohio* 21 (1963): 267–72.

Baum, Bruce. *The Rise and Fall of the Caucasian Race: A Political History of Racial Identity.* New York: New York University Press, 2006.

Baum, Dale. "Know-Nothingism and the Republican Majority in Massachusetts: The Political Realignment of the 1850s." *Journal of American History* 64 (1978): 959–86.

Bean, William G. "Puritan versus Celt, 1850–1860." *New England Quarterly* 7 (1934): 70–89.

Bensel Richard F. *Yankee Leviathan: The Origins of Central State Authority in America, 1859–1877.* Cambridge: Cambridge University Press, 1990.

Bertaux, Nancy. "Structural Economic Change and Occupational Decline among Black Workers in Nineteenth-Century Cincinnati." In *Race and the City: Community, Work, and Protest in Cincinnati, 1820–1970*, edited by Henry Louis Taylor Jr., 126–55. Urbana: University of Illinois Press, 1993.

Betz, Gottlieb. "Die Deutschen und die Sklaverei." In *The German Language Press of the Americas*, edited by Karl J. R. Arndt and May E. Olson, 565–615. New York: K. G. Saur, 1980.

Biesele, Rudolf L. *The History of the German Settlements in Texas, 1831–61.* Austin: Von Boeckmann-Jones, 1930.

———. "The Texas State Convention of Germans in 1854." *Southwestern Historical Quarterly* 33, no.4 (1930): 247–61.

Blackett, Richard J. M. *Building an Antislavery Wall: Black Americans in the Atlantic Abolitionist Movement, 1830–1860.* Baton Rouge: Louisiana State University Press, 1983.

Blight, David. *Race and Reunion: The Civil War in American Memory.* Cambridge, Mass.: Belknap Press of Harvard University, 2001.

Blue, Frederick J. *No Taint of Compromise: Crusaders in Antislavery Politics.* Baton Rouge: Louisiana State University Press, 2005.

Brancaforte, Charlotte L., ed. *The German Forty-Eighters in the United States.* New York: Peter Lang, 1989.

Bruns, Claudia. "Towards a Transnational History of Racism: Interrelationships between Colonial Racism and German Anti-Semitism? The Example of Wilhelm Marr." In *Global Dimensions of Racism in the Modern World: Comparative and Transnational Perspectives*, edited by Manfred Berg and Simon Wendt. New York: Berghahn Books, forthcoming.

Burtis, Mary Elisabeth. *Moncure Conway, 1832–1907.* New Brunswick, N.J.: Rutgers University Press, 1952.

Butler, Diane S. "The Public Life and Private Affairs of Sherman M. Booth." *Wisconsin Magazine of History* 82 (1999): 166–97.

Butler, Leslie. *Critical Americans: Victorian Intellectuals and Transatlantic Liberal Reform.* Chapel Hill: University of North Carolina Press, 2007.

Campbell, Randolph. *An Empire for Slavery: The Peculiar Institution in Texas, 1821–1865.* Baton Rouge: Louisiana State University Press, 1989.

Chused, Richard H. "Married Women's Property Law: 1800–1850." *Georgetown Law Journal* 71 (1983): 1359–1425.

Conzen, Kathleen Neils. "Ethnicity and Festive Culture: German-Americans on Parade." In *The Invention of Ethnicity*, edited by Werner Sollors, 44–76. New York: Oxford University Press, 1989.

———. "German-Americans and the Invention of Ethnicity." In *America and the Germans: An Assessment of a Three-Hundred-Year History*, edited by Frank Trommler and Joseph McVeigh, 1:148–59. Philadelphia: University of Pennsylvania Press, 1985.

———. "Germans." In *Harvard Encyclopedia of American Ethnic Groups*, edited by Stephan Thernstrom, 405–25. Cambridge, Mass.: Belknap Press of Harvard University, 1980.

———. *Immigrant Milwaukee, 1836–1860: Accommodation and Community in a Frontier City.* Cambridge: Cambridge University Press, 1976.

Craig, Gordon A. *The Triumph of Liberalism: Zürich in the Golden Age, 1830–1869.* New York: Scribner, 1989.

Davis, David Brion. *Inhuman Bondage: The Rise and Fall of Slavery in the New World.* New York: Oxford University Press, 2006.

———. *The Problem of Slavery in the Age of Revolution, 1770–1823.* Ithaca, N.Y.: Cornell University Press, 1975.

———. *The Problem of Slavery in Western Culture.* New York: Oxford University Press, 1988.

D'Entremont, John. *Southern Emancipator: Moncure Conway, the American Years, 1832–1865.* New York: Oxford University Press, 1986.

Diedrich, Maria. *Love across Color Lines: Ottilie Assing and Frederick Douglass.* New York: Hill & Wang, 1999.

Douglas, Ann. *The Feminization of American Culture.* New York: Knopf, 1976.

Downey, Matthew T. "Horace Greeley and the Politicians: The Liberal Republican Convention in 1872." *Journal of American History* 53 (1967): 727–50.

Drescher, Seymour. *Capitalism and Antislavery: British Mobilization in Comparative Perspective.* New York: Oxford University Press, 1987.

Easton, Lloyd D. "Hegelianism in Nineteenth-Century Ohio." *Journal of the History of Ideas* 23 (1962): 355–78.

———. *Hegel's First American Followers: The Ohio Hegelians; John B. Stallo, Peter Kaufmann, Moncure Daniel Conway, and August Willich.* Athens: Ohio University Press, 1966.

Efford, Alison Clark. "German Immigrants and the Arc of American Citizenship during Reconstruction, 1865–1877." *Bulletin of the German Historical Institute* 46 (2010): 61–76.

Fahs, Alice, and John Waugh. *The Memory of the Civil War in American Culture.* Chapel Hill: University of North Carolina Press, 2004.

Faust, Drew Gilpin. *The Ideology of Slavery: Proslavery Thought in the Antebellum South.* Baton Rouge: Louisiana State University Press, 1981.

Finkelman, Paul, ed. *His Soul Goes Marching On: Responses to John Brown and the Harpers Ferry Raid*. Charlottesville: University of Virginia Press, 1995.

———. "Lincoln, Emancipation and the Limits of Constitutional Change." *Supreme Court Review* (2008): 349–87.

Fladeland, Betty. *Men and Brothers: Anglo-American Antislavery Cooperation*. Urbana: University of Illinois Press, 1972.

Foner, Eric. *Forever Free: The Story of Emancipation and Reconstruction*. New York: Oxford University Press, 2005.

———. *Free Soil, Free Labor, Free Men: The Ideology of the Republican Party before the Civil War*. New York: Oxford University Press, 1971.

———. *Reconstruction: America's Unfinished Revolution, 1863–1877*. New York: Oxford University Press, 1987.

Foner, Philip S. *American Socialism and Black Americans: From the Age of Jackson to World War II*. Westport, Conn.: Greenwood Press, 1977.

Franz, Eckhart G. *Das Amerikabild der deutschen Revolution von 1848/49: Zum Problem der Übertragung gewachsener Verfassungsformen*. Heidelberg: Winter, 1958.

Frederickson, Mary E., and Walter Herz. "A Matter of Respect: The Religious Journey of Peter H. Clark," *AME Church Review* 68 (2002): 25–36.

Fredrickson, George M. *The Arrogance of Race: Historical Perspectives on Slavery, Racism, and Social Inequality*. Middletown, Conn.: Wesleyan University Press, 1988.

Freitag, Sabine. *Friedrich Hecker: Biographie eines Republikaners*. Stuttgart: Franz Steiner Verlag, 1998.

Gemme, Paola. *Domesticating Foreign Struggles: The Italian Risorgimento and Antebellum American Identity*. Athens: University of Georgia Press, 2005.

Gerber, David A. "Peter Humphries Clark: The Dialogue of Hope and Despair." In *Black Leaders of the Nineteenth Century*, edited by Leon Litwack and August Meier, 173–90. Urbana: University of Illinois Press, 1988.

Gienapp, William. *The Origins of the Republican Party, 1852–1856*. New York: Oxford University Press, 1987.

Grant, Susan-Mary. *North over South: Northern Nationalism and American Identity in the Antebellum Era*. Lawrence: University Press of Kansas, 2000.

Green, James. *Death in the Haymarket: A Story of Chicago, the First Labor Movement, and the Bombing That Divided Gilded Age America*. New York: Pantheon Books, 2006.

Grossman, Lawrence. "'In His Veins Coursed No Bootlicking Blood': The Career of Peter H. Clark." *Ohio History* 86 (1977): 79–95.

Gurda, John. *The Making of Milwaukee*. Milwaukee: Milwaukee County Historical Society, 1999.

Gutman, Herbert G. "Peter H. Clark: Pioneer Negro Socialist, 1877." *Journal of Negro Education* 34 (1965): 413–18.

Handlin, Oscar. *Boston's Immigrants, 1790–1880: A Study in Acculturation*. Cambridge, Mass.: Belknap Press of Harvard University, 1991.

Hansen, Karen. *A Very Social Time: Crafting Community in Antebellum New England*. Berkeley: University of California Press, 1994.

Harding, Leonard. "The Cincinnati Riots of 1862." *Bulletin of the Cincinnati Historical Society* 25 (1967): 229–39.

Harsham, Peter M. "A Community Portrait: Over-the-Rhine, 1860." *Cincinnati Historical Society Bulletin* 40 (1982): 63–72.

Hausen, Karin. "Die Polarisierung der 'Geschlechtscharaktere': Eine Spiegelung der Dissoziation von Erwerbs und Familienleben." In *Sozialgeschichte der Familie in der Neuzeit*, edited by Werner Conze, 363–93. Stuttgart: Klett, 1976.

Herz, Walter. "Influence Transcending Mere Numbers: The Unitarians in Nineteenth Century Cincinnati." *Queen City Heritage* 51 (1993): 3–22.

Herzig, Arno. "Judenhass und Antisemitismus bei den Unterschichten und in der frühen Arbeiterbewegung." In *Juden und deutsche Arbeiterbewegung bis 1933*, edited by Ludger Heid and Arnold Paucker, 1–18. Tübingen: Mohr, 1992.

Hinners, Wolfgang. *Exil und Rückkehr: Friedrich Kapp in Amerika und Deutschland, 1824–1884*. Stuttgart: Akademischer Verlag Stuttgart, 1987.

Hochgeschwender, Michael. *Wahrheit, Einheit, Ordnung: Die Sklavenfrage und der amerikanische Katholizismus, 1835–1870*. Paderborn: Schöningh, 2006.

Hofstadter, Richard. *The American Political Tradition and the Men Who Made It*. New York: Knopf, 1948.

Horsman, Reginald. *Race and Manifest Destiny: The Origins of American Racial Anglo-Saxonism*. Cambridge: Cambridge University Press, 1981.

Horton, James Oliver, and Lois E. Horton. "The Affirmation of Manhood: Black Garrisonians in Antebellum Boston." In *Courage and Conscience: Black and White Abolitionists in Boston*, edited by Donald M. Jacobs, 127–54. Bloomington: Indiana University Press, 1993.

———. *Black Bostonians: Family Life and Community Struggle in the Antebellum North*. New York: Holmes & Meier, 1979.

Hunt, Lynne. *Inventing Human Rights: A History*. New York: W. W. Norton, 2007.

Ignatieff, Michael. *Blood and Belonging: Journeys into the New Nationalism*. New York: Farrar, Straus & Giroux, 1993.

Ignatiev, Noel. *How the Irish Became White*. New York: Routledge, 1995.

Jacobs, Donald M., and Hartmut Keil. "African Americans and Germans in Mid-Nineteenth Century Buffalo." In *Free People of Color*, edited by James Oliver Horton, 170–83. Washington, D.C.: Smithsonian Institution Press, 1993.

Jacobson, Matthew F. *Whiteness of a Different Color: European Immigrants and the Alchemy of Race*. Cambridge: Cambridge University Press, 1998.

Johannson, Robert W. *Stephen A. Douglas*. Urbana: University of Illinois Press, 1973.

Jordan, Terry G. "Germans and Blacks in Texas." In *States of Progress: Germans and Blacks in America over 300 Years*, edited by Randall M. Miller, 89–97. Philadelphia: German Society of Pennsylvania, 1989.

———. *German Seed in Texas Soil: Immigrant Farmers in Nineteenth-Century Texas.* Austin: University of Texas Press, 1966.

Kamphoefner, Walter D. "German Texans: In the Mainstream or Backwaters of Lone Star Society?" *Yearbook of German-American Studies* 38 (2003): 119–38.

Kantrowitz, Stephen. "Fighting like Men: Civil War Dilemmas of Abolitionist Manhood." In *Battle Scars: Gender and Sexuality in the American Civil War*, edited by Catherine Clinton and Nina Silber, 19–40. New York: Oxford University Press, 2006.

Keil, Hartmut. "German Immigrants and African-Americans in Mid-Nineteenth Century America." In *Enemy Images in American History*, edited by Ragnhild Fiebig-von Hase and Ursula Lemkuhl, 137–57. Providence, R.I.: Berghahn Books, 1997.

———. "German Working-Class Radicalism after the Civil War." In *The German-American Encounter: Conflict and Cooperation between Two Cultures, 1800–2000*, edited by Frank Trommler and Elliott Shore, 37–48. New York: Berghahn Books, 2001.

Keller, Christian B. *Chancellorsville and the Germans: Nativism, Ethnicity, and Civil War Memory.* New York: Fordham University Press, 2007.

Kistler, Mark O. "German-American Liberalism and Thomas Paine." *American Quarterly* 14 (1962): 81–91.

Klement, Frank L. "Sound and Fury: Civil War Dissent in the Cincinnati Area." *Cincinnati Historical Society Bulletin* 35 (1977): 98–114.

Knobel, Dale T. *Paddy and the Republic: Ethnicity and Nationality in Antebellum America.* Middletown, Conn.: Wesleyan University Press, 1986.

Lader, Lawrence. *The Bold Brahmins: New England's War against Slavery, 1831–1863.* New York: Dutton, 1961.

Lankevich, George J. *Boston: A Chronological & Documentary History, 1602–1970.* Dobbs Ferry, N.Y.: Oceana Publications, 1974.

Lattek, Christine. *Revolutionary Refugees: German Socialism in Britain, 1840–1860.* London: Routledge, 2006.

Levine, Bruce. "Community Divided: German Immigrants, Social Class, and Political Conflict in Antebellum Cincinnati." In *Ethnic Diversity and Civic Identity: Patterns of Conflict and Cohesion in Cincinnati since 1820*, edited by Henry D. Shapiro and Jonathan D. Sarna, 46–93. Urbana: University of Illinois Press, 1992.

———. "Conservatism, Nativism, and Slavery: Thomas R. Whitney and the Origins of the Know-Nothing Party." *Journal of American History* 88 (2001): 455–88.

———. *The Spirit of 1848: German Immigrants, Labor Conflict, and the Coming of the Civil War.* Urbana: University of Illinois Press, 1992.

Linden, W. H. van der. *The International Peace Movement, 1815–1874.* Amsterdam: Tilleul, 1987.

Logan, Rayford W., and Michael R. Winston, ed. *Dictionary of American Negro Biography.* New York: Norton, 1982.

Lupo, Alan. *Liberty's Chosen Home: The Politics of Violence in Boston.* Boston: Little, Brown, 1977.

Marten, James A. "Drawing the Line: Dissent and Disloyalty in Texas, 1856 to 1874." PhD diss., University of Texas, Austin, 1986.

Martyn, Carlos. *Wendell Phillips: The Agitator.* New York: Funk & Wagnalls, 1890.

Mayer, Henry. *All on Fire: William Lloyd Garrison and the Abolition of Slavery.* New York: St. Martin's Press, 1998.

McCarthy, Timothy P., and John Stauffer, eds. *Prophets of Protest: Reconsidering the History of American Abolitionism.* New York: New Press, 2006.

McFeely, William S. *Frederick Douglass.* New York: Norton, 1991.

McKivigan, John, and Mitchell Snay, eds. *Religion and the Antebellum Debate over Slavery.* Athens: University of Georgia Press, 1998.

McManus, Michael J. *Political Abolitionism in Wisconsin, 1840–1861.* Kent, Ohio: Kent State University Press, 1998.

McPherson, James M. *Abraham Lincoln and the Second American Revolution.* New York: Oxford University Press, 1991.

———. *Battle Cry of Freedom: The Civil War Era.* New York: Oxford University Press, 1988.

———. "Grant or Greeley? The Abolitionist Dilemma in the Election of 1872." *American Historical Review* 71 (1965): 136–57.

———. *The Struggle for Equality: Abolitionists and the Negro in the Civil War and Reconstruction.* Princeton, N.J.: Princeton University Press, 1964.

Menand, Louis. *The Metaphysical Club: A Story of Ideas in America.* New York: Farrar, Straus & Giroux, 2002.

Messer-Kruse, Timothy. *The Yankee International: Marxism and the American Reform Tradition, 1848–1876.* Chapel Hill: University of North Carolina Press, 1998.

Metzner, Heinrich. *A Brief History of the American Turnerbund.* Pittsburgh: National Executive Committee of the American Turnerbund, 1924.

Moltmann, Günter. *Atlantische Blockpolitik im 19. Jahrhundert: Die Vereinigten Staaten und der deutsche Liberalismus während der Revolution von 1848/49.* Düsseldorf: Droste, 1973.

Morrison, Michael A. "American Reaction to European Revolutions, 1848–1852: Sectionalism, Memory, and the Revolutionary Heritage." *Civil War History* 49 (2003): 111–32.

Musgrave, Marian. "Heinrich Heine's Anti-Slavery Thought." *Negro American Literature Forum* 6 (1972): 91–94.

Nadel, Stanley. *Little Germany: Ethnicity, Religion, and Class in New York City, 1845–80.* Urbana: University of Illinois Press, 1990.

Nagler, Jörg. "Deutschamerikaner und das Liberal Republican Movement 1872." *Amerikastudien/American Studies* 33 (1988): 415–38.

———. *Fremont contra Lincoln: Die deutsch-amerikanische Opposition in der Republikanischen Partei während des amerikanischen Bürgerkrieges.* Frankfurt: Peter Lang, 1984.

Noll, Mark, ed. *God and Mammon: Protestants, Money, and the Market, 1790–1860.* New York: Oxford University Press, 2001.

Oates, Stephen B. *To Purge This Land with Blood: A Biography of John Brown.* Amherst: University of Massachusetts Press, 1984.

O'Connor, Thomas. *The Boston Irish: A Political History.* Boston: Northeastern University Press, 1995.

Öfele, Martin. *German-Speaking Officers in the United States Colored Troops, 1863–1867.* Gainesville: University of Florida Press, 2004.

Ortlepp, Anke. *Auf denn, Ihr Schwestern! Deutschamerikanische Frauenvereine in Milwaukee, Wisconsin, 1844–1914.* Stuttgart: Franz Steiner Verlag, 2004.

Osofsky, Gilbert. "Abolitionists, Irish Immigrants and the Dilemmas of Romantic Nationalism." *American Historical Review* 80 (1975): 889–912.

Palmer, Robert R. *The Age of the Democratic Revolution: A Political History of Europe and America, 1760–1800.* 2 vols. Princeton, N.J.: Princeton University Press, 1959.

Paludan, Phillip Shaw. *The Presidency of Abraham Lincoln.* Lawrence: University Press of Kansas, 1994.

Paul, Heike. *Kulturkontakt und Racial Presences: Afro-Amerikaner und die deutsche Amerika-Literatur, 1815–1914.* Heidelberg: Winter, 2005.

Piepke, Susan L. *Mathilde Franziska Anneke (1817–1884): The Works and Life of a German-American Activist.* New York: Peter Lang, 2006.

Quarles, Benjamin. *The Negro in the Civil War.* New York: Oxford University Press, 1988.

Randers-Pehrson, Justine Davis. *Adolf Douai, 1819–1888: The Turbulent Life of a German Forty-Eighter in the Homeland and in the United States.* New York: Peter Lang, 2000.

Reinhart, Joseph. *August Willich's Gallant Dutchmen: Civil War Letters from the 32nd Indiana Infantry.* Kent, Ohio: Kent State University Press, 2006.

Reiß, Ansgar. *Radikalismus und Exil: Gustav Struve und die Demokratie in Deutschland und Amerika.* Stuttgart: Franz Steiner, 2004.

Reynolds, David S. *John Brown, Abolitionist: The Man Who Killed Slavery, Sparked the Civil War, and Seeded Civil Rights.* New York: Knopf, 2005.

Rice, Alan J., and Martin Crawford, eds. *Liberating Sojourn: Frederick Douglass & Transatlantic Reform.* Athens: University of Georgia Press, 1999.

Rippley, La Vern J. "German Assimilation: The Effects of the 1871 Victory on Americana-Germanica." In *Germany and America: Essays on Problems of International Relations and Immigration,* edited by Hans L. Trefousse, 122–36. New York: Brooklyn College Press, 1980.

Roberts, Timothy Mason. *Distant Revolutions: 1848 and the Challenge to American Exceptionalism.* Charlottesville: University of Virginia Press, 2009.

Roediger, David. *The Wages of Whiteness: Race and the Making of the American Working Class.* New York: Verso, 1999.

Roper, Laura, Wood. *FLO: A Biography of Frederick Law Olmsted.* Baltimore: Johns Hopkins University Press, 1977.

Samuels, Shirley, ed. *The Culture of Sentiment: Race, Gender, and Sentimentality in Nineteenth-Century America.* New York: Oxford University Press, 1992.

Schmidt, Klaus. *Mathilde und Fritz Anneke: Aus der Pionierzeit von Demokratie und Frauenbewegung*. Cologne: Schmidt von Schwind, 1999.

Schneebeli, Robert, ed. *Zürich: Geschichte einer Stadt*. Zürich: Verlag Neue Züricher Zeitung, 1986.

Sherwin, Oscar. *Prophet of Liberty: The Life and Times of Wendell Phillips*. New York: Bookman Associates, 1958.

Shields, David S. *Civil Tongues & Polite Letters in British America*. Chapel Hill: University of North Carolina Press, 1997.

Silber, Nina. *The Romance of Reunion: Northerners and the South*. Chapel Hill: University of North Carolina Press, 1993.

Sollors, Werner. *Neither Black nor White yet Both: Thematic Explorations of Interracial Literature*. New York: Oxford University Press, 1997.

Spevack, Edmund. *Charles Follen's Search for Nationality and Freedom: Germany and America, 1796–1840*. Cambridge: Cambridge University Press, 1997.

Stange, Douglas C. *Patterns of Antislavery among American Unitarians, 1831–1860*. Cranbury, N.J.: Fairleigh Dickinson University Press, 1977.

Stauffer, John. *The Black Hearts of Men: Radical Abolitionists and the Transformation of Race*. Cambridge, Mass.: Harvard University Press, 2002.

Stewart, Charles D. "A Bachelor General." *Wisconsin Magazine of History* 17 (1933): 131–54.

Stewart, James Brewer. *Holy Warriors: The American Abolitionists and Slavery*. New York: Hill & Wang, 1996.

——— . *Wendell Phillips: Liberty's Hero*. Baton Rouge: Louisiana State University Press, 1986.

Stowe, William W. *Going Abroad: European Travel in Nineteenth-Century American Culture*. Princeton, N.J.: Princeton University Press, 1994.

Stuecher, Dorothea D. *Twice Removed: The Experience of German-American Women Writers in the 19th Century*. New York: Peter Lang, 1990.

Taylor, Clare, ed. *British and American Abolitionists: An Episode in Transatlantic Understanding*. Edinburgh: Edinburgh University Press, 1974.

Taylor, Henry Louis, Jr. "On Slavery's Fringe: City-Building and Black Community Development in Cincinnati, 1800–1850." *Ohio History* 95 (1986): 5–33.

Taylor, Henry Louis, Jr., and Vicky Dula. "The Black Residential Experience and Community Formation in Antebellum Cincinnati." In *Race and the City: Community, Work, and Protest in Cincinnati, 1820–1970*, edited by Henry Louis Taylor Jr., 96–125. Urbana: University of Illinois Press, 1993.

Taylor, Nikki M. *Frontiers of Freedom: Cincinnati's Black Community, 1802–1868*. Athens: Ohio University Press, 2005.

Taylor, Steven. "Progressive Nativism: The Know-Nothing Party in Massachusetts." *Historical Journal of Massachusetts* 28 (2000): 167–85.

Thomas, Herman E. *James W. C. Pennington: African-American Churchman and Abolitionist*. New York: Garland, 1995.

Tolzmann, Don Heinrich, ed. *The German-American Forty-Eighters, 1848–1998.* Indianapolis: Indiana German Heritage Society, 1998.

Tompkins, Jane. *Sensational Designs: The Cultural Work of American Fiction, 1790–1860.* New York: Oxford University Press, 1985.

———. "Sentimental Power: *Uncle Tom's Cabin* and the Politics of Literary History." In *Sensational Designs: The Cultural Work of American Fiction, 1790–1860,* edited by Jane Tompkins, 122–146. New York: Oxford University Press, 1985.

Trefousse, Hans L. *Carl Schurz: A Biography.* Knoxville: University Press of Kentucky, 1982.

———. "The German-American Immigrants and the Newly Founded Reich." In *America and the Germans: An Assessment of a Three-Hundred-Year History,* edited by Frank Trommler and Joseph McVeigh, 1:160–75. Philadelphia: University of Pennsylvania Press, 1985.

Tuchman, Arleen Marcia. *Science Has No Sex: The Life of Mary Zakrzewska, M.D.* Chapel Hill: University of North Carolina Press, 2006.

Überhorst, Horst. *Turner unterm Sternenbanner: Der Kampf der deutsch-amerikanischen Turner für Einheit, Freiheit, und soziale Gerechtigkeit, 1848–1918.* Munich: Moos, 1978.

Van den Berghe, Pierre L. *Race and Racism: A Comparative Perspective.* New York: Wiley, 1967.

Vogel, Stanley M. *German Literary Influences on the American Transcendentalists.* New Haven, Conn.: Yale University Press, 1955.

Von Frank, Albert J. *The Trials of Anthony Burns: Freedom and Slavery in Emerson's Boston.* Cambridge: Cambridge University Press, 1998.

Vorenberg, Michael. *Final Freedom: The Civil War, the Abolition of Slavery, and the Thirteenth Amendment.* Cambridge: Cambridge University Press, 2001.

Wagner, Maria. "Feminismus, Literatur und Revolution: Ein unveröffentlichtes Manuskript aus dem Jahre 1850." *German Quarterly* 50 (1977): 121–29.

Wagner, Ralf. "Turner Societies and the Socialist Tradition." In *German Workers' Culture in the United States, 1850 to 1920,* edited by Hartmut Keil and John B. Jentz, 221–39. Washington, D.C.: Smithsonian Institution Press, 1988.

Walters, Ronald G. *American Reformers, 1815–1860.* New York: Hill & Wang, 1997.

Wellenreuther, Herrmann. "Die USA: Ein politisches Vorbild der bürgerlich-liberalen Kräfte des Vormärz." In *Deutschland und der Westen im 19. und 20. Jahrhundert,* edited by Jürgen Elvert and Michael Salewski, 23–41. Stuttgart: Franz Steiner, 1993.

Welter, Barbara. "The Cult of True Womanhood: 1820–1860." *American Quarterly* 18 (1966): 151–74.

Wiebe, Robert. "Framing U.S. History: Democracy, Nationalism, and Socialism." In *Rethinking American History in a Global Age,* edited by Thomas Bender, 236–49. Berkeley: University of California Press, 2002.

Wilentz, Sean. *The Rise of American Democracy: Jefferson to Lincoln.* New York: W. W. Norton, 2006.

Williams, T. Harry. *Lincoln and the Radicals.* Madison: University of Wisconsin Press, 1965.

Wittke, Carl. *Against the Current: The Life of Karl Heinzen (1809–80)*. Chicago: University of Chicago Press, 1945.

———. *The German-Language Press in America*. Lexington: University of Kentucky Press, 1957.

———. "The Germans of Cincinnati." *Bulletin of the Historical and Philosophical Society of Ohio* 20 (1962): 3–14.

———. "The Ninth Ohio Volunteers." *Ohio Archeological and Historical Quarterly* 35 (1926): 402–17.

———. *Refugees of Revolution: The German Forty-Eighters in America*. Philadelphia: University of Pennsylvania Press, 1952.

Zucker, A. E. *The Forty-Eighters: Political Refugees of the German Revolution of 1848*. New York: Columbia University Press, 1950.

INDEX

abolitionism, 3–9, 23–34, 78–81, 108–10, 147–54, 160–61, 169–71; and disunionism, 149–55; in Europe, 1–3, 15, 114, 121–25, 132–33; and evangelicalism, 4, 31, 53–54, 78–80, 145, 196n40 (*see also* revivalism); female participation in, 23, 115, 150, 176; literary representations of, 58, 127–33; and nonviolence, 53–54, 94–95, 142, 148; relationship of, to antislavery, 10

Achenbach, Hermann, 39

African Americans, 27, 76–77, 140, 149; and emancipation, 5–6, 101–3, 131–33, 159–61; fight for the Union, 101–2, 131–32, 148, 163; interact with German immigrants, 33, 37, 72–73, 80, 95–96, 152–54, 157–58; and racial discrimination, 7, 24–25, 77, 95–96, 186–88

Agassiz, Louis, 60, 196n52

American and Foreign Anti-Slavery Society, 15, 144

American Anti-Slavery Society, 24, 150

American exceptionalism, 15–16, 55–56, 125, 179, 188; European criticism of, 55–56, 88–89, 124–25, 144

Anglo-Saxonism, 7, 16–18, 26, 186

Anneke, Fritz, 83, 99, 104–34, 182, 204–5n27

Anneke, Mathilde Franziska, 8, 104–36, 171, 176, 182; abolitionist fiction of, 127–33; antireligious views of, 113; champions women's rights, 112–13, 127–33, 135–36;

and revolutionary violence, 115–17; and transatlantic democracy, 122–23, 134

Anthony, Susan B., 136, 176

anti-Catholicism, 17–18, 76, 82, 113, 146. *See also* Know-Nothings; nativism

anti-Semitism, 184

aristocracy, 3, 6–7, 13–14, 39, 54, 178, 182; slaveholders as members of, 7, 28, 50, 56, 59–60, 99, 123, 156, 174–75. *See also* feudalism

Assing, Ludmilla, 119, 181

Assing, Ottilie, 22, 32, 35–36, 119, 173–74, 180–81

Bates, Edward, 162

Baum, Martin, 74

Becker, August, 80, 84

Beecher, Henry Ward, 20, 44

Bell, John, 20

Bigelow, John Prescott, 141

Bird, Isabella Lucy, 74–75

Bismarck, Otto von, 178, 181–83

Bleeding Kansas, 49, 51, 64, 67–69, 71, 81, 142

Blenker, Ludwig, 121, 157

Blum, Robert, 94

Bondi, August, 64

Booth, Mary H. C., 12, 104–36, 183–84, 206n; abolitionist fiction of, 127–33; and evangelical reform, 113–14, 122; as expatriate, 118–36; as "true woman," 113–14, 126

231

RACE IN THE ATLANTIC WORLD, 1700-1900

*The Hanging of Angélique: The Untold Story of Canadian
Slavery and the Burning of Old Montréal*
by Afua Cooper

*Christian Ritual and the Creation of British
Slave Societies, 1650–1780*
by Nicholas M. Beasley

*African American Life in the Georgia Lowcountry:
The Atlantic World and the Gullah Geechee*
edited by Philip Morgan

*The Horrible Gift of Freedom: Atlantic Slavery and
the Representation of Emancipation*
by Marcus Wood

*The Life and Letters of Philip Quaque, the First African
Anglican Missionary*
edited by Vincent Carretta and Ty M. Reese

*In Search of Brightest Africa: Reimagining the Dark
Continent in American Culture, 1884–1936*
by Jeannette Eileen Jones

*Contentious Liberties: American Abolitionists in
Post-emancipation Jamaica, 1834–1866*
by Gale L. Kenny

*We Are the Revolutionists: German-Speaking Immigrants
and American Abolitionists after 1848*
by Mischa Honeck

9 780820 338231